COLLECTED TARTS AND OTHER INDELICACIES

COLLECTED TARTS

&

Other Indelicacies

TABATHA SOUTHEY

 Douglas & McIntyre

· · · · ·

For my two perfect children, for whom every word was written

·

DOUGLAS AND MCINTYRE (2013) LTD.
P.O. Box 219, Madeira Park, BC, VON 2HO
www.douglas-mcintyre.com

Cover design by Anna Comfort O'Keeffe
Text design by Shed Simas / Onça Design
Printed and bound in Canada

Douglas and McIntyre (2013) Ltd. acknowledges the support of the Canada Council
for the Arts, which last year invested $153 million to bring the arts to Canadians
throughout the country. We also gratefully acknowledge financial support from
the Government of Canada and from the Province of British Columbia through the
BC Arts Council and the Book Publishing Tax Credit.

LIBRARY AND ARCHIVES CANADA CATALOGUING IN PUBLICATION

Southey, Tabatha
[Newspaper columns. Selections]
    Collected tarts and other indelicacies / Tabatha Southey.

Issued in print and electronic formats.
ISBN 978-1-77162-167-0 (softcover).--ISBN 978-1-77162-168-7 (HTML)

    I. Title.

PS8587.0977A6 2017   C817'.6   C2017-904409-5
                                            C2017-904410-9

Contents

Introduction

I'll never know exactly why I wrote this first column; it was certainly not in the hopes of getting published in a newspaper. I think I wrote it as a sort of answer-I'd-never-give to a new friend, a neighbour of mine, who looked at me quizzically (that's the kindest word for it) in his kitchen one night when I made some fairly obscure musical reference over wine.

I was newly single with two young children, one under two, one barely four, and my friend's face said, "Oh, dear, how did you know that? What good will it do you? Where are you coming from and where will you go?"

I had fairly recently moved back to Toronto from Los Angeles, where I'd been living for just less than a year, but in that time my best friend, Karen, had accepted a postdoc in Dublin, my good friend Cindy had moved to New York, others had moved on and it felt as if everyone had scattered. Although I had a house in Toronto, in many ways returning there, somewhat shell-shocked as I was, felt a bit like moving to a strange town. My new friend, I thought, was perhaps right to wonder where I belonged, how I fit in.

When I was married I once joked with my husband, a comic by trade, and a fine one, that the job I was best qualified for was writing the column that then ran in the back of the *Toronto Star*'s TV guide. The weekly feature involved an actor being taken out to a local restaurant where he was interviewed about his latest project; the instructions for the establishment's signature dish were always printed below. The column was called "Dinner Date" and I read it faithfully.

"Look, I go out for dinner, pretend to be interested in your career, I get a recipe," I said to my man. "This is perfect for me." And that is what

I had in mind when I wrote what would become my first column, a piece I called "Drunk with Men."

"Drunk with Men" found its way to the *National Post* via a smart, funny woman named Jane Thompson, who I would sometimes drive home from the half-day preschool my eldest was attending.

"Do you write?" she had said to me on one of these drives, in much the same way you might say, "Do you ever shut up?" I said that while I told stories to my children, I did not write.

She told me to send those stories to her friend at Key Porter and I did. I mailed them a few stories and was not in the least surprised when time went by and I did not hear back from them. I knew people did not just get published. And yet about three months later I received an email saying, essentially, "We love your stories and would like to publish at least one of them, but you did not put your name on them so we have had a hard time tracking you down." I have never been good with paperwork.

The book, *The Deep Cold River Story*, was in the works, and yet I would have thought it very presumptuous to call myself a writer. I believe I showed my first attempt at a column to no one but a therapist I was seeing at the time.

About a year later Jane began working as an editor at the just-launched *National Post* and emailed, suggesting I write something for her, and I sent the column. That same week my therapist asked if she could show the piece to a friend. That friend turned out to be the editor of *Toronto Life*.

"Drunk with Men" was thus accepted by two publications in one day. The excellent Ellen Vanstone, then editor of the *National Post*'s weekend section, said, "Give it to us and we'll give you a column." While I did not think I would ever write much, I agreed.

So here is "Drunk with Men" pretty much as I submitted it. A slightly edited version of it ran and really did change the course of my life.

Drunk with Men

National Post, June 19, 1999

•

At the age of 15 I was taken from the suburbs and abandoned in the woods. There I was found and raised by a pack of feral single men aged 15 to 26 who didn't get a date until they were 30. They took me in as one of their own, taught me their ways, dressed me and fed me individual pizza slices. The experience has truly left me with sympathy for, and an understanding of, the entire species.

Although it has left me unsuited for any normal job, I now realize that all my early training has rendered me uniquely qualified to undertake an important research project: I would like to be employed to get drunk with various men, and document my experiences, so that I may bring some of the wonders I have seen back to the general public and possibly raise some awareness of single-men-aged-15-to-26-who-will-never-get-a-date-until-they're-30, and not just of them but of other groups—for example, men 32-to-40-with-bastard-brats-from-a-fuck-at-a-frat-party-who-still-think-they-can-dance.

The data I collect may well have as profound an influence on society as it already has on me. For example, despite the alarming increase in their numbers, I remain firmly opposed to the legalization of the single-men-aged-15-to-26-who-will-never-get-a-date-until-they're-30 hunt. In spite of their encroachment on more vulnerable populations (e.g., single-women-aged-28-to-35-still-working-at-The-Body-Shop-but-hoping-to-break-into-the-music-business), I believe this species deserves our protection. Not only for their natural grace and beauty but also because they remain an important archival source for Academy Award Best Supporting Actress nominee information. I am, however, in favour of more humane and government-sponsored means of culling their numbers and relocation, specifically heroin and Canada World Youth.

My credentials are flawless. Using my cover as a neurotic teenage girl, I explored every aspect of their secretive world. Following my 18th year, which I now refer to as my *"Good morning. What instrument did you say you played?" year*, I spent several years studying "the jazz guys," sweet, educated men who, armed with a copy of *Our Bodies, Ourselves* and a tape of *Sketches of Spain*, were determined to right the real or imagined wrongs of the previous group of guys. As if the poetic phrase, "I sold my comic book collection to buy you a Christmas present but I lost the money playing poker. Did you buy any hash?" could ever be erased by "I need you to know that you don't have to shave your legs if you are not comfortable with it politically"—(ooh, yuck)—"Did you buy any hash?"

Do I have any regrets? Yes, I wish I hadn't let the guys pierce my ears that one night. They're crooked.

Following tradition, I married within the pack and bore two children who already show a precocious interest in how my stereo is wired, so I've done my part to preserve the culture. But my reintroduction to the real world, necessitated by their births, has been a traumatic one. I find myself alone and completely unemployable, not just by virtue of my odd socialization (the Eaton Centre subway level proves that no one's too bizarre for retail), but because I am dyslexic, a vague term applied to numerous learning disabilities, mine being perhaps the most crippling: I don't understand daylight savings, I don't know why we do it, I can't remember when to do it, I can't figure out how it works, nor can I perform the necessary mechanical alterations on my clocks or appliances to make it happen. The truth is that for six months of the year I have to go out to my car to check what time it is.

I have almost no formal education. My high school experience was brief but diverse, covering 18 months, during which time I quit, was thrown out of, or forgot the location of three separate high schools.

Sadly, this does not look as impressive on my resume as I had calculated it would at the time.

During my very brief stint at university I majored in film, but I hate it when people talk when you're trying to watch a movie, so I dropped it. I tried women's studies, but while the professors made many very good points, I clung to my belief in pornography, polygamy and short skirts, preferably worn with heels.

These beliefs have endured, although in retrospect I now regret my controversial thesis proposal in which I attempted to prove that menstruating women *are* actually unclean and can in fact spoil crops.

There are certain things I've never had to do: roll a joint, alphabetize my own CDs or go on a "date," per se; I have never been out to dinner and a movie with an individual, single male with whom I have not had sex at least twice

What do I have to offer these potential drinking companions? I have been in a monogamous relationship for 14 years, which, by my calculations, makes me body fluid gold. My blood is like a time capsule from the mid-eighties. Scientists should be hauling it out in vats, putting it under microscopes, seeing if it coagulates faster when they play Culture Club. I know the lyrics to every song ever written. I can correctly identify all the Marx Brothers—yes, including Gummo. I can make people think that you're not gay. I can interpret the language of single men—not just the common phrases used by dull men universally, but the dialects of several cities. For example, in Toronto the correct phrase for "I'm lonely, over 30 and I drink too much" is "Hey, there's always a band at the Horseshoe."

I'm not a female Uncle Tom. I am not one of the guys. I know nothing about sports. I enjoy the company of women, but in my experience, getting drunk with women almost always involves Bonnie Raitt and cheese. It never fails—without the civilizing influence of at least one man, someone brings a brie and then someone goes and puts on *The Glow* and the whole night is shot. I love cheese, I like Bonnie Raitt, just not while I'm drinking.

Men get drunk and talk about important things, like sex and whether *The White Album* should have been a double album or a single album. No guy has ever got me drunk and tried to get me to more accurately define my relationship with my mother. Sure, every once in a while some sweaty bastard will have a little too much, put on *Pet Sounds* and try to convince you that Brian Wilson is a genius, but you learn how to handle them eventually.

I miss them. Fortunately, I know where to find them as they graze free in their natural habitat: the used record store. Against the background metronomic click of cds being flipped, I hear that voice. I barely understand it anymore but it still makes me thirsty.

"Hey, this is something you might want to see, this guy was the original bass player for T. Rex, Bolan fired him before they recorded the first single, but these are some tracks that he did with a guy that had played with a guy Bowie auditioned for Davy Jones & the Lower Third. They've just been re-mastered and re-released by the Yardbirds' ex-manager's ex-wife, pretty neat huh?"

Hmm . . . I wonder what he's doing after work. Take only pictures, leave only footprints, Vortex Records, don't crowd me in the folk section, and make mine a double.

Increasingly, when confronted with social reality, if that's what you can call a baby shower, I long for complete isolation. Anyone who's been drunk with single men in their mid-twenties has a ten-album, ten-movie list they'd take if they were stranded on a desert island, but I'm the only one I know who's packed.

Like many women of my generation, even those raised in normal families, I took the easy way out, deciding early that love, commitment and responsibility were the answer. I now realize that I just didn't try drinking hard enough. I want to go back. I could get drunk with good bands, with bad bands, with good but derivative bands with great bass players but overrated lead guitarists, with politicians, and writers, the Long Range Planning Division of the un and the guys from the bar with the bricked-in windows near my house.

• • • • •

The Most Boring
Adventure Story
Ever Written

National Post, November 20, 1999

This is one of my favourite pieces, mostly because it really captures a time in my family's life. I never did write a regular column for the *National Post*—with the children taking up most of my time—but for a few years they ran everything I sent them and while it existed, Ellen let me edit the kids' page. This meant that for a few months I got to attend the weekly editorial meetings and pick up promotional movie tie-in toys from a box under someone's desk. These meetings were my journalism school and I am deeply grateful to Ellen and to Jane for the chance.

•

In the year of our Lord 1999, I began reading *The Swiss Family Robinson* to my four- and six-year-old children. It is now November of that same year and there is still no sign of rescue. Our lonely and forsaken condition weighs heavily upon me. I have surveyed the pages for some spark of character development or intrigue, but, alas, have found none.

In vain, I have tried losing the book. Dropped it behind the sofa. The children fetched it. It found its way into the bottom drawer . . . of the fridge. They rescued it. I did something of which I am extremely ashamed. I said, "Take it to your grandmother's. She'll love it."

It came back.

I've tried distracting my children from the many virtues of the good *Swiss Family Robinson* with other books—books with great pictures or books that I had refused to read to them, such as *Animorphs*. I put a big pile of candy all around *Finn Family Moomintroll*. I put delightful accompanying music on for *Stuart Little*. I did a wacky character voice for *The Little Prince*. I installed a laser light show for *A Wrinkle in Time*. They just looked at me with their eager little faces: "Hey look, Mummy, we found *Swiss Family Robinson*. It was in the liquor cabinet." I guess I have to, you know, trust in God and keep reading the damn thing.

The Robinsons, for those who don't know, are a family shipwrecked on an island in the 19th century and they really make the best of it. They make a tent, a fire and eventually, a tree fort. They find food, item by item: they hunt, they gather, they cook, they garnish. They spend a whole page getting salt. Everything is methodically done, efficiently, piously, and then laboriously documented in Father's journal. They make the Ingalls, the austere pioneer family of *Little House on the Prairie* fame, look like *Party of Five*. Father Robinson just never stops building things around the tree fort, full of bravado and sanctimonious good cheer, rigging up conveniences for "my good, brave wife." He's like an out-of-work actor.

Chapter 16: Father decides to make candles. Merciful God, I think, please don't. Or, hey, why not go down to the beach again, maybe some candles washed up there as well. Everything else a Swiss family needs seems to turn up, including, in Chapter 24, a trunk of appropriated jewels and money.

No, not Father, he's going to make the candles for what must be seven bone-chillingly dull pages, starting with:

"The idea of candle-making seemed to have taken the fancy of all the boys; and the next morning they woke, one after the other, with the word candle on their lips. When they were thoroughly roused they continued to talk candles; all breakfast-time, candles were the subject of conversation; and after breakfast they would hear of nothing else but setting to work at once and making candles."

Both my children are breathless with excitement. You see, *we don't know if the candles will work*. Father has no tallow. We must read on, for days.

Now, in the *Little House on the Prairie* books they make their own soap, cure ham, put up preserves, pray religiously and yes, make their own candles, but it's all really interesting. Why, I wondered, are the Robinsons so dull and insufferable about the whole thing? And then it hit me: they're the *Swiss* family Robinson.

I don't know how much of the story is true. Perhaps the author, Johann Wyss, based his tale on a real, incredibly boring family and their, uh, "adventures." In which case, he certainly captured the flat, self-obsessed tone of the average journal keeper.

No, I think it more likely that the antics of Mother, Father, Fritz, Franz, Ernest and Jack are the actual trials of a real family whose ocean voyage went awry. Except, now that I think of it, we really only have their word for it. In terms of a book, movie or TV deal, "shipwrecked" sure sounds a lot better than "dropped off."

I refer to Chapter 3: "At the mention of an excursion, the four children were wild with delight, and, capering around me, clapped their hands for joy. 'Stop!' I exclaimed. 'We have not yet joined in morning prayer. We are only too ready, amid the cares and pleasures of this life, to forget the God to whom we owe all things.'"

Absolutely, dropped off. In fact let's now refer 700-odd pages back, back to page two, on which the lifeboat leaves the sinking ship: "The last of the seamen spring into her and push off, regardless of my cries and entreaties that we might be allowed to share their slender chance of preserving their lives."

I'm right there with you, men. By page 50, I was hoping the seamen would come back, with guns.

Also Fritz is 18 at this point. Isn't he a little old to be capering, if you get my meaning? Does he really *want* the girl who is so conveniently going to wash ashore in Chapter 42? Okay, I've been skipping ahead for the dirty bits. Perhaps Fritz might be happier with a different companion—say, that really great guy Robinson Crusoe found.

By the way, that girl, Jenny, has been living alone, on another, smaller island, for three years—without Father, without running water, since she was 17. Nothing washed up from *her* wreck. She didn't introduce any non-indigenous species to her colony, just Jenny. Jenny never beat a whole colony of apes to death. She seems to have gotten by fine, just fishing. There was no book deal for Jenny, though. "Jenny's Lonely Island" is not a popular Disney attraction. No one ever merchandized "Jenny's Pole, String and Hook." If there is a message here about self-reliance, I hope my children are missing it.

We reach Chapter 6: Mother Makes a Suggestion. It's as good as it sounds. Chapter 7: We Build a Bridge. Guess what happens? I quote: "Adopting my son's idea, we speedily ascertained the distance across to be 18 feet. Then allowing three feet more at each side, I calculated 24 feet as the necessary length of the boards . . ."

I don't want to spoil it for you, but I don't think I'm giving too much away when I tell you that six full pages later, "They danced to and fro on the wonderful structure, singing, shouting and cutting the wildest capers."

Last week, I had a babysitter read to the kids while I went down to the Winchester and listened to some guys complain about their good, brave wives for a few hours. Anything to get out of "New Switzerland" for a while.

The next morning I asked, "So what happened in *The Swiss Family Robinson*?" My youngest child looked at me, tears welling up in his eyes. "Their faithful donkey, Grizzle," he said, "was eaten by a boa constrictor." Bet that took a long time.

What are my children getting from *The Swiss Family Robinson*, I asked myself, that I'm not giving them at home? Maybe I should buy a monkey.

It's Friday night, 7:15. I leave you now. The children have found the book. I had burnt it, but they've downloaded another copy off the internet. It's a new translation. They want to start at the beginning. All hope is lost. The Robinsons are hungry again. They will have to find food. Prepare a meal, praise God for it and affirm their strength as a family unit. Seventy pages later, they'll blow out those damn candles, maybe recap the jolly time they had making them, thank their merciful Lord for that time and finally go to sleep.

Maybe, I turn the page hopefully, there'll be some friendly natives in this chapter, maybe the natives run a little tiki restaurant, maybe tonight the Robinsons will get some take-out and eat it in front of the television. But for the moment, as Father says, "patience and courage."

• • • • •

On an Alleged Personality Flaw

Open Letters, July 11, 2000

Here's an oddity I found when going through my clippings. I wrote this for a website the excellent Paul Tough ran for about a year. I include it partly for his introduction—which I have reprinted here—because I found it immensely encouraging at the time, and partly because I like it.

> Dear Readers,
> [. . .] I have never met Tabatha Southey, author of today's letter. I have, however, admired her as a writer and a mother ever since she published a mean and funny article (in the form of a letter, no less) in the *National Post* about how much her young children loved, and she despised, *The Swiss Family Robinson*. And so when Ian Brown and I first began casting around for open-letter-writers, we tried to track her down, but found the task unexpectedly difficult. She became a talisman, a grail, an unreachable—and then she just wandered into Ian's living room one night, and that seemed like a good sign.
>
> I love the way she writes about her not-quite-intact family, and life in Toronto. I hope she'll do more of it for Open Letters. And I trust she'll take these sentiments entirely the wrong way.
>
> Yours truly,
> Paul Tough

•

To Whom It May Concern,
The other day someone suggested to me that I might be defensive.

"Me?" I said. "I am not. I really don't think so. What gives you the right to make that judgment?"

"Well," she said, "I am your therapist."

"Oh," I said, "and that somehow gives you insight into my personal life?"

"I've been your therapist for two years," she replied.

"Big deal," I responded, wittily.

"Twice a week."

"Oh yeah, right, 'doctor.' That's impressive."

"It's simply been my observation that you might be somewhat defensive in your personal relationships."

What an idiot. She knows nothing about me, I thought. But later on I started wondering about it. What if she's right? What if I *am* defensive? That's not a good thing to be, "defensive," is it? That's not an attractive personality trait. Actually it's pretty much a fault. I felt vulnerable. It was just possible that I could legitimately be criticized for my defensive posturing. Damn it. Something had to be done. I must, I reasoned, become less defensive, *today*, before someone else figures it out and cruelly blindsides me.

This was a breakthrough.

Strategically, I knew that until I had this minor personality flaw ironed out, it would be best if I retreated to a more defensible position. My house is tall, and when under siege, I occupy the upper floors. As a last resort I have determined that the third-floor shower, with me armed with a bottle of wine, a good (though wet) book, and a razor, is by far the most defensible position in my house. "I can't talk now," I can say if anyone calls. "I'm in the shower, at the end of a really good book, and I have to shave my legs, and you can't take any of this seriously because I'm drunk."

Twice a week my therapist and I get together and examine that core question of modern psychoanalysis: "What the fuck is wrong with Tabatha?" And when I think of the progress I've made I'm, well, I'm defensive, but still, progress, it's there, *okay?*

Consider this: about a year after we separated, my ex-husband took me out for a lovely dinner by the ocean, at one of our favourite restaurants. After the main course, he looked up at me from the dessert menu and asked, knowingly, "So, are you going to order the crème brûlée?" That *bastard*. I was very upset but I couldn't figure out exactly why, until my therapist suggested to me that the level of intimacy the question implied bothered me. After 11 years of marriage, that man had the nerve to assume that he knew what my favourite dessert was.

That was another breakthrough.

My therapist and I talked it through for a while, and I was able to use my new self-awareness to arrive at a solution. Next time I'm in a long-term relationship with a man, I'm always going to order the almond torte with orange sherbet. That way, when we split up after 11 years and he takes me out for dinner and says, "So, are you going to order the almond torte with orange sherbet?" I can say, "No, I *hate* almond torte. I don't *like* orange sherbet. You know *nothing* about me." My therapist asked whether 11 years of bad dessert and self-denial would be worth this "small victory."

Sometimes I wonder if she's even listening.

Although I rely on geographic isolation, living as I do at the top of a fully detached late-Victorian alp, I am still capable of strategic advances. It's another Saturday night, and I've not only maintained my position, I also opened last week's mail. Greenpeace is asking if I want to renew my support. What the hell is that supposed to mean? My Clinique bonus is waiting for me at Holt Renfrew. I knew that. And you, the Committee of Adjustment, have turned down my application for a portcullis at the front door. It's against the stupid building code.

Idiots.

Love,
Tabatha

Summer Camping

Explore Magazine

Here's the piece I thought was my big break. Not yet writing for *The Globe*, I came back from a camping trip to an email from an editor at the *New York Times*, asking if I'd like to submit for a new "slice of life" type feature they were about to start running. Boy, did I. I wrote this right away, sent it in and got an email saying, "Great, we'll be running it soon."

I was pretty excited! And then a few days later I got an email from a fact-checker. He had been unable to locate the study I cite, he wrote. Could I please direct him to the research that indicated that the majority of branches in a forest had been urinated upon by a bear.

I could not, I explained, because it was a joke.

Well, said the *New York Times*, we don't run things that aren't true. And that is how my big break went bust.

A while later I sent it to *Explore Magazine* and they kindly gave a home to my lie.

•

In the summertime, when the living is easy, I like to go camping and make it really difficult again. I like to cut cheese with a fish-gutting knife directly onto a rotten picnic bench for my two eager children and then perhaps cook up a hot dog over an open fire on a stick that in all statistical likelihood has been pissed upon by a bear. I like to stand outside my tent wearing a mid-length cotton nightie over some stained sweatpants and a smart pair of yellow flip-flops, wave at my fellow campers and exchange insights with them about the weather, even though—all the while I am doing this—I am brushing my teeth.

When the earth is at its most bountiful and the trees are dense with fruit I like to abandon the lushness of the fruit belt and drive as far north as I possibly can. Here, I buy up the shrivelled end of last year's apples, a loaf of Wonder Bread, some ash-grey hamburger meat and a few pounds of that really inexpensive brand of bacon that is entirely white because you know what? *You just never see bacon like that in the city.* I like to down all of that, oh, and some bear piss.

I like to pretend that I am alpha-tent.

I like to sit peacefully with my trusty dog by the campfire reflecting Thoreau-like on the higher laws and Nature with a capital N as opposed to nature with a lower case n. And then, on the subject of lower cases, I like to wonder about the sleeping arrangements of the ubiquitous trio of mixed-sex campers who always take the site one over from me and who never fail to have between them nine children named Madison and four burly Akitas. And then I like to get up and move my plastic lawn chair to dodge the smoke from the fire and then I like to poke the fire with a wet stick. Then I like to move my chair again and then I start to wonder exactly what Thoreau meant by *"hoary* blueberries" and whether he might have chosen a similar word for those leggy girls over at site #455 who don't seem to understand what the higher law "no radios" means. And then I like to get up and move my plastic lawn chair again . . . and then more bear piss . . . move chair . . . bed.

I bring a bag of frozen milk to the wilderness. It melts and goes off in less than two hours. I buy fresh ice for the cooler every day, driving 25 miles to find a store that sells only ice, tent pegs and vanilla fudge that I have never actually eaten but that looks suspiciously *exactly* like the bacon. I put the ice in the cooler where it melts the second it has punctured the bag of milk and squished the tomatoes. "Mission accomplished," I tell my two young children. "Dinner tonight will be a sour milk–based gazpacho . . . oh, and some bear piss."

"Hey kids," I like to yell loudly to my offspring, "get the hell over here before the dog eats your burger!"

Late at night I like to stoke up the campfire good and strong, boil some water over my camp stove, crack open a beer and then wash blue metal dishes for three hours. The soft clinking of wet blue metal dishes spills out from every other site in the park like blue metal crickets (being washed) and then the sound reverberates through the forest. Nearby, close to the lake, someone strums a guitar and sings Joni Mitchell. I hate Joni Mitchell, and off in the distance I hear someone call out, "Hey kids, get the hell over here before the dog eats your burger!"

You should know that the Coleman Exponent lightweight lantern is, as the box says, "bright enough to read by." It is impressively bright, *really, truly bright*, I think admiringly. Certainly, it seems to me that the flame is even more luminous than the 75-watt bulb it is compared to on the box. Very, very easy to read by, I realize, *so* much brighter than a mere puny little 75-watt bulb, certainly bright enough for me to eventually read the words, "CAUTION: Flames other than at the mantle indicate a fuel leak. TURN FUEL VALVE OFF, allow flames to burn out and lantern to cool before re-lighting." We sit, my children and I, and then we move our chairs, and then we sit and we watch the blackened lantern cool, and before we know it—it is morning.

In the autumn, I return to the land of plenty, of flush toilets and meat-ed bacon. It is good to be home and realize just how much your sleeping bags stink. You appreciate how bright and modern everything is, at the laundromat . . . for three hours, where the change machine is invariably out of order and you run out of coins before that crucial fifth drying cycle and then you walk home with three wet sleeping bags in a bundle buggy, meeting your ex-lover on the way, a man you haven't seen in some years, and he stares at you, still in your sweatpants, pushing your bundle buggy bulging with sodden blue poly-fil, and he shakes his head a bit and then he says meaningfully, "How *are* you?"

And you say helplessly, "I have a washing machine. And Chanel boots!" But he knows that what you really have is an unquenchable thirst for bear piss.

• • • • •

Underwear
by Edith Wharton

National Post, July 19, 2003

After a while I was asked to review books for the *National Post* and I couldn't have been happier about that. Books were something to do.

I still wasn't sure what it was I wanted to write about, and in fact had very little time in which I could write, but I knew I did not want to write exclusively, or all that much, about myself. Although somehow mostly oblivious to the Bridget Jonesing of women journalists that was then in full swing, I knew that when someone at an editorial meeting said, "Hey! We should send Tabatha speed-dating!" I should say "no," and I did. What I still believe to be a virtual dead end was avoided.

One night at a friend's movie opening I met Martin Levin, who, although I did not know it when we were introduced, was at the time and for many years *The Globe and Mail*'s books editor, and something of a legend.

Martin asked me what I did, as one does at parties, and I told him that I was "sort of a writer." When asked what I wrote I said, "I just started writing book reviews."

I never did send Martin the clippings he kindly invited me to send (paperwork issues again) but I'd given him my business card which read "Tabatha Southey, Single Mother, phone ____ fax ____ cell ____ email ____" and on the basis of that card, as he later said, Martin sent me this book and asked me to review it.

•

Trading Up
By Candace Bushnell
Hyperion
404 pages, $36.95

> *"Above all, you must illumine your own soul with its profundities*
> *and its shallows, and its vanities and its generosities, and say*
> *what your beauty means to you or your plainness, and what is*
> *your relation to the ever-changing and turning world of gloves*
> *and shoes . . ."*
> —Virginia Woolf

I already had reading plans for the weekend. I'd just been given a book about the Donner Party that I was very much looking forward to. Yet, when a copy of Candace Bushnell's (*Sex and the City*, *4 Blondes*) new novel, *Trading Up*, arrived at my door on Friday evening with a note suggesting I might review it, I knew immediately that the Donners would have to wait.

I've never much recommended the other chick lit books assigned to me and the response to my reviews from friends has always been frustration. "But Tabatha," they explain to me, "those books aren't meant to be good. They're meant to be read at the beach." And so on Saturday morning I rose eagerly, wrapped the book in a towel, jumped on my bike and went straight down to the lake. I so wanted to get this one right.

Trading Up is the story of the vain and manipulative Janey Wilcox, a top Victoria's Secret model who will stop at nothing to claw her way to the pinnacle of New York society and . . . I've never really understood the beach. It's very sandy, but lulled by the soft-tongue lapping of Lake Ontario, toes buried in the sand, kept awake by the sounds of the many people seemingly enjoying the sorts of sports routinely organized in POW camps, that all sounded reasonable enough to me.

The beach isn't so bad, I decided, reading on. After all, it's near the water. Janey goes to a party in the Hamptons and there's a handsome polo player and she pretends to make friends with a woman who we are told wears "her birthright as easily as a fashionable woman wears designer dresses." Now, just for a second I thought, aren't fashionable women fashionable women *because* they wear designer dresses? So, I thought, concentrating hard, isn't the author saying, "she wore her birthright as easily as people with a birthright wear that birthright." But then I thought, hey, is that a one-legged seagull?—and went off to get a closer look.

Trading Up begs to be compared to the works of Edith Wharton. Bushnell is obviously a fan and, although the gap between "reads like" and "likes to read" is a staggering one, I sat up on my towel, ignored the seagulls and tried sombrely to consider the difficulties inherent in writing a contemporary "society novel."

Is it still possible for a writer to draw tension from a character's disgrace (Janey is disgraced) when "society" is no longer insular, scandal is often lucrative and the worst fate society women risk is that of having to work at a real job? Would Tolstoy's novel have endured, I wondered, if Anna Karenina had merely been driven to get her real estate licence, the fear of which pushes poor Janey into a loveless marriage? Can one rewrite *The Age of Innocence*, I wondered, in the age of . . . and then I just wondered how far I'd have to walk to buy ice cream . . . and then, lying back on my towel, enormous pink book in hand, I abandoned myself to my own vanity and imagined that every man walking by me was sighing sadly to himself and thinking, "Now that would be my ideal woman, if only she were reading a book about the Donner Party."

Trading Up is not a sexy book—but for the many past-tense references to career-move blow jobs specifically given in bathrooms, there's almost no sex at all. Maybe it was the sun, but I began to get obsessed.

When I lived in New York, I went to the kinds of clubs and restaurants in which our heroine professes to have performed these acts. Almost without exception, what passes for a bathroom in these places is a very tiny room involving a good-sized bathroom attendant, an even larger floral arrangement, one toilet and an inevitably star-studded lineup outside the door. Nobody's doing anybody in the bathroom. You don't have the time. You don't have the space, and to my mind it'd be difficult to stay properly engaged in something like that with Kate Winslet banging on the door because she's desperate for a pee.

Maybe it's different in the men's. Maybe there's a waifish attendant in the men's, a rose in a stem vase and acres of wide-open country. Maybe there's an orgy in the men's. I won't speak for the men's, but I promise you everyone's pretty hard up in the ladies'. I never saw any sex in the ladies' room. Even the conversations are a bit chilly.

Is it believable, I asked myself, gazing at the horizon, that a woman would be catapulted into overnight underwear model fame in her thirties? How does a 6 × 9–inch book manage to have an 8 × 10–inch glossy of the author on the back cover? Are the characters shuffled artlessly about as if that 8 × 10 author were a parking attendant in a full lot trying to get to the red van? Is the novel's relentless cynicism just boring, I wondered, watching a fistful of hot sand pour through my fingers like a fistful of hot sand pouring through my fingers? I can't say, I thought, but those kids over there sure look as if they could use some help with that sandcastle.

Sunday it rained. I took the book to bed, opened it and, of course, got the bed full of sand. Clearly, I have a lot to learn about beach reading. In Book 3, Janey leaves Manhattan for Paris and recalls her former life there as a naive, young, money-grubbing prostitute, and then an incomprehensible dream involving the rescue of a sad dolphin makes her reflective. Janey is 33 years old, after all (that's 56 in underwear model years), and this maturity causes her to wonder if "somewhere down the road of her life she might have made a wrong turn and if that wrong turn was like a tree trunk, spawning a series of branches that had also become wrong paths." Now, I'm all confused. Is it a road or a tree, and why, if it is either or both of these things, is it spawning?

Why was I so willing to desert the Donner Party for Candace Bushnell? Because I think these books are meant to be, and deserve to be, judged on a case-by-case basis. I'm convinced that from somewhere in that big pile of pink books a few worthwhile ones will emerge. One day, a woman will sit down and write the "sentimental histoire" of an underwear model, a vh1 vj and a polo player, and in the sum total of its trivial detail and petty love affairs that novel will break our hearts. From the frenzy of chick lit, a few writers will stand up alongside Nancy Mitford and Clare Boothe Luce, Edith Wharton, George Eliot, Jane Austen and all the other smart, sexy, candid women who wrote the chick lit of their generations, and I don't want to miss them.

Stay with me one last minute, while having lost the battle fought on the beaches, I fight the chick lit war. Imagine that Shakespeare had a sister . . . no, not that sister, another sister, the kind of sister who put boy band posters up all over her walls and was always borrowing your clothes. Supposing that sister one day, having done everything possible with her friend's hair, concluded that she too had a genius for fiction and "lusted to feed abundantly upon the lives of men and women and the study of their ways." Shouldn't we give her a room as well?

A Day in the Life of a Flighty Urbanite

Elle Canada, March 2005

My Bushnell book review is what led *Elle Canada* to offer me a monthly column in the character of "Elle Girl." Columns from that gift of a gig, a gig I did for over 10 years, are dotted throughout this book, and this is one of them.

•

I was parking the other day and just as I pulled into the space—a legal parking space—I heard a sound. It was a loud sound and a new sound to me and I would like to be able to say that it sounded like *something*. I would like to be able to say that it sounded like a pudding-filled balloon exploding or like a piece of bubble wrap bursting in a sewer, but it didn't. It didn't sound like anything except exactly what it was: a great big snow tire rolling over a live pigeon. There was another aspect to the sound, a resonance I couldn't put my finger on until I stepped out onto the curb and the teenage girl who was sitting on the bench nearby said, "Hey, you just ran over the pigeon that was eating my hot dog."

She then turned to her boyfriend and, throwing her leg over him, began necking passionately. I can't explain why this girl had abandoned her hot dog in the only parking space available in a four-block radius or why she and her man seemed to find the sad but, I would like to point out, reasonably predictable death of this bird so erotic. I only know that the entire city block seemed to go into mourning.

"Did you see what you did?" the nearby hot dog vendor said to me. "You killed that pigeon."

"I know," I said. "I didn't see the pigeon. I feel terrible," I added truthfully.

"You ran right over it," the teenage boy said, taking a breather. "It was just eating my girlfriend's hot dog," he said in shock.

"It was a *tofu* dog," the girlfriend added pointedly.

"A vegetarian dog," the vendor confirmed.

I wondered if I was expected to look under my car. "I didn't see it," I said. "Pigeons are grey and small and the streets are slushy. I just saw a parking space," I said. "I was just running into the butcher's . . ."

"Figures," a passerby said, joining the gathering crowd, and I realized that I was wearing my vintage mink coat.

"I'm having a friend to dinner," I said for no reason at all, and at this point I have to confess something. I drive an suv. That's right, I drive a big gas-guzzling, pigeon-killing, four-wheel drive truck, in the city. So there I was, standing beside my suv, which was parked on top of a dead bird, and, okay, I also happened to be wearing my—no, not, I'm afraid, my demure brown Miu Miu Mary Janes; not on this, the day of the great pigeon slaughter—I was wearing my patent-leather, four-inch-high, spike-heeled, pigeon-blood-red Christian Louboutins and, of course, my mink coat. I was Cruella de Vil.

"He's married," I blurted out for no reason. "The man who's coming for dinner is married. We're just friends, but you might as well know that I'm an suv-driving, pigeon-killing, mink-coat-wearing woman who's just popping into the *butcher's* for some chicken, chicken that I'm planning on brining and marinating in really good wine, not cooking wine, but good wine, good South African wine that was bottled in the de Klerk era, which I've been saving for the right married man, and then I'll be cooking that chicken and serving it to that married man, who also happens to be the father of three children."

Gasps from the crowd, a raised pitchfork.

"They're all under the age of six months and . . . hey, does anyone have a cigarette?" I continued. "One of them is in a wheelchair."

"Who would put a six-month-old child in a wheelchair?" someone cried out from the back.

"He would," I said. "Which may be why his wife doesn't understand him. Now if you'll excuse me," I said, "there's an endangered squirrel up in Forest Hill with my name on it."

• • • • •

Whores, Hamsters
and Head-Butts

The Globe and Mail, August 5, 2006

Coming almost full circle, it was in fact my "Elle Girl" column that eventually landed me my column in *The Globe and Mail*. I was daunted by the idea of weekly humour when offered the chance and, mostly just to prove to myself that I could, I swore I'd do Tart, as I named my column, for one year.

One thing I had not considered at that point—*Elle* did not include my email address in each issue—is that writing means readers, and they are why I let that one-year thing drop.

It is the unfailing support, feedback, wit, wisdom and flat-out kindness of my *Globe and Mail* readers, many of whom email me, from all parts of the country and from many parts of the world, some almost every week, that has kept me at the Tarts.

It's a privilege to sometimes be a part of our national conversation, or just to be a moment of someone's weekend morning, and then to have so many readers drop me a line means everything. I owe my readers so much, but I can only offer this book, which they sometimes enquire about, and a sincere thank you to all of you who have read and written and kept me at this fun and rewarding job for more than 10 years.

Here is what was basically my first Tart. For those who have forgotten, what happened was this: With France and Italy locked at 1–1 and the match in extra time, the legendary Zinédine Zidane had walked past Azzurri defender Marco Materazzi. The two exchanged words and then Zidane head-butted Materazzi with alarming force. What, exactly, those words were was the subject of many rumours and much speculation.

Three weeks after Italy took the World Cup from France, after wit-nessing first-hand the joy on College Street in Toronto, having heard the chart-topping head-butt song (*Coupe de Boule*) with which the French are currently consoling themselves, and after considerable reflection, I realized that there was a lesson to be drawn from all of this, and I called my two young children to my side.

Basically I said, "Look kids, there's something I have to tell you, and I want you to listen carefully. If it should ever happen, and I know it seems unlikely, that either one of you should find yourself playing for Canada, final game, in extra time for the World Cup, and someone from the opposing team should sidle up to you and call me a whore—*don't* dismiss it out of hand.

"All I'm saying is, at least consider the possibility. After all, do either one of you really know where the money comes from? No, you don't, do you?

"This is certainly not a confession, and I don't mean to alarm you. But I do want you to promise me that, if someone, particularly in a high-stakes situation, ever calls me a whore, you will, before you lower your head and ram it directly into your fellow sportsman's chest, take a second to consider whether your worthy opponent is perhaps employing the word in its less literal sense.

"Perhaps the other player does not really mean that I am a woman who sells sexual favours on the street to strangers for cash, although again, what do you really know about my finances?" I said, looking at their sweet, bashful faces. "Exactly, that's what I thought.

"Perhaps the player means it in a more metaphorical sense, as in, 'Your mother has no firm values and has debased herself by do-ing things for purely monetary reasons.' You know, like shopping at Costco.

"Perhaps he just thinks I look slutty. So, maybe we should agree now that your strategy could be to just play out those last 10 minutes, and then later, after the game, ask if he has any first-hand knowledge of my whoring. Does he have tapes—or receipts?

"Also," I continued, "you two don't have an older sister, but if you ever did and she was on the game, I would have to say that's her perfectly reasonable life choice and no reflection on you. Do you understand?

"After all, you are good enough to play for your country, so if your mother and older sister were both 'whores,' then that would only make you look better. You would have overcome some pretty tough odds, my little darlings, and your big sister and I would be total lost causes—just a couple of no-good whores, walking the streets to keep you in cleats.

"There'd be nothing to be gained by defending our honour," I assured them, "except—considering Zinédine Zidane's punishment—a three-game suspension and a £3,260 fine.

"Do you have any idea," I chided, wagging a finger at them, "exactly what I would have to do to earn £3,260? Don't even think about it.

"Finally," I added, "and I think this should be all I need to say on the subject—if, supposing, with 10 minutes left to play in the match that may well decide your legacy—will it be twice a World Cup winner or mere novelty song subject—someone should call me, your sweet mother, a hamster, I would want you to let it go, kids, let it go.

"It could be that he's calling me a hamster because he knows that, in all your years in bad neighbourhoods and then pro sports, that might be the one thing you have never heard me called before. Which is why, from now on, just to be on the safe side, as a pre-emptive measure, I want you to start calling me 'Hamster.'

"That's right. No more 'What's for dinner, Mum?' Not if you want an answer in this house. From today forward, I want to hear, 'What's for dinner, Hamster?' Or maybe even 'What's for dinner, Hamster, you whore?'

"Have I made myself clear?" They nodded, and I thought I'd done my duty, but after a wee bit more reflection on the FIFA judgment, I had to call them back in one last time.

"Kids," I said.

"Yes, Hamster," they replied.

"Sit down and listen up. I have to cover yet another base with you. When Marco Materazzi apologized for provoking Zidane and accepted his own £2,170 fine, I recall now that he maintained that his comments were not racist, religious or political, and that he'd said nothing about his mother. Which means, kidlets—and this is women's intuition here and it has been eating away at me all week—that whatever he did say must have had something to do with the size of Zidane's penis.

"Now there's no need to press me on the whys and wherefores of this one, but well, my darling," and I looked straight at my little boy, "it just so happens—long story—that I've seen a fair number of penises in my time and if, in the decisive moments of a World Cup match, in the final game of your remarkable career, someone tries to provoke you by saying something about the size of your penis . . . well," I said, with a breezy gesture of my hands, "based on a random, and I do mean random, sampling, you certainly have nothing to worry about in that department.

"So please promise me now that, if it happens, you'll just let it go, kid, let it go."

• • • • •

The Subprime Mortgage Crisis for Idiots

The Globe and Mail, August 25, 2007

•

Forgive me if I seem preoccupied as I try to explain the subprime mortgage crisis to you. I'm distracted by the fact that you're an idiot. You know how sometimes you'll be talking to an idiot and you'll think, "Hey, does this person know he's an idiot?" and you lose your train of thought? Oh no, sorry, of course you don't. You're an idiot. Never mind.

If I were trying to explain the subprime mortgage crisis to, say, a crazy person, and he began nodding his head slowly up and down, there would always be a chance he was nodding because he believed this rhythmic motion was soothing to the little, soft monkey who lives on the top of his head. That would be challenging too. However, you can usually tell the difference between actual comprehension and mere soothing monkey-rocking by looking the crazy person straight in the eyes—and of course listening for offhand comments addressed to the monkey.

Unfortunately, with an idiot (like you), it's more complicated. Sometimes an idiot will nod because he has seen someone else nod while something was being explained, and sometimes it's because his mind is miles away and what he's actually thinking is, "Yeah, why are teabags square when cups are round? What are those corporate hotshots trying to pull? They'll never fit. I should buy round teabags." So he's nodding, but he has learned next to nothing about subprime mortgages.

Let me try to put the subprime mortgage crisis in the simplest possible terms. Say you're driving the wrong way down the one-way street that I live on. Say you're driving a bronze Range Rover, talking on your cellphone. Say you've turned onto Sumach Street from Winchester Street, failing to notice the "No Right Turn" sign. Say you've already driven past the third Victorian house, the one that was recently re-landscaped using only pea gravel, five granite boulders and less-than-winter-hardy bamboo (idiots), before you notice your error. Do not speed up.

Driving your Range Rover the wrong way down a one-way street really fast so that you spend less time in the act of driving the wrong way down a one-way street (like an idiot) is not necessarily the best solution. I can see why you might think it would be (the idiot thing again), but, in fact, it's not. Cars turning north off Carlton Street won't be expecting you. They'll turn legally (and with average intelligence) straight into you—speeding and still on your cellphone. The vehicles will collide, totalling your car. Your insurance will go up and the point is you probably can't afford this because of the subprime mortgage crisis. Get it, you idiot?

Let me explain another way. Say you're an idiot, which I'm assuming you are because this article is called "The Subprime Mortgage Crisis for Idiots" and you're reading it. So say you're an idiot, unless—and this might just be true—you're reading this just in case you're approached by a real, live, walking, talking (though not at the same time) idiot who asks you to explain the subprime mortgage crisis to him in language that he will understand and you want to be prepared. In which case please disregard the fact that I keep calling you an idiot. You're not an idiot. None of this "you're an idiot" talk is addressed to you, and don't actual idiots drive you crazy, the way they have no comprehension of the subprime mortgage crisis? Me too!

Oh, sorry, did I offend you, Idiot? That wasn't something you wanted to hear, Idiot? Well, take your fingers out of your ears. You're reading this. Plugging your ears won't work.

Anyway, as I was trying to say, liquidity in the market is reliant upon . . . oh, good Lord. You're holding your nose now, aren't you? You idiot.

• • • • •

The Strain on Brains
Comes Mainly
Near the Planes

The Globe and Mail, September 8, 2007

On June 11, 2007, Larry Craig, then a Republican senator from Idaho, was arrested on suspicion of "lewd conduct" at the Minneapolis–Saint Paul International Airport. A police officer staking out a bathroom stall as part of an undercover operation investigating complaints of sexual activity in the restroom arrested Mr. Craig. The arrest and his subsequent plea to a lesser charge of disorderly conduct meant his career was effectively over.

•

In defence of Larry Craig, airports are boring. You do things that maybe you shouldn't do. I, for example, bought a bottle of Yves Saint Laurent perfume at the duty-free a few months ago that I really shouldn't have. We all feel a bit reckless and entitled in an airport—especially if our flight is delayed.

Senator Craig, the poor lost soul, was arrested in an interstate airport where they don't even have a duty-free. His options for misbehaviour were more limited.

At the airport, you watch traveller after traveller try on a pair of sunglasses, read the back of a Tom Clancy novel, consider and reject a shoeshine and then head for the Western-themed bar—demoralized, trundling a suitcase, three gates from the hostess stand, resigned already to the nachos. Airport hours feel like hours that don't count against you, like hours not deducted from your life. You're carrying all your identification, dangling the odd label, but you feel at your most anonymous. Seems that way to me. Might have seemed that way to Larry Craig on June 11th, the day he was arrested.

Larry Craig made a bigger, costlier airport mistake than most of us make, bigger than the Yves Saint Laurent perfume, bigger than the nachos and scotch I ordered at Pearson—but still, on balance, smaller than one of those Gucci scarves. Mr. Craig gave two versions of what that mistake was. There's a signed confession of guilt and there's a police transcript recording both his "I have a wide stance" explanation for his stall-based toe-tapping and the assertion that far from signalling under the divider, Mr. Craig was merely picking up toilet paper from the bathroom floor.

I'm not particularly pro-bathroom-sex—personally, I don't even like cars—but the sting was cruel and unfair. Police seldom stake out the Western-themed airport bars of the world where straight men make endless overtures, oblivious to the fact that they have something akin to a bundle buggy propped up against their bar stools, which turns me right off. Of Mr. Craig's two accounts, only one provoked actual revulsion in me: who picks up toilet paper from a public bathroom floor?

Much this week was written about the elaborate bathroom-sex code in which Mr. Craig appeared well versed. He has done for loo cruising what Monica Lewinsky did for the blow job. As an outsider, I'm fascinated. Women are never still or alone in a bathroom. We're forever passing toilet paper under, throwing tampons over, holding each other's doors, watching each other's drinks, tucking each other's labels. Often there's some freaky girl who thinks you'll let her borrow your lipstick.

Anyone trying to read a code into ten minutes of commonplace women's bathroom interaction might conclude we'd just covertly arranged to steal spoons from the cafeteria, organize a choir to disguise the sound of the digging and tunnel out at midnight.

Probably when Mr. Craig says, "I am not gay," and the odder, "I never have been gay" (as in "Are you now or have you ever been a member of the Communist Party?"), he believes it. He's not gay. He's gay-in-an-airport, a limbo where, I concede, something peculiar overcomes one in regards to character and ability: once, at Charles de Gaulle, I bought a pocket book of Sudoku.

Democrats are wisely silent on Mr. Craig, but, judging from GOP response to the enduring scandal, it's safe to say that should he continue to fight to overturn his guilty plea, they'll merrily contribute to his defence fund.

When I look at Mr. Craig, his polonium-210'd face makes me sad. He looks lost, as if he's scanning the crowd. It's the familiar, apprehensive expression one sees on a traveller's face as he comes through the opaque-glass doors just after clearing customs, the look of a man headed through the arrivals gate after an exhausting journey—an old man in a foreign country, who needs now more than ever to be picked up at the airport.

Harper's "Ethnic Outreach Team" and the "Festival of Another Man Tarring My Driveway"

The Globe and Mail, October 20, 2007

•

The absence of any Conservative MPs at my door this week leads me to believe that white Zimbabweans are not on the list of immigrant populations that the Conservatives recognize as sharing their party's values. This comes as a bit of a surprise to me. White people of African descent have a long history of racial profiling.

Earlier this week, *The Globe and Mail* obtained documents outlining the Tories' policy of using a designated "ethnic outreach team" to identify and target specific ethnic and religious groups for their votes. Conservatives are being encouraged to attend "major ethnic events" held by the 79 percent of those groups identified as "accessible communities," which I guess my family and I are not, because the Conservatives never come to any of our events or send us anything in the mail. We never get biltong on July 5 (Cecil Rhodes's birthday) and no one has ever promised us an investigation into why Loblaws no longer carries Mrs. Ball's chutney.

Possibly I've misread how untargeted my family is. Maybe we're one of the groups Conservatives (understandably) take for granted. Or maybe Conservatives, who've been told to "look outside your normal comfort zone," feel that my family lies outside even their not-so-comfortable zone—you know, that zone that's right next to their comfort zone, that's also white and straight and comfortable, but offers a bit less legroom.

Possibly, we reside six zones from the Conservative comfort zone, beyond their I'm-sure-I-can-be-made-comfortable-if-I-have-a-stiff-drink-in-my-hand-and-oh-my-God-these-aren't-the-people-who-don't-drink-are-they-and-will-that-mean-I'm-going-to-have-to-eat-barbecued-dog zone. Or maybe, because we're one of the more minor minorities, they're not sure how to approach us.

So, as a service, I'm offering a few tips.

Any candidate vying for my dad's vote would be wise to take some time this autumn to actively celebrate with him the traditional Zimbabwean "Give Me a Hand with the Gutters, Will You, Mate? Weekend."

It's not a festival I remember fondly from my childhood—involving as it does a surprisingly dense compound of bird droppings and wet leaves—but, as expat Zimbabweans know, it falls close to our more charming "Bag Those Leaves for Me Will You, Love? Sunday," a day when children get five dollars or "a good clip 'round the ear."

Similarly, savvy Canadian politicians should learn that in our native land it is a long-established ritual that shortly after the harvest, ambitious politicians show up at constituents' homes carrying sturdy ladders and offering to put up the constituents' storm windows. This is generally done while all eligible voters are in the house watching boxing.

A more informed politician might question the veracity of my statements here on the grounds that Zimbabwe is a very hot country and it's therefore curious that a festival involving eligible voters and storm windows should evolve, and he'd be right. It's damn hot in Zimbabwe. Which is why, tradition also has it, the ambitious politician brings cold beer.

Canadians of Lebanese origin might recognize similarities between this Zimbabwean holiday and their own spring "Festival of Another Man Tarring My Driveway"—a joyous occasion, not unlike the more secular "Sure, You Clean My Car and I'll Read Your Damn Pamphlet Day," observed by many Hindus.

Honestly, New Canadians, you mustn't be shy. Invite your local candidates to these events—show off your heritage. Why, the Scots have had the Tories round to celebrate their annual "Change the Bulbs in My Christmas Lights Eve" for generations.

Also, a final tip for Tories: in Estonia, a campaigning politician would never kiss a baby. Instead, he'd take the baby from its mother's arms, change it, feed it, burp it, put it to bed, tidy the kitchen and then fold laundry until the mum came home.

Now that you know, join in these festivals, Tories. Don't worry yourselves so much. Everything tastes like chicken.

The Conservatives have stated that there's "growing anecdotal evidence that New Canadian values are more aligned with the values of the Conservative Party of Canada." Well, perhaps, but I'm cautious. Anecdotal evidence concerning ethnic groups often begins: "A Jew, an Arab and an Irish guy walked into a bar . . ."

It's better to send the same message to everyone and then walk in the streets, go to work or go to school. You're in Canada. The country itself is a "major ethnic event."

Lust, Revenge, Intrigue— Ah, the Pleasures of Summer Reading

Elle Canada, April 21, 2005

•

When I was about 14 years old, I read a book that I now recognize as Kate Millett's *Sexual Politics*, which contained a chapter on the sexual subjugation of women in literature, and I thought, "*That* is hot." Later, I read all the works of Henry James, looking for the works of Henry Miller (Henry James . . . *Daisy Miller* . . . Henry . . .). Well, that's just the sort of mistake you make when you're reading in the dark.

I read in the dark or the near-dark in my bedroom, down a short hall from my parents' room. I feigned a humiliating fear of sleeping in the pitch-black after my big brother left our shared bedroom and ran off to live in the basement.

The post-bedtime reading calculation, involving the amount of light needed (hall light or just bathroom?) and the width my bedroom door had to be ajar, was a challenge. If the door was open too wide, I lost the split-second lead time it took to hide the book under the covers should one of my parents check on me. If the door was shut too far, I misread Roald Dahl's *Danny, the Champion of the World* and believed that it was possible to write a funny, sweet story about a boy and his father who live in a caravan behind their semi-rural car garage and hunt and eat *peasants*.

The agreement we hammered out allowed the bottom corner of my bedroom door to be left open to the point where it lined up with the northern corner of my rug, which I later shifted a few inches in my favour. The bathroom light could stay on, my mum agreed, but the bathroom door had to be closed. The hall light was a given, and sometime during my John le Carré phase, I fetched the ladder and secretly switched it to a 100-watt bulb.

Our house was small although, inexplicably, the basement—to which I eventually lost all my brothers—was big. But in the sloped-ceiling upstairs part of the house, the sound of a page being turned travelled like bad news, and the door–light–speed calculation had to account for this. Even now, when I'm reading by the light of my choice in my own home, I catch myself pausing after each page turn, straining my ears for a sign that I've been caught. I listen fearfully for someone to shout, "It's bedtime!" or, worse yet, the still horrifying, "You have school in the morning."

I learned to make a covering-up noise at the end of every page. Yawn. Turn page. Cough. Turn page. Snuffle. Turn page. My parents thought I was asthmatic. I later learned this was the reason why I was never allowed to join the warren of brothers in the damp basement where, hidden away, I could have switched on the bedside lamp and tackled all those Russian names and French marriages on surer ground.

It's not that my parents were anti-reading parents. They weren't. The before-bedtime reading of English books by English writers was encouraged. My mother believes the world of books can be summed up this way: English writers good; North American writers bad. It's much the same with television: English television good; North American television bad. *I, Claudius* good. *Are You Being Served?* equally good. No further distinction was made. I read the semi-pornographic multi-volume novelization of *Upstairs, Downstairs* in full view of my parents. Yet I may have been the only child in the world with Farley Mowat hidden under the mattress. I would lie over him waiting for the perfect bulb-watt-open-door-full-moon-drape-gap alignment, always half hoping for the baby brother to cry and smother the sound of the pages recklessly flipped over. So that to me is the promise of summer. It's the day stretched out long like an exhausted animal, the light still coming in through the pale curtains and me in my bed—knees camping in my cotton nightie—reading, pleading with the sun so suddenly patient to stay with me until the end of the last chapter.

Pitch In to Keep
This Country Dirty—
and Its Obscenely
Creative Spirits Free

The Globe and Mail, March 8, 2008

When I filed this column I did not expect it would earn me the honour of being the writer with the word "fuck" used more times in a single story than any writer in *The Globe and Mail*'s history—a record I still hold. I assumed the word would be presented as it was being used in the promotional material for the film I was discussing, like this: "F_ _ cking."

I was told, however, to *The Globe*'s credit, that they don't "bleep." It was fucking or nothing, bless them. I was asked to cut the number down, to give less fucks, and I did, negotiating for as much fucking as I could get.

I got seven fucks in the end, but here the column is printed as it was written, in all its fucking glory.

•

It's ironic that evangelist Charles McVety gleefully took credit for influencing the government on Bill c-10, a bill that would allow the heritage minister to withhold tax credits if a film is judged, upon completion, to be "contrary to public policy."

After all, it's not as if the churches in Canada don't receive a number of tax breaks of their own, and not upon their work's completion, either. No one says to Canada's evangelists, "Keep up your good works, people, and all of your donors will indeed get tax receipts—just as soon as Jesus shows up and believers are saved."

Predictably, provocatively, almost every newspaper article written about Bill C-10 mentioned the film entitled *Young People Fucking*. I'm glad, though, because it underscores just how arbitrary this censoring process would undoubtedly be.

Such smaller, easily red-flagged films would be the ones least able to afford the lawyers needed to fight their case or to offer skittish investors assurances that the film tax credit wouldn't be withheld. They would fail first.

Under C-10, the onus could fall upon filmmakers to prove to financers that "public policy" did not currently prohibit young people (say, Romeo and Juliet) from fornicating—and, what's more, that this public policy wouldn't change over the couple of years the film was in production.

Heritage Minister Josée Verner has argued that Bill C-10 is not about censorship. It was intended, she claims, to ensure that the government "won't fund extreme violence, child pornography or something like that."

Many brilliant films contain sex, extreme violence and heroes robbing banks. The term "contrary to public policy," apart from having a retro, Soviet ring to it, is only slightly less vague than Ms. Verner's "something like that." I'm not sure what either phrase might exclude, but I'm definitely afeard for David Cronenberg—and ditto for Theodore Tugboat.

One hopes Ms. Verner knows that child pornography is already illegal in this country and that child pornographers (being criminals) generally file as few government forms as possible.

Child pornographers are not on the phone to the bank first thing Monday morning saying, "I think we can get four 11-year-olds, a dingy motel room and an Akita, provided we can recoup some of the labour costs through a 25-percent tax credit." They don't apply for arts grants, either.

Trying to end child pornography through Bill c-10 is like trying to end pot smoking by cutting off tax relief to farmers or university loans to agricultural students, while simultaneously banning corner-store sales of salty snacks.

Bill c-10 is a "Norwegian Wood" law—like the Beatles song, its wording invites endless interpretation. After hiding the measure within a complex tax bill and passing it without a reading, the Conservatives can hardly expect the public to have faith in its interpretation. "Norwegian Wood" is a solid pop song, but I wouldn't want to hear it covered by REO Speedwagon—or Mussolini.

Several years ago, when the desire to kill Salman Rushdie didn't seem almost prescient, people rightly rallied to his cause as he went underground. Among other things, people wore "I am Salman Rushdie" buttons. Let us see Canadian filmmakers and their supporters take a similar stand.

Bill c-10, because of the public outcry, will probably die in the Senate, but lest this tactic be tried again, let's boldly mark all of our films as obscene—because undoubtedly, of course, to someone, they are.

Let's ask Canadian filmmakers to say proudly that they made *Nobody Fucking Waved Good-bye*, *The Fucking Decline of the Fucking American Empire*, *My Fucking American Cousin*, *The Sweet Fucking Hereafter*, *My Fucking Uncle Antoine*, *The Saddest Fucking Music in the World*, *Atanarjuat: The Fast Fucker*, *Les Boys et le Fucking*, *I've Heard the Mermaids Fucking*, *Thirty Two Short Films About Fucking* and yes, the brilliant *Get the Fuck Away from Her*.

The point is, a law that chokes off some of our films will ultimately kill off all of them. If so, the government would continue to award lesser tax credits to foreign productions, as they should (this industry creates a lot of jobs). But Canadian filmmakers are making it clear they have something to say about this bill—just as they have a lot to say about much else.

Maybe It's Because My Dad Wouldn't Give Me One That I'm So Attracted to Those Little Monkeys

The Globe and Mail, April 12, 2008

•

A study released this week revealed that, when offered a choice, male monkeys played exclusively with toy cars and trucks while female monkeys played with both of these things and stuffed animals as well. I'm reasonably certain that this study won't alter my life either way because the only things I've ever wanted to play with are monkeys.

Obviously, when assessing the depth of mankind's innate preferences, we should avoid weighing the findings of a study like this too heavily. After all, regardless of their individual toy situations, monkeys of both sexes often prefer to play with their own poo. Yet, because I do spend a fair amount of time thinking about monkeys, the study has been on my mind.

I've also been wondering a lot about that other recent monkey study, of course—the one that was published several weeks ago, in which scientists proved conclusively that depressed monkeys with low self-esteem and inadequate accommodations were more likely to use cocaine.

That study was probably a really bad idea. That is definitely a combination laden with its own unique set of problems. You really don't have to be a monkey scientist to see what you're going to end up with once you start going down the depressed-monkey-crap-apartment-low-self-esteem-cocaine road. Everyone knows what you're going to end up with if you give depressed monkeys cocaine. You're going to end up with some insufferable monkeys. But still I would have played with them.

I would have played with the toy-truck-playing monkeys or the stuffed-animal-playing monkeys. Whatever. I would even hang out with the lowest-of-the-low-depressed-cocaine monkey when all of the happy-cool monkeys had ditched him by pretending they were going home to their great condos when really they were going on to another club.

I can just see some hipster monkey signing all that information (all Koko-the-Gorilla-clever) to sad-loser-basement-dwelling monkey.

"Sorry, man," hipster monkey would sign to strung-out monkey, while ducking out. "Missed your message. My machine's been acting up, but sure we should do something sometime, hang out, play with toy trucks, throw poo, bite people, whatever. I'll call you."

Okay, now honestly, readers, is something feeling slightly wrong to you right about now? Wrong with me and this particular aspect of my monkey fantasy? You know, because I'm here, totally latching onto this depressed, addicted monkey like this? Laughing at all his sophomoric, stoned-monkey-eating-with-his-feet jokes? And lending him money?

Does it make you uncomfortable that the entire time that I'm peeling more bananas for him (just trying to get him to eat something), I'm actually wondering if Monkey knows that I'm doing all of this just because he's a monkey? Does Monkey realize that I wouldn't sit around his ugly, smelly apartment (on wet straw) listening to Miles Davis, or help him nail that stupid pot-leaf flag over his one window if he were, say, a large marsupial? Let alone perform all that euphemistically termed "social grooming" I'm asked to do when Monkey's coming off one of his crying jags.

Does Monkey accept that even though I act like I'm his friend, I would so dump his bald pink ass if I ever got introduced to, say, a nice bonobo? Ah, who knows? Who cares? Right now, he's my monkey and he needs me.

As long as I can remember, I've wanted to play with monkeys. Once, as a child, I became terribly ill with something that was incorrectly diagnosed as malaria and in the thick of that illness, while lying in my hospital bed, I turned to my dad and asked him if, when I was cured, he would buy me a monkey, and he said, "Yes."

The thought of that monkey carried me through several months of illness and recovery, but when I was up and well again and I went to see my dad to collect, he said, "Jesus, no, are you crazy, woman? I thought you were delirious. There's no way I'm going to buy you a monkey."

And I understand. I know that he meant well and wild animals are not pets and I still love him, but, God's truth, I can't look at my father without thinking deep down inside, "That man owes me a monkey."

I think this monkey promise may have damaged our relationship. I think it may have damaged me. I think I just might have a higher level of simian-companionship entitlement than is healthy, than is normal, even here in the entitled city of Toronto.

Salty Ol' Hills, Make Sure She Keeps the Safety On! See You, Me and Hillary Down by the Squirrel Trap

The Globe and Mail, April 19, 2008

•

Hillary Clinton was politic this week. She refused to answer a par-ticular query: when was the last time she went to church or fired a gun? That "is not a relevant question in this debate," she said, which sounded stuck-up.

But, really, she's not like that. The Hillary I know was different when we went out duck hunting last weekend, early Sunday, before the sun hit the lake—right after we did the flowers for Father Packham down at Our Lady of the Blessed Cross.

I understand why Hillary said that. She doesn't want to exploit our friendship and, besides, ducks are out of season. (Hush now.) Also, both of us missed confession that day. Drudge would've gone to town on that one, even though we bought the father a beer down at the bar later, right before we shot some pool, kicked the shit out of the jukebox until it played non-stop Johnny Winter and then hauled our drunken asses over to the bar stools.

There, Hills flashed her tits at the bartender and told him to "turn up the goddamn game" so she could shout obscenities at the officials, until I had to say, "Settle down, girl. They'll call the cops on us again—

and stop hollering for him to turn up 'the game' because technically, with tennis, Hillary, they usually call it 'a match.'"

After that, Hillary belted down her usual Crown Royal and pounded on the bar while intermittently shouting, "Set 'er up" and "Swear me in."

Hills and I are friends because of our similar childhoods. My dad—who, in an effort to sound more approachable, I'll call "daddy" (whilst affecting a southern accent, quilting, spitting and eating live squirrel)—my daddy mightn't have been able to teach me to read and write, on account of his being at work all day long lecturing on economic policy down at the university, just like all the other daddies did back before the lecturing ran dry.

But my daddy still taught me how to fire a gun—in the hills, on the bayou, down in the mines, south of the picket lines, on the wrong side of the tracks, uphill, near the mansion on the hill, while under sniper fire (from Martin Luther King) in Guelph, Ontario.

My gun was only an air rifle, but it might surprise some people to learn that, among my other skills, I can shoot the bar code off a ketchup bottle at 20 paces. You sneer as much as you want, but should the condiments ever attack, I know who you'll come running to. Me. Maybe Hillary.

"Tabatha and me, we're going deer hunting next weekend," Hills said later, when Bill came looking for her. She was spoiling for a fight, but Bill is used to it. He barely glanced up from rolling her another smoke.

"She's fine on the beer, but crazy on the whisky," he told me once. You can tell he loves the bones of her. "She ain't been right since they shut down the mine."

"Really?" I'd said, surprised. "Even though she's Yale-educated and the junior senator from New York State?"

"Only till she can get back to coal mining," he said sadly. "Or Nam."

"All I ask," Bill said to Hillary—manoeuvring a coaster under her bourbon while she begged the barkeep to pass her the "remote to the friggin' idiot box"—"is that you be careful out there hunting, babe."

"Hell, you know I will," Hillary replied, spinning her lighter on the beer-puddled bar, flicking ashes into her discarded nachos. "Why'd you think I own that yellow pantsuit?"

I asked her once if everything was all right with her and Bill. "We'll be fine," she told me, before giving me her "you can pick your pastor, but you can't pick your family" line again.

"Well, except the husband part," I said.

"Oh. Yeah. Right. Well, if we ain't fine, I'll get a do-over."

She was referring, I understood, to the "Who's the man?" tattoo with Bill's image that graces the small of her back—with an arrow pointing downward.

People get Hillary wrong. They trash her for saying, "Pull my finger," "Better out than in," or that her mom named her after Sir Edmund Hillary even though Hillary was six when the explorer climbed Everest.

Girlfriend was obviously misquoted. Why, I heard her tell a nine-year-old girl that she was actually named after Hilary Duff.

"Hey, spark me up a doobie, Tabatha," Hillary said, long after last call, back at the house.

"Jesus, Hills, ain't you had enough?" said Bill, pulling off one of her beloved camouflage hip waders while I, having dutifully passed her a spliff, began tugging at the other.

"Ah, one of these days, Bill," Hillary said, raising her one un-doobied fist without a hint of actual menace, "straight to the moon, Bill, straight to the moon."

• • • • •

Oooh, Irish Immigration to Newfoundland— It Just Screams "Sexy," Doesn't It?

The Globe and Mail, May 17, 2008

•

I've been trying to imagine what the Canada Border Services Agency was expecting when, suspicious that it was pornographic, it confiscated undeveloped footage from the Canadian film *Love & Savagery* on its way from Ireland to Montreal.

The film, "a romantic tale of passion and longing," is set in Ireland and Newfoundland—so perhaps there'll be two comely Irish immigrant girls, tatting, naked. A knock at the door. And then . . .

"Why, Aiofe, I didn't order fiddleheads!"

"No, Bridgid, 'tis the man come about mending the roof," Aiofe says as the male lead, Allan Hawco, steps into the cabin wearing nothing but a tool belt.

"Well," says Bridgid, rising, a-tremble, eyes pinned on Hawco's belt, "he'd best get to it. If the winter comes before the roof's patched, there's a good statistical chance we'll die of pneumonia."

Hawco attends to his roofing duties—palpable disappointment from Canada Border Services. It has never noticed that porn films don't have words like "love" or "savagery" in the title. They're called *Star Whores*, *On Golden Blonde* or *Hannah Does Her Sisters*, because that's what happens when you live in a society increasingly desensitized to puns.

The narrative within Californian porn developed to take advantage of California's natural light—lots of exteriors. Certainly a drive through the Mojave Desert suggests that the vast number of porn film orgies set in deserts fails to reflect the reality of American sex lives and the near asexual landscape of America's deserts.

My male friends complain that, broad-minded as their girlfriends may be, there's never a good time to approach a partner about possible sexual liaisons involving six of her best-looking friends, your absolutely gayest-looking friend, cacti and sand.

Perhaps Border Services thought Irish/Newfoundland porn would have lots of mist-based storylines: "Sorry, I thought you were my husband . . ." Or the weather suddenly turns: "Might I come in . . .?"

In porn films, whenever a group of women are alone, one of them always suggests that they should shower together. Feel free to throw this "let's shower" idea out there, ladies, when next your book club meets. Report back to me. I've always wondered how the suggestion would go over in real life. I know how it plays out in Irish immigrant porn: "Well lassies, what say we shower?" the buxom Nola giggles, beginning the laborious process of unlacing her boots. "There're no menfolk about for miles but for that handsome 18-year-old lad turning the potato bed outside the window . . ."

Canada Border Services leans forward eagerly, but this being a masterpiece of the Irish-immigration-to-Newfoundland porn genre, it'll take the girls two hours to get their clothes off and six hours to boil the bathwater. Naturally, there'll be a cow that needs milking, by which time the bakeapples will have come into season and the girls will choose to go berry-picking instead.

How's this for a scene? Three men are standing on the wharf. A tall, full-breasted woman approaches them, wearing fishnets. Actual fishnets.

"Could you mend these nets for me, lads?" she says, eyeing the brawniest of the men while he stands there, shirtless, as the sunlight— and then, seconds later, the hail—bounces off his chest.

"Sure, Siobhan," he says.

And then the men fix the nets so that Siobhan and her family of 18 won't starve to death come winter.

Why is our government currently fussing about protecting adults from porn anyway? We have the internet now and in that medium, a man could probably find porn specific to the Irish immigrant experience if he wanted to, anyway. In fact, I'll bet that there's a site where he could watch another man have sex with a potato.

I was just reaching the end of this column when, coincidentally, my friend Martha Burns called me from Newfoundland to convince me that I must come out there.

"It's heaven," she said. "I'm doing a few days on *Love & Savagery*. Have you heard of it?"

Why, bless you Canada Border Services. "Yes."

"I play a nun," she said, "which is something I've always wanted to do."

"Me too," I said. "And I'm not even an actress."

I learned that the film is set in 1968, not 1768, so I've altered my vision wardrobe-wise, but now, well, nuns . . . I'm thinking Border Services was onto something.

Martha, I won't miss this one.

What About the Humane Treatment of Humans?

The Globe and Mail, August 2, 2008

•

*"Would Jesus have condoned such brutality for the sake of
entertainment? Do you?"*
—A Humane Society anti-rodeo advertisement in
Victoria's *Times Colonist*

I've never wondered where Christ stood on the rodeo, although I like
to think that he didn't line dance. The mere fact of his occupying a
manger doesn't necessarily make him an ideal spokesman for animal
welfare. But I'm sure he would have done better by my cat than I did.

In my defence, I'm allergic to cats. So when a cat arrived mid-
winter on my cat-magnet front porch, I put out food and blankets and
looked for "Lost Cat" posters. It had worked before, but not this time.
The cat quickly overran the house. My children were as happy as my
dog was pissed and I got very ill but went into denial about why. Maybe
I was allergic to vacuuming, I thought, since that's all I was doing.

But when I developed asthma, my doctor insisted that I find the
cat another home. Which is how I arrived, cat in hand, at the Humane
Society, along with two other cat-carrier-carrying people.

We were all of us vying for the attention of the attendant, who
was aggressively focused on the layout of the "Bad People Surrender
Cats" posters on her "People Don't Even Deserve Animals" corkboard.

Eventually, after much ostentatious flourishing of my inhaler, a
complaint from the first man (who was Russian) and cursing from the

second, we were given clipboards. They contained several forms about the cats' medical history and a dozen pages demanding our personal information, after which apparently we were contractually obligated to ghostwrite gripping memoirs of our cats' lives.

It was clear that we would be there for the better part of the day. They weren't going to make this easy. If they could bore/bully/torment/ guilt one person into assuming permanent cat custody, they would.

In retrospect, it's the Russian I feel sorry for. When he was eventually questioned by the woman as to why he wanted to offload something as precious as a huge cat, he answered carefully, with considerable embarrassment, in a thick accent: "This cat," he gestured toward the carrier. "This cat, she shit where she sleep."

The woman barely glanced up from reading his cat's extensive bio.

He tried again. "I buy cat here. They say 'good cat,' but cat she shit where she sleep, forever."

Here, I have to almost credit the attendant. She merely nodded, looking him straight in the eye. "I'm waiting," her movements implied. "I've asked you why on earth you want to surrender your cat."

"She shit where she sleep," the Russian repeated, in confusion, s-l-o-w-l-y. I sensed he had carefully researched these words in order to make this case and now he was worried that he had got them wrong.

"Where she sleep, she shit," he tried, looking at us now for support. But the whole event had taken on a cutthroat reality TV feel, as if only one of us was going to be allowed to dump a cat that day, so baseball cap man and I just nodded expectantly. "Your point?" we indicated, smiling back at him.

No prisoners, buddy, I thought. I'm here to lose a cat.

"She wake, leave, return, shit. Where she sleep . . . in my bed . . ." he said. "Only shi . . ."

Clearly, he was thinking, What kind of a land have I immigrated to where they think that a cat should defecate where she sleeps?

"This is my buddy's cat," the other man interrupted as if that first case had all been sorted. "He shipped out to Afghanistan and . . ."

Oh, nice one, I thought. Play the Afghanistan card.

"This isn't my cat," I tried to interject, sucking back on my inhaler like a porn star.

Suddenly everything resembled a scene from *The Wire*.

"Oh, really?" The woman faced me as if leaning across a desk. *And whose cat is it, sister?* she seemed to say. It was if they had found cocaine in my pants.

I told her my story—sold that cat like a screenplay. "He's a great cat," I pitched. "Uses a litter box," I whispered proudly. "Loves dogs." This must be what speed-dating is like, I thought. "But I'm dying," I said earnestly. "I've got two children who'll be made wards of the state if I keep . . ."

At which point the Russian's enormous cat awoke in its carrier and made it obvious even to me (who hadn't been able to smell anything in weeks) that his owner wasn't lying.

"I'm leaving this cat!" I cried and bolted out the door, wondering then, as I do now, where the Humane Society lost its way—and whether we should put up posters.

The Great Line Dance
Is Over, Buckos—
Time to Pay the Band

The Globe and Mail, September 27, 2008

•

I sometimes buy things on eBay. Until about a year ago, I found myself distracted by a banner ad at the top of the page. It featured a row of line-dancing animated cowboys in silhouette. Occasionally there was a kick line of Broadway dancers instead.

The cowboys and the kick line dancers were selling mortgages. Impossible-sounding sums flashed while they danced. The cowboys were offering to lend eBay shoppers in the US sums in the range of $250,000 for a payment of $693 per month or some similarly modest figure.

The siren cowboys of eBay aren't there anymore—they rode off as soon as the subprime mortgage crisis hit. But I think about them whenever I hear anyone condemn those who have defaulted for buying homes that they couldn't afford, even though it's easily possible that many of those buyers, within their adult lifetimes, had never seen housing prices fall.

I thought about those cowboys when I read the amended rules on mortgage lending approved this summer by the Federal Reserve System. I couldn't understand how many of these "innovative lending practices" had ever been legal. It was like opening the paper and reading that you weren't allowed to juggle babies anymore.

I sometimes wonder if Americans ever use the word "cowboy" in the pejorative sense, the way people raised in a British tradition sometimes do. My father would occasionally use the word that way when I was growing up: "Some cowboy came by offering us a free estimate on new eavestroughs," he might say. Or, "I'm not getting the engine mended at that place on Speedvale anymore. They're cowboys."

This always excited my imagination. As a child, I went places with my dad—across town to the hardware store, out of town to the dump. I accompanied my father more often then I accompanied my mother because, to my ear, she didn't offer nearly the same odds of seeing cowboys.

Traditionally we've had more oversight in Canada in most areas (the listeriosis outbreak is an example of what happens when it's whittled down). And I'll admit that sometimes our inclination to view every choice as a potential disaster first and an opportunity second can be frustrating. But the cowboys we most celebrate have cows.

I realized eventually that my father intended "cowboy" to mean someone reckless—part of a fly-by-night operation. Perhaps better to go with my mother, I decided, who offered at least a 20 percent certainty of cake.

America's banker-cowboys were stripped near to naked this week. They danced around trying to explain why raising the national debt by $700 billion was at once a dire necessity and a once-in-a-lifetime opportunity.

Over at the *Wall Street Journal*, the editorial board even insisted, "The $700 billion isn't spending per se, like Medicare." Lord, no.

There was a familiar ring to the sentiments bankers voiced as they railed against the core principle of the market: something is worth only what someone else is willing to pay for it. Anything above that is aid. I've heard similar arguments at yard sales. Simply put: how much it cost you, how long you've had it, what you predict it'll be worth in 10 years, what you believe it's worth now (only in the south of Spain) or the fact that it doesn't go with your new kitchen but is otherwise a quality item are all irrelevant.

One man's "troubled asset" is still another man's ceramic salad spinner with a broken string. Similarly, one man's "innovative lending practice" is another's loan sharking.

I have a mortgage at my staid bank. The branch I use is old-fashioned, by which I mean that they never put up balloons and the manager has been there for all 10 years of my mortgage. I applied for a modest credit increase once and she asked me a lot of sensible questions while suspiciously eyeing my shoes.

The closest they get to bling at my bank is a card on the counter listing the nine languages in which one can expect to be served. I know the fees are high and their profits higher, but I can get quite patriotic about the whole arrangement.

Sometimes you want all hat and no cowboy.

Thrilling Tales of Truly Terrible Parenting

The Globe and Mail, October 25, 2008

·

As a child, I had a recurring nightmare about being put in the position of having to steer a car. Sometimes I'd wake up crying. And so when my own children were born, I decided to spare them the disturbance of this nightmare by teaching them both, while they were very young, how to drive.

As soon as my children demonstrated any interest, I showed them how to operate a car. I taught them the rules of the road. Eventually I allowed them to sit on my lap and steer around empty off-road spaces of Northern Ontario whenever we went camping.

I reasoned that this way, when they were forced in their dreams to escape from flying monkeys (another childhood concern of mine) by taking the wheel of a truck, they would be ready. Properly prepared, my children would be able to enjoy their dream driving much the way I enjoy driving now.

Honestly, it only recently occurred to me that my childhood dream of finding myself behind the wheel, often with beloved passengers on board and mostly in heavy traffic, was symbolic of some other fear— likely of growing up, having to know everything and be responsible.

I meant well, but by teaching my children how to drive, I have deprived them of a useful and protective metaphor.

Now my children come to me in the night, saying, "Oh, Mummy, I dreamt that I was heavily invested in an Icelandic bank and mortgaged to the hilt in Florida when suddenly the Canadian dollar dropped below

80 cents. This meant that I couldn't afford to get a divorce and was stuck forever in a stifling marriage to . . ."

"A flying monkey?" I ask.

"Yeah. Can I sleep in your bed?"

I scooch right on over.

My children come to me with wild, I'm-in-over-my-head, Sarah Palin eyes—their faces have that same expression: Hey, am I allowed to make a right-hand turn on a red light here? Hell, I'll just gun it and see what happens.

I'm confident that they will check their mirrors and signal, but that won't be much help to them when they're dreaming that they're carrying $70,000 in student debt and failing the bar exam, naked.

Last week, I read about a mother who, concerned that she was too tipsy to drive herself home from a weekend function south of Ottawa, allowed her nine-year-old daughter to drive her home instead.

I'll admit that in designating the driving this way, the woman was irresponsible, but she kind of made my week: I love a story about any mother who is a worse mother than I am. I'm planning someday to publish an inspirational book of shockingly bad tales from true-life parenting.

Someone got the idea that exemplary parents inspire parents, forgetting that, in most things, humans are inspired by the bad, not the good. We would always rather hear about the mother who backs the car over her child's foot than about the one who lifts the car off her child's body.

How many novelists-to-be have finished reading a book and thought, "There's no way I can do any worse than that," do you think? A hell of a lot more than ever closed *War and Peace* and thought, "Hey, great, I should give that a whirl."

Try telling a True Tale of Crap Parenting to a group of parents and watch their little faces shine.

Day to day, parents heave a sigh of relief, thinking, "Well, say what you want, maybe I did"—for example—"teach my five-year-old to drive but at least I never"—for example—"asked my nine-year-old to drive me home from a party."

And thus they find the will to go on.

This week, when accused of infractions such as serving shepherd's pie three nights in a row, all I had to do was twist open a bottle of scotch, toss the nearest child my car keys and say, "Mummy's feeling tired tonight. She wants to go and visit Grandma." And peace was restored. Even to me.

And so I applaud you, South of Ottawa Mum, along with every other misguided mum with tiny offspring at the wheel—those mums whose names are usually withheld in order to protect their children.

• • • • •

What My Barbies Understood about Hard Times That the Media Apparently Don't

The Globe and Mail, November 15, 2008

•

When we were young girls, my friends Nadine and Patricia and I read all of Laura Ingalls Wilder's Little House on the Prairie books over and over, but the book that we enjoyed the most was *The Long Winter*.

There was something, as I recall, about eight feet of snow, living on a potato a day and burning all the furniture for warmth that really put all of those endless interpersonal conflicts with that stuck-up Nellie Oleson into perspective.

The three of us played Little House on the Prairie with our Barbie dolls. Our mothers sewed doll-sized gingham pioneer dresses with coordinating bonnets and aprons—in which Barbie still managed to look hot.

And then one happy Christmas my father built a prairie dollhouse for me, and Nadine and Patricia's father built a covered wagon for them. I don't think we came out of the basement for a year. We had tiny oil lamps and dishes. We built Barbie-sized tables and chairs, which we would pile up in the middle of the cabin and happily pretend to burn— for warmth. And of course, in order to cook the potatoes.

Sometimes our dolls would be forced, because of some calamity, to abandon their home and trek across the basement. And then life became still harder for them.

The journey was long, and around about the time they left the carpet and began to make their way across the desolate parquet floor, the Barbies would often have little choice but to eat their last good oxen (at which point Pa would have to pull the covered wagon). Usually they would do this only after they had eaten their beloved donkey, a souvenir from the Athens airport that we believed to be covered in real donkey fur.

The point is, young and well-fed as we were, we understood the importance of constructing a hard-times narrative.

Nadine, Patricia and I never considered serving up Mary Ingalls's favourite gelding at the fall of the first snowflake. We waited. We held off. Just as we resisted cooking up the family's faithful china dogs (they came from the Red Rose Tea box) until the Ingalls were at least midway over the parquet, on the far side of the baseboard heater.

There, in the shelter of the large recliner (Pa having failed yet again in his hunting), we would mournfully throw all of the china poodles and corgis in a shoebox with the other already-eaten animals and the battered miniature papier mâché apples that had been the first to go.

Then we would have young Laura Ingalls sombrely ponder the fate of tiny, rubber, still rosy baby Grace.

Of course, we were normal little girls too. Which meant that our Barbies had sex pretty much all the time. Pa was a G.I. Joe and couldn't actually stand up for long—there were too many movable joints on a G.I. Joe to offer any stability. He couldn't hold an axe either. However, periodically we would unlean him from the fireplace or unhitch him from the wagon and some Barbie or other would have what we imagined to be her way with him.

It was a time of almost-innocence and pioneer Barbie survivalist porn in the Swidinsky basement back then. But our hardship stories had an arc to them that the media have failed to give the current recession.

So far in this crisis, I've been told how to dress, eat, get married, decorate and work out in a recession. The media have predicted, heralded and then bemoaned the return of Velveeta, undersized muffins and child labour—and we're only six weeks in.

The average newspaper reader has gone from learning the benefits of having a carp give them a pedicure to "never have a pedicure again" to "how to serve that same cuticle-eating carp grilled on a bed of steamed lawn clippings" in just over a month.

It's like *The Long Winter*, if it began with the burning chairs. Or if page one of *The Grapes of Wrath* presented us with a broken woman breastfeeding a starving man. Or if Cormac McCarthy . . . okay, it just is like Cormac McCarthy.

It's like Bruce Springsteen's "The River," but Mary's pregnant in verse one—and eating a donkey.

Pace yourselves, press. This recession may have years to run. Build an arc.

• • • • •

The Latest Secret
O.J. Manuscript:
"If I Wrote It (Your Kid's
Book Report, That Is)"

The Globe and Mail, December 13, 2008

•

"I know these guys. These guys have eaten in my home. I've done book reports with their kids."
   —O.J. Simpson at his sentencing for armed robbery that took place last week

Here are some excerpts from book reports submitted to Florida schools since Mr. Simpson relocated to that state:

JANE EYRE

In the book *Jane Eyre* by Charlotte Brontë, a man has the great idea of locking his wife up in his attic so that he can still control her while doing whatever he wants. Thornfield Hall had to be way cheaper than any of the real estate in Brentwood.

I think it's a good book. I wonder if Mr. Rochester ever slashed Mrs. Rochester's tires? Because that would be a totally understandable thing to do.

I am happy to live in a country where it's not as damp and grey as England, and where evidence from a dead person who says someone is going to kill them is inadmissible because they are dead.

MADAME BOVARY

In *Madame Bovary* by Gustave Flaubert, the character of Emma Bovary sleeps with men other than her husband. It is boring. Except for the end, where she dies in agony.

THE LORD OF THE RINGS

I think this is a great book although it has a sad ending. The character I like best in this book is Sauron because he does not want other people to have his ring because the ring is part of his stuff. It is very believable to me that when someone takes Sauron's stuff, he wants to get his stuff back. The question this book asks is, "What kind of an asshole has a goddamn problem with someone wanting to get his own goddamn stuff back?"

I think the short, useless people are prejudiced against Sauron because he is evil and trying to cover the world in darkness.

CRIME AND PUNISHMENT

What I want to know is what kind of advance did Fyodor Dostoyevsky get to write this book in which a guy confesses to murder? No one had a problem with *his* book, did they?

Dostoyevsky must have had a pretty good lawyer because my teacher, Mrs. Lipman, said the first draft of this book was written in the first person. After that, maybe a lawyer said, "No, write it like it's happening to a guy named Raskolnikov—then they can't touch you." Smart. Also, if a guy gets 33 years for, say, taking his stuff back, how is he going to feel when he reads that Raskolnikov got only eight years for two murders?

Like stabbing more people, I bet that's how he is going to feel.

THÉRÈSE RAQUIN

Thérèse Raquin is a novel by Émile Zola. It is about two people who are having hot sex who decide to kill the woman's husband so they can have more hot sex. The woman is named Thérèse, the man is named Laurent. The guy they kill is called Camille. So, like, no wonder.

I did not find this book very believable because after they go through all the trouble of ridding the world of a worthless guy (who couldn't play football and seldom procured light acting work) by drowning him, Thérèse and Laurent feel so tormented by "guilt" that they can't enjoy life anymore. Not even golf.

IN COLD BLOOD

This book is about a family in Holcomb, Kansas, who all shoot each other one day, probably because the whole family is heavily involved with the LA mafia. Also, I think the pretty girl, Nancy Clutter, had a boyfriend! It's also about two absolutely, 100 percent not guilty guys.

The thing I did not like about this book is the blood. The blood is everywhere. I see it when I close my eyes. The blood. Always the blood.

ANNA KARENINA

This book by Leo Tolstoy is about a beautiful, lively woman who is not allowed to get a divorce, love other men or see her child just because her husband says so. I think that a good title for this book would be "Article 3, Section 7 of the California Divorce Code."

THE STRANGER

My favourite character in this book by Albert Camus is Meursault. At least at the beginning. I would recommend this book to anyone who has ever just decided to kill someone. Or maybe two people.

• • • • •

On the Fine Literary Line between Christmas Spirit and Complete Idiocy

The Globe and Mail, December 20, 2008

•

If there's a less satisfying and more badly written short story than O. Henry's Christmas story "The Gift of the Magi," I've never found it.

That's the story in which a wife, Della, sells her hair to buy her husband, Jim, "a platinum [watch] fob chain, simple and chaste in design, properly proclaiming its value by substance alone and not by meretricious ornamentation" while her husband sells his watch to buy her combs for her hair.

These gifts always seemed like inexcusably poor purchases for the financially strapped couple to be making, and they're so mindlessly chipper to one another at the end. "My hair grows so quickly," she says to him. It always struck me that there was something deeply disturbing about their relationship.

They speak to one another as if they were children. O. Henry describes them as "children." When they reveal their misguided purchases to one another they seem unable to address the situation with frankness and (nowhere to be found) humour. The story may have endured for 100 years but I give the marriage six months.

The message is supposed to be that they are ideal spouses because they've each sacrificed the things dearest to themselves for the other. I've never bought it.

I mean, first of all, how much hair did this woman have to begin with? It sounds as if she had an awful lot of hair. Is the hair maybe the reason she couldn't go out and get a job? Did she have to sit around all day brushing it? Sticking pretty things in it?

Also, given the treacly tone of the rest of the story, it's sort of less than Christmassy that Della, looking at her newly shorn head in the mirror, trying to convince herself that all will be fine, thinks, "If Jim doesn't kill me . . . he'll say I look like a Coney Island chorus girl."

Coney Island chorus girl would at least be a job, I'd like to point out, and arguably a more honourable way to save a few pennies than Della's usual scam of "bulldozing the grocer and the vegetable man and the butcher until one's cheeks burned with the silent imputation of parsimony that such close dealing implied." But mainly, where does the "kill me" come from? It seems to trip off her mind's tongue too easily. What exactly is going on in this marriage?

When Jim comes home it's explained that he's young to be "burdened with a family." Although they have no children, just Della who "flops" down on a couch to "howl" and can only "wriggle" off a table and "cry." As well as, one assumes, comb her hair, put sparkly things in it and sometimes rip off the butcher.

He sells his watch for her (watch equals time, his life), accepting that he's condemned to come back day after day to their dark, oppressive, almost grotesquely hair-filled apartment. She sells her hair (hair, Samson-like, equals power) for $20. His life's hours earn him a set of rather awful-sounding combs. Putting this in perspective it's as if, in today's terms, her husband had bought her a solid gold scrunchie.

He's a hair-combing enabler and potential psychotic killer. O. Henry gives his age as 21, never hers. But given her flopping, howling, wiggling and chronic unemployment, either she's just a complete pain in the ass, or she's nine.

The level of creepiness in this story haunts me every Christmas. It's more of a cautionary tale than *A Christmas Carol*.

I asked both my children separately if they knew the story "The Gift of the Magi."

"The one with the hair?" said one child.

"The one with the combs?" said the other.

"I hate that story!" they both said angrily.

"Good," I said, "but there are lessons to be drawn from it. First of all, as much as possible, write like a Russian, and never trust a man who doesn't appreciate the chorus girl in a woman. Don't surrender the things most precious to you, even for love. It'll only lead to resentment.

"And while this might arguably be my own, very subtle interpretation of the story, if you must venture into consumer goods at Christmas, never buy a woman underwear. Even if you get the size right, odds are you'll drastically underspend."

Okay, Okay, I Will Finally Admit It— It's Been an Act All Along

The Globe and Mail, December 27, 2008

•

Twenty-odd years ago, I moved to the city. Sweet 16—the world was at my feet. I remember dumping my change into the fare box of the city bus and hearing it tumble down, sounding just like music as it fell. I remember swinging my body around the pole, past the driver, onto the first available seat, my World Famous bag swinging behind me. It felt as if I were flying.

And then what I really remember is the big-city bus driver shouting out, "Hey, you! Those seats are for the handicapped! Get your ass to the back of the bus!" Which is when I stood up and limped all the way to the very last row of seats.

Reflecting on this moment on Christmas Day, my birthday, I realized that I've changed since then. I've grown. I've matured. And I've decided it would probably be okay if I stopped limping now.

They say it takes a big man to admit his mistakes. Well, yeah, I say—easy for the big man.

"Hey," the big man just has to say, "I made a mistake."

"Hey, that's okay," the world replies. "You're a big man, bound to happen. Here, take my seat, I'm gonna go beat the crap out of that little guy."

Society celebrates the fallibility of the big man, but I've always believed that the five-foot-three woman needs to be more cautious about admitting her mistakes. However, as I've said, I've matured. I'm ready.

For starters, I shouldn't have chosen such a big limp. It has been absolute hell on my shoes. Just possibly I needn't have limped at all. I could've taken a cab or walked. I was only going eight blocks—hardly any great distance at all, unless, of course, you're limping.

Indeed, at various times these past years I've wondered, as I limped to, say, Nick's Shoe Repair, if I shouldn't have made a clean breast of it, simply stood up and said, "I'm sorry, I didn't see the sign. I am in fact able-bodied and happy to take a different seat." Or maybe I should've pretended to be blind.

Secondly, I now concede that my need to appear invulnerable in the eyes of my fellow men, most of whom on this and many other nights of my life have been drunk, asleep or ignoring me, demands a disproportionate share of my energy. No one was paying attention to me, so why did I have to be the one with the perfect limp?

It's true: it's a perfect limp. You see, as a child, I had 13 years of ballet training—would've turned professional except I was really bad at it—and the training allowed me to master a compelling limp. And, oh yes, I don't deny that my big, perfect limp has opened some doors for me—although never metaphorically.

Indeed, just the other day, I was dipping out of Starbucks, an unlidded hot chocolate balanced in my hand, the subtle movements of my arms and upper body expressing my struggle for life—my Dying Swan of a limp—when an enormous, great woman hove into view, spilling her own cocoa and dropping her purse, so great was her need to open just such a door for me.

"You're so kind," I said demurely. "And when is the baby due?"

"Tomorrow," she said, plummeting to collect the contents of her purse.

"Good luck with that," I said. "I do so hope he's born without a limp."

I didn't catch her reply, but of course we're all born without a limp. It comes later, as does the police record. They spring from the same source really. The impulse to limp down the aisle of the city bus is akin to the impulse to announce to the sales clerk at the liquor store, should your card happen to be declined, "Yes, well, you might as well cut that card up, sir. I must have stolen it. *My* card is certainly never over the limit."

But I wonder, would simple Starbucks Lady have understood this? Her face betrayed a weariness that's familiar to me. I've seen that look on the face of many a pregnant woman as she has risen to give me her seat on the subway. And yet there was joy in her reckless abandonment of decorum—splayed out on the floor in a pool of mint cocoa, so walrus-ish beside my penguin-like dignity.

I couldn't help but wonder if I should take a page from her book. But then I thought, "Heavens no, it's a Maeve Binchy novel and it's absolutely drenched in mint cocoa."

No, there was some other aspect of this woman I coveted, something that spoke to me and said, "Lose the limp." Possibly it was the remarkably fine condition of her shoes.

Two Strikes and I'm Out (of Ingenious Garbage-Disposal Schemes)

The Globe and Mail, June 27, 2009

•

The strike this week by Toronto municipal employees, including gar-bage collectors and child-care and park workers, and a separate, threatened strike at Ontario's liquor stores didn't bring out the best in people.

My own enterprise, Tabatha Southey's New Private Daycare Where We Teach the Children to Make Garbage into Booze, was obviously a sensible attempt to respond to and capitalize on a changing market. Not hysteria, the kind of thing on display in the local papers, which ran pictures of the lines outside liquor stores, pre-strike, and of the stark, denuded shelves.

My favourite photo showed a man crouching beside one of six remaining bottles in a cavernous store. He was studying the label, for the cameras, obviously—as if, having waited five hours to get in, he was suddenly concerned about tannins.

He probably tripped an elderly woman to reach that bottle, I thought. It's possible I nicked her on the shin myself, with my heel, as I stepped over her. Honestly, after witnessing our liquor store mobs, Health Canada should have banned the sale of hand-sanitizing gel in the entire province.

Now, however, the Liquor Control Board of Ontario strike has been settled and we at Tabatha Southey's New Private Daycare Where We Teach the Children to Make Garbage into Booze are stuck with a house full of kids, and I only had one actual activity planned, damn it. (I was going to teach the children to make garbage into booze.)

When I put up posters inviting my neighbours to drop by and investigate Tabatha Southey's New Private Daycare Where We Teach the Children to Make Garbage into Booze—well, not "investigate" in any official "what's with all the tangled power cords stapled up over the sink?" sense, or at least so I hoped—it seemed like a viable business plan.

"Come on over, look around," I wrote, "and then consider enrolling your child in Tabatha Southey's New Private Daycare Where We Teach the Children to Make Garbage into Booze, especially if your child has, in his few short and enchanting years of life, managed to acquire a working knowledge of how to make hard liquor or wine from kitchen peelings."

Sadly, my frequent and increasingly desperate Google searches yielded very limited information on the subject.

Still, here at Tabatha Southey's (now rather purposeless) New Private Daycare Where We Teach the Children to Make Garbage into Booze, your children will be cared for (but not, you know, coddled) in a (relatively) safe environment.

They will be taken on frequent and exciting field trips, mostly to visit Tabatha Southey's parents, who live out of town, pleasantly situated in a city where there is no garbage strike. There, we'll explore the workings of my parents' compost heap, which needs a good turning, kids, so "Lift with your knees," as my dad used to say to me, "Lift with your knees!"

However, separate trips will also be organized to one of Toronto's exciting, heavily picketed official disposal sites, where children over the age of 18 months will be offered a chance to earn their Garbage-Disposal-Site-Line-Placeholder Badge—a badge that may *look* like an unwashed, empty one-litre milk bag with "badge" written on it in black marker. But isn't.

Participating parents are asked to please sign, but not return, the enclosed permission form, a form that may appear to be an empty toothpaste tube but really isn't, and which is enclosed, obviously, in a watermelon rind.

Here at Tabatha Southey's New Private Daycare Where We Teach the Children to Make Garbage into Booze, we understand that placing your child in daycare isn't about warehousing your child—or your garbage, so pack a litter-free lunch, please, next time. Bitch.

Also, parents are obliged to accept any "science projects" that your children bring home, which will be constructed from cans, paper towel rolls, mango pits and chicken bones from the barbecue I had last night.

Here at Tabatha Southey's New Private Daycare Where We Teach the Children to Make Garbage into Booze (most parents said they were attracted by the name), we realize that daycare is about teaching children social skills (and, I'd hoped, oenology) and random crafts if necessary, as well as the knowledge and confidence needed to flush whole onions down the toilet—an activity that, for multiple reasons, is best done only once the onions get pretty soft.

We're still here at Tabatha Southey's New Private Daycare Where We'll One Day Teach the Children to Make Garbage into Booze. And we're giving out applications.

Which aren't old newspapers. Because we said so.

• • • • •

The Tories May Be Upset about Gay Parades, but I Object to Publicly Funded Sax and Violins

The Globe and Mail, July 11, 2009

•

Much like Conservative MP Brad Trost—who, in a statement to LifeSiteNews.com, claimed that Tourism Minister Diane Ablonczy's decision to fund Toronto's Gay Pride events had come as a shock to most of the Conservative caucus—I, too, am troubled by some of the choices that our government has made in supporting cultural events.

In fact, I'm glad that we're finally talking about this issue, because I really don't enjoy jazz music.

Our government funds many cultural events, but it always seems to me that they fund a lot of jazz festivals. What with the CBC playing so much jazz, one could easily start to believe that our government has a pro-jazz agenda.

Not that I consider myself anti-jazz, you understand, any more than the group to which Mr. Trost directed his comments is necessarily anti-gay. They're just pro-family. And I'm just pro-music.

I don't mind other people liking jazz. What people listen to behind closed doors is their own business. I accept it: jazz happens. I just don't see why we need to use tax dollars to promote it.

I'm not saying that jazz should (necessarily) be illegal—I just don't want to see bands in the streets or hear jazz emanating from some depressing beer tent, ruining an otherwise perfectly nice city park.

In contrast to my stroll through this year's Gay Pride celebration, during which I saw exactly two sets of naked breasts (which because of a sadly underutilized legal ruling is permissible in Ontario) and one exposed penis (which is par for the course on any long walk through downtown Toronto; at least this one wasn't pissing on any public property), I'm shocked by the outfits people wear to these "jazz" events.

I just can't see how dressing that way helps their cause.

Jazz fans have just begun to reach a level of societal acceptance—not that you'd want them near your children with their Ken Burns box sets, or near your stereo at a party. But with their ill-fitting Dockers, they're only setting themselves back.

My children don't need to see that sort of thing. And by "that sort of thing," I do mean those shorts, sir; yes, those shorts. They are in opposition to our values.

And can't jazz fans buy one pair of adult shoes?

Oh, I know: "it's a stereotype," they claim. They'll always tell you that most of them don't really dress like that—it's just that it's always the most flamboyantly unstylish participants that get shown on the evening news.

Honestly, if the government wants to use cultural events to stimulate the economy (just because it works), maybe they should bypass that nodding Thelonious Monk fan, smugly nursing a cranberry juice in some misguided bar, and give the money straight to the makers of Wallabee shoes.

Or let's restrict jazz to brunch. They deserve each other.

Now, I don't know what my bitching about jazz festivals can achieve here. Once, I'd have assumed that the answer was: Nothing. Don't go if you don't get it. Go to the Stampede instead.

But then the tourism minister, Ms. Ablonczy, was relieved of the task of distributing the funds for the Marquee Tourism Events Program shortly after she supported Toronto's Pride events—with funds used primarily to hire entertainment and increase accessibility.

It appears that she was caught running what fellow Conservative MP Dona Cadman has since called "an inclusive and responsive portfolio," and the party couldn't let that stand.

Just shortly before, the Institute for Canadian Values, run by Reverend Charles McVety (the champion of that ridiculous attempt at film censorship, Bill C-10), called on "the prime minister to reverse the path he has chosen" of supporting "spiritually destructive . . . sex parades."

So maybe I'm wrong and there'll be no more jazz festivals next year.

I don't find them very inclusive. Pride, in contrast, is full of gay, lesbian, straight, bisexual and transgender people and diverse families from across North America, with strollers and kids hoisted up on their parents' shoulders, all celebrating what is arguably the most inclusive event in Canada.

Pride is for everyone who doesn't hate gay people. Or parades, I guess.

I maintain that most Canadians don't hate gay people. And I do hate parades, but I make an exception for Pride because, with the good-natured police officers and the army recruiting booth and some members of Canada's armed forces marching and the hotels full, the bars brimming, the DJs playing and people celebrating, it makes me feel blessed to be Canadian now.

I Do Not Like It at a Fest.
I Do Not Like It as a Test.
I Do Not Like Jazz, Boys.
Deal with It

The Globe and Mail, August 8, 2009

•

I received lots of email in response to my July 11 column, in which I defended federal funding for Toronto's Gay Pride parade by writing that jazz festivals also receive support—and, I wrote, I don't like jazz.

Some of the emails were kind (invitations to jazz festivals, links to radio stations), but many of the angrier ones accused me of having an irrational, emotional bias against jazz.

"You must've had a bad experience with a man who loved jazz," they wrote. Repeatedly.

Their assumption is that a woman's tastes evolve entirely through her romantic encounters. We just can't figure that stuff out on our own.

It's true. That's how it works. Once I dated Broken-Glass-on-a-Baking-Hot-Sidewalk, it ended badly, and now I avoid contact with broken glass on a baking hot sidewalk. For a while, Falciparum Malaria and I kept company, but he turned out to be kind of weird and clingy, and now I stay away from falciparum malaria.

And for six months, I was hot and heavy with Banging-My-Head-into-a-Big-Old-Piece-of-Barn-Board, until I left him for Stepping-on-a-Rusty-Nail. They both went nuts and now I don't like banging my head on barn boards or stepping on rusty nails.

Lord, but it is hard to be a woman. We're such creatures of the heart. How could we possibly know what we don't like?

Which brings me to the next line of jazz defence in these emails and presented to me at parties: "Whatever it is you don't like, that's not jazz."

Try it. When next jazz-grilled, start by saying, "I really don't like Joe Zawinul."

"That's not jazz," they'll say.

"I'm irritated by Pat Metheny."

"Ha! Not jazz."

"I don't like Chet Baker."

"Not jazz." (Really?)

"Miles Davis makes me itchy."

"Oh you mean late Miles Davis," they'll say. "That's not jazz."

So certain are they that you like jazz that anything you don't like stops being jazz.

It's like when you're in Spain and whenever you reach a new town, your guidebook essentially says, "No, you idiot, they don't speak Spanish here. Speaking Spanish here will get you beaten up."

There's no Spanish in Spain, no jazz in jazz and also, before you try it, any emails containing the questions "What kind of music *do you like*?" (the answer is punk, rap, country or techno—whatever makes you angriest) or "What about Ella?" will be redirected to my junk folder.

Apparently Ella Fitzgerald is the gateway drug to jazz. Obviously I just haven't met her properly yet.

And there's another thing I dislike about jazz. When I go to the symphony, they don't tell me the full name (and nickname and city of origin) of the third cello or the cool guy on the bassoon. When I go the opera, they don't introduce me to Valkyrie 7 or Fallen Warrior 12. So why is it that during a jazz performance the announcer names every single dinkus in the entire ensemble every bloody time they play?

I wouldn't mind so much if they stopped playing while they did this, because it takes a good half-hour, which in jazz years is one song, and it would give us all a break. But they don't. They keep playing. They noodle. It's their noodling that I hate the most.

Also, jazz fans, stop trying to out-jazz one another (Michael Enright) with your jazztistics. You know, people, if your music were louder, you wouldn't have to talk about it so much. I blame the *Playboy* Jazz Poll of the 1960s for convincing men (whose taste in music is inextricably tied to their sexual experiences) that, plied with enough candles, Chianti, Coltrane and jazz banter, a woman would kick off her kitten heels when a man peeled off his ascot. *Playboy* made jazz the new "come up and see my etchings."

I like etchings and honestly I can forgo the respected music happily, and save me from candles anyway. I mean what are we trying to do here, have sex or contact the dead?

I've heard that someone conducted a study that proved that as people age, they become more responsive to jazz. This worries me. I check my music collection weekly for signs of the early onset of jazz.

Sometimes I think, sadly, "One day I shall be very old, it won't be much fun, I won't get out much and then that's going to happen to me."

I imagine this is what it was like being in prison and hearing that Garth Drabinsky's coming in.

"Oh, great," the prisoners sighed, on hearing of the *Phantom of the Opera* producer's sentence for fraud. "On top of everything else that's wrong with this place, now the music is going to suck."

Don't Start In with Me about the Bounty of the Harvest Season

The Globe and Mail, September 5, 2009

•

It was around this time of year, September, in my hometown when I was growing up, that our neighbours would begin arriving bearing baskets brimming with zucchinis harvested from their gardens. And it was around this time of year, when I was growing up, that I began to hate our neighbours and wonder what it'd be like to live elsewhere, somewhere with less green space, where you didn't know most of your neighbours anyway.

It's true what they say about small towns: we answered the door to strangers. But not to people that we knew. At least not in September, when my mother used to say, pulling the curtains closed, "Pretend we're not home."

Acquaintances would come by our house, empty-handed. "Just to chat." Sure.

"Looking forward to going back to school?" they'd say.

As if. And as if they'd come by just to ask me that riveting question. And then, just as they were leaving, they'd run out to their cars and return with a shoebox full of zucchini. "Oh, I almost forgot, picked fresh this morning . . ."

"We have . . ." my mother would start to say, but they'd be gone.

Sometimes people gave zucchini to innocent kids as they dropped them off from, say, ballet lessons. "Not a problem," they'd say. "I'll drive."

"It's our turn," other, weaker, parents would protest, but those aggressive-gardening-carpooling-monster-parents would happily dump a daughter on the curb outside her house with her little pink shoes in one hand and half of hell's harvest in the other and take off down the street, tires screeching, whooping for joy.

Some people feigned medical emergencies so their children would dial that special number by the phone. Over that good neighbour would rush and then, wham! Zucchinied! Sometimes, after checking that no one was lurking around the back door of course, my mother would hand a plastic Zehrs bag to me. "Nip over on your bike and leave that for Mrs. Gordon," she'd say.

And I'd do it—as if I didn't know what was in that bag. Even though Mrs. Gordon was so tiny and frail that I'm pretty sure she survived for 12 months entirely on the two boxes of Brownie cookies that I guilted her into buying from me every year. And yet I knew better than to argue with my mother.

One did not argue with one's mother. Not in September—unless one wanted to feel a hard, fresh zucchini across the back of one's hand.

Instead, I'd just step over the inevitable bushel of zucchini left, with ninja-like skill, outside our screen door and do what I was told—which was to give a woman I believed to be 250 years old a cash-crop-sized amount of vegetable matter and then peel out of there before she caught me.

My mother, meanwhile, would set to work retaliating for that bushel of zucchini by baking up a nice, fat whole wheat zucchini loaf for Mrs. McLachlin, who'd apparently left the bushel basket there, and "whose mother had passed away."

"Eighteen years ago," my father reminded her.

"Still, she's our neighbour. In fact, I'll double the recipe," my mother said, shredding away. "Gill's mother's not looking too robust these days!" she added, brightening.

Zucchini is prolific. One zucchini plant can meet the zucchini needs of an entire block—accepting the fallacy that humans even have zucchini needs. Still, gardeners feel compelled to plant an entire row and then to share the inevitable bounty with everyone they can corner.

Gardening-wise, zucchini's relatively easy, yet it looks impressive. People like to show their zucchini off—it's the "Smoke on the Water" of vegetables.

Rhubarb is the "Louie Louie."

The Zucchini Wars continued until October. The loaf would draw zucchini muffin fire. We'd respond with zucchini pie. They'd deploy fritters. "Kids will eat anything if you put it in Jell-o!" people shouted as they hurled zucchini tied to other zucchini through someone's living room window.

Who started that rumour, I wondered. Had there been actual research? It gave me nightmares. Even if it's true, I thought, surely this behaviour shouldn't be encouraged?

Once *Canadian Living* mainstreamed ratatouille, it was best to avoid dinner invitations. You'd sit through a meal while they played a little cat-and-mouse with you: The appetizer? No? The soup? A zucchini casserole? Or the cruellest deception ever practised on a child—the zucchini chocolate cake?

Why, I remember once driving back from just such a dinner. We were all wondering how we'd escaped it, when my father, who'd been smacking his lips uncomfortably from the driver's seat, sighed. "Those bastards," he said—"the wine."

He shook his head sadly. "The wine."

Don't Try to Horn In on the "Acting Like Humans" Racket, Pussycat— That's Monkey Business

The Globe and Mail, October 10, 2009

●

The interesting part of the findings reported in the October 2009 edition of the journal *Animal Behaviour* isn't that spotted hyenas out-performed chimpanzees in co-operative problem-solving tests. It's that researcher Christine Drea of Duke University discovered this in the mid-1990s, but only now found a publisher for her results.

Big Primate has a lock on anthropomorphic research.

Shortly, I predict, the local police will find that Professor Drea's car has been driven off a cliff. Some chimps at a nearby bar will insist that she was depressed and had been drinking.

Oh, there'll be questions. For a while. The journal *Primate* will be asked why they declined to publish Professor Drea's findings in 2006, choosing instead to run with their all-Danish-cartoon issue at the last moment.

The publisher will read a terse statement, caked in straw and banana, citing Professor Drea's "*eeeek-eeek-eeek*, insufficient sample size," while pounding his chest for emphasis and glancing nervously offside.

The four-fingered editor will decline to comment. Local monkeys, of course, will stick to their story.

"But her colleagues report that she was satisfied with her personal life . . ." a persistent detective will say, flipping open a notebook—earning himself only a shrug from the gathered primates, and some hurled feces.

"And looky here, boys, a little item from *Nature* says: 'Orangutans can learn to cut the brake cable on a Chevrolet Impala and make it look like an accident.' Know anything about that, boys?"

"Hell, no," an ape will respond, winking at a rhesus macaque perched on the light fixture above the pool table. "Hey, little Martha, why don't you show the nice detective one of your babies. You like monkey babies, detective?

"Hey, Bombo," he'll gesture to a majestic lowland mountain gorilla, leaning on the bar in the shadows. "Why don't you buy the detective a drink?"

"Sure. Say, detective, what kind of car do you drive?" Bombo will ask, loping over, holding up two fingers to the bartender. And then a prehensile thumb. Just, it will seem, to make a point.

"Ever actually seen a hyena cub?" Martha will ask as she sidles up, sweet babe in arms, bypassing two young gibbons who, almost as if on cue, will undertake some impossibly endearing shtick involving an empty bucket and a hula hoop.

"Here, wanna hold him?" she'll coo, dangling herself upside down by her tail from a bar stool.

"Didn't Drea discover that experienced hyenas helped inexperienced partners learn to do the research trick?"

"Possibly, but we teach our partners to do food-earning tricks and then pretend that we can't do them."

"Me too," the detective will concede.

"They'll never usurp us, anthropomorphism-wise," a handsome bonobo will say.

"No one's interested in non-primate social cognition. Why?" the detective will ask.

"Haven't got a clue," the ape will say, "but maybe you remember that old TV show *B.J. and the Bear*? Anyone here remember that show?"

A chorus of *eeeks* will be heard around the bar.

"It was about an itinerant trucker named B.J. . . ." The entire bar will break into howls of laughter. Understandably.

"And B.J."—more laughter—"hauled a big rig with a chimpanzee companion named Bear by his side. They were close, those two. Real close.

"Why, I recall one episode where B.J."—shrieks of pure monkey glee, banging on tables—"sang all of Billy Joel's 'Just the Way You Are' to that chimp. Those were some pre-PETA days, let me tell you.

"No one ever established what exactly the relationship was between these two, B.J."—yes, more laughter—"and Bear, but surely no network official would've green-lit that show if it had been about an itinerant trucker and his spotted hyena driving around, encountering doe-eyed, plush-lipped ladies."

"Nope," the bonobo will interject. "The pilot episode would've gone something like this: 'Hey, B.J., who's your friend?' asks Cindy in her cut-off shorts, turning toward the fully grown spotted hyena hunched in the passenger seat. 'Why, isn't he the cutest—agggh, agggh! My leg! My leg! That ugly-ass dog of yours just ate my leg!'"

"You seriously think that any show would've run for two seasons and spawned a spinoff if the leading man's 'best buddy' had possessed a penchant for devouring small ungulates in the open grassland?" the ape will interject as the bonobo returns, thoughtfully, to his whisky.

"America's not ready for veld-dwelling co-stars in their comedy-dramas yet. Nor does anyone want to see too many parallels drawn between themselves and hyenas.

"So are we suppressing research, detective? Is that what you're asking? Perhaps, but we're not—as with that crap you make us do with primitive tools—finding it all that hard.

"Now, please, detective, allow us to escort you to your car."

Let Me Tell You How My Dad Would Have Burst Balloon Boy Dad's Pathetic Little Bubble

The Globe and Mail, October 24, 2009

On October 15, 2009, six-year-old Falcon Heene's father reported that his son was drifting 2,100 metres up in the air in a helium balloon. The story, of "Balloon Boy," as he was quickly dubbed, turned out to be a hoax—the father was, apparently, hoping to get a reality TV show from the stunt—but for a few days it was everywhere.

•

The difference between my dad and Balloon Boy Story Dad is that my dad would have built a real spacecraft—not like the one Balloon Boy Story Dad built out of cardboard and duct tape, covered in tinfoil.

And if my dad had decided that it was a good idea for our family to have a reality TV show, there's no way in hell he would've let me hide in the attic while his spacecraft drifted across the country—the way candy-ass Balloon Boy Story Dad supposedly allowed his kid to hide.

We were expected to work for things, just like my dad, who couldn't take us camping without digging a First World War–style trench around our tent. One drop of rain and my dad would dig a trench so deep that it required a bridge to cross it, which he also built, from iron—and then he rigged up tarpaulins over our entire campsite anyway.

In my family, we drove upward of 500 miles just to live under a thick, green layer of plastic. For our holiday, we basically camped out inside a Marks & Spencer shopping bag all summer because that's what my dad wanted. And we liked it.

Now, does that sound like the kind of dad who'd wimp out and let his kid hide inside a box? No, sir, my dad, a professor of economics, would've sent me up in that balloon and he'd have expected me to have my homework completed when it landed.

In order not to let my dad down, I'd have had to pilot that spacecraft, repair it in mid-air and master polynomials while doing it, not sit inside a box.

Obviously I've internalized those high expectations: I became depressed last week when I realized that now, thanks to Dr. Elinor Ostrom, I'll never be the first woman to win the Nobel Prize for economics.

Balloon Boy was hiding in an empty cardboard box, his dad said, after his publicity stunt had wasted a day of America's time and left the entire country muttering, "Hey, say what you want about O.J. Simpson, at least he turned out to be *in* that white Ford Bronco. Not hiding in an empty box."

The empty-box thing should've tipped off the media right there. "Hold on," I said. "Who has an empty cardboard box in the attic? What family of five has the space for empty boxes?" I didn't buy it for a second.

What, no Christmas lights in the box? No faded art from kindergarten? No punch bowl with 107 matching cups and a broken plastic ladle?

Empty cardboard box? Not in my day. If there was a cardboard box in our attic, it had grout or roofing tiles in it and we kids had moved it up there ourselves, in winter.

And even if I'd emptied out a box, my dad wouldn't have let me hide in it, or even let me go up in that balloon peacefully, or alone, for that matter.

No, he taught me that if you wanted a reality TV show, you worked for it. "No one owes you a reality TV show," he used to say.

My dad would've sent me up there with all of my brothers and my cousins and then he would've had us vote one child off the balloon every few days.

At some point, he would've had me land and get myself inseminated with eight embryos, re-board and give birth pioneer-style and then raise them up on the balloon, taking the time to hold a pageant to determine which one was the prettiest.

And then—when I'd mastered some recipe involving seven specific and incongruous ingredients, using a flambé technique that I observed at a struggling restaurant, which I'd hovered over long enough to re-decorate and thus render entirely characterless—and only then, would I have been considered worthy of a reality TV show and allowed to get out of the balloon.

And so there'd be me, dancing out of my spacecraft, belting out a show tune, pivoting gracefully on four-inch heels in a backless gown of my own design, my tiara-wearing angel baby in one arm and a Cajun-inspired lamb and penne dish made with star anise, candy floss and soup in the other—and there, standing amid the throng of admiring supporters and journalists, all yelling questions, would be my dad.

And he'd be saying exactly what I always imagined he'd say, should I ever win a Pulitzer Prize for journalism (okay, I haven't thought that one through yet). He'd be saying, "Ask her about the math."

Cardboard box, you say? Poor boy was hidden in a cardboard box? Well, children, cry me a river. I dreamt of a cardboard box.

• • • • •

Roll Over, Ebenezer— There's a New Classic Christmas Tale. I Heard It from My Neighbour

The Globe and Mail, December 19, 2009

•

I used to have a neighbour who was a repository for all the world's urban legends.

Legends landed with her when they had reached their apex. Certainly one might hear a story about a couple who had five boys, tried for a girl one more time and had triplet boys. But not from Rachel. From Rachel, one would hear about a couple who had 15 boys, tried once more for a girl and were "surprised" with sextuplet boys, that very morning.

She was a sincere person. I'm not suggesting that she embellished these stories. It just seemed to me that after a story had wended its way through the story circuit, when it was plumped and full to bursting—when, for example, every business card ever handed out by a helpful stranger at a gas station was coated with a disorienting drug designed to make one faint at the exact moment that one pulled into one's garage—it came to Rachel.

One didn't hear from Rachel when there were alligators in the sewers. One heard from Rachel when hitherto unidentified Crocodilia poured from the faucet every time one turned the handle on the kitchen sink.

In fact, by the time the story of the 21-boy-childed family reached Rachel, all the boys had *hooks for hands!* Myths were archived with Rachel.

Rachel had a story about a couple who went on holiday to Florida with their two young children. They were friends of friends of Rachel's, which comprised an extraordinarily unlucky group of people. The couple met another couple with two children ("just like them," Rachel said) and, after a few afternoons by the pool, it was agreed that the couples would swap babysitting duties.

This went on for a week. One couple took the children one night, the other couple the next, and then, on the last night, her friends' friends went out for dinner and then dancing and, when they came back to their hotel, *the other couple and all of the children were gone.*

You'll note that Evil Couple took full advantage of all the free babysitting first. Just the worst kind of criminals. And also that the Good Couple had gone too far that night—not just dinner, but dancing!

Rachel had a Christmas story. Likely it didn't begin life as a Christmas story, but by the time it entered Rachel's Treasury, it went like this:

A divorced man was living in a motel, while his ex-wife lived in the house with their children. By Rachel's time, the ex-wife hadn't just met another man, nor had she just left her husband for another man, but—and I believe this was the detail, the tweak, that finally placed the story with Rachel—she had left her husband for his best friend.

As part of their "arrangement," as these things are called, the ex-husband still had to shovel the driveway of his old house. And in this story, it wasn't just winter, it was Christmas Eve. While the ex dutifully shovelled the snow as it was coming down, he looked up and saw his ex-wife and his former friend drinking champagne together and dancing, and he had a heart attack and he died.

And it kept snowing and they never found him until spring.

I'll admit this was my favourite of Rachel's stories.

"But how'd they know that he saw . . .?" I gently asked.

"So tragic," interrupted Rachel.

"But didn't she run into his body when she tried to take the car out?" I asked. "Or was he shovelling the front garden? Which is called stalking."

Rachel never answered me. She just said, "So sad," lost in—well, I won't call it thought. Lost in sad.

Every Christmas now, I try to puzzle this story out on my own.

Maybe this ex-wife and her new lover were having such a good time that they never thought to leave the house until the spring, in which case, I'm sorry, more power to them.

Or perhaps (and understand that in Toronto, where all of Rachel's friends' friends lived, we seldom get more than 10 inches of snow) the ex-husband wasn't a large man—a mere hint of a snow dune on his former front yard, really.

He was shoebox-sized, which likely made for a trying marriage. And yes, he died an ungraceful death but . . . no, wait, that's not true. It was a beautiful death. I love this story. It's a Christmas story. It's so very Hans Christian Andersen.

The ex-husband is there, you see, in the snow, outside the window. He's the Little Match Girl for our time.

Did he strike three matches, the Little Match Ex-Husband? Did he have three visions? Did his ex-wife wear red shoes? Did the bitch get up in the morning and say, "Idiot forgot to salt the steps"?

Yes, of course she did. Merry Christmas.

• • • • •

She Parcelled Out Love with Tinned Fish and Egg Coddlers

The Globe and Mail, December 24, 2010

•

The Christmas season in our family began early. It began with the arrival of the Christmas parcel from my maternal grandmother in South Africa.

Because my family has an imagined adversarial relationship with any organization that claims to be in the business of getting objects from point A to point B (airlines, the post office and anything connected to the disreputable profession of cartography), the parcel usually arrived in mid-October.

The parcel arrived only after many blue, folded airmail letters concerning this year's parcel strategy had been exchanged. Its arrival was preceded by an anxiety vigil that began in early June.

My parents believe that—just as airlines labour, through fine print, luggage restrictions and witchcraft, to ensure that their planes leave with as few passengers burdening them as possible—mail is a system to be gamed.

My parents arrive 12 hours before international flights. They sit and study the departure board as though they are trying to break a Cold War code. They rise with each flight announcement, check and recheck their tickets and generally behave as if awaiting a reprieve from a particularly hard-assed governor, not a plane.

They never doubted my grandmother's belief that the post office is an even cannier opponent. My grandmother took no risks with the parcel. It came wrapped in brown paper, addressed at least 15 times in chemically different inks, secured with string and covered in sealing wax.

I had, and still have, a poor understanding of sealing wax—its origins and purpose. As a child I imagined that, like the slaves building pyramids, thousands of bees died in the making of those Christmas parcels.

The parcel's substructure was fabric stitched over plastic, followed by a protective layer of the *Durban Mercury* and then straw (yes, straw), covered in heavier plastic in case the straw attracted donkeys, and each gift inside was separately wrapped and labelled.

In the early days of my childhood, the parcel waited under the tree like a second Christmas—stockings, gifts, parcel! But over the years its contents changed. Earlier, there were exotic chocolates, Marks & Spencer's pyjamas, fancier tights than my mother approved of and pencil boxes with secret drawers. Then the gifts grew weirder, darker.

Sometimes it was as if my grandmother were mailing things that she had found in her apartment. Or on a bus. Sometimes the gifts were themed—all medical supplies, or various egg coddlers. After a few years, we began to look at the parcel less in wondrous expectation and more in the way people now look at unattended luggage.

Just as it sometimes feels as if children born far apart in the same family are raised by different parents, my younger brothers grew up with a different Christmas parcel from the parcel of my early childhood.

My youngest brother hit his prime years of Christmas awareness during my grandmother's obscure-canned-goods phase. And in the way that even the youngest members of an older generation seek to keep the pleasures and mysteries of a holiday alive for the next, my big brother and I would watch him unwrap his gift and then say, "Oh! Wow, pilchards! You're so lucky!"

After opening the gifts, we'd call my grandmother to wish her a happy Christmas, tossing the phone from family member to family member as if it were on fire, as we'd practised, while my dad whispered his mantra: "Long distance is expensive."

Later we'd write cards: "Dear Grandmother, thank you for the green china cat, the wool vest and the box of marzipan and lemon-flavoured rusks . . ."

And still the gifts grew weirder. When I was 14 (exactly 14—I was born on Christmas Day), my family watched me unwrap an entirely sheer, tiny baby-doll nightie. It was as if my grandmother had sent me a G-string and pasties.

I blushed, and my parents jumped in, as I'd done on the tinned fish: "Oh, look! It's lovely! Go try it . . . oh. Never mind."

My grandmother died this past spring at 92, in her sleep, in her own bed, in apparent perfect health. "She just switched herself off," my mother told me.

Despite the airlines' best efforts, she'd been spending winters with my grandmother, bringing a Christmas cake wrapped like a Fabergé egg and returning with gifts, mostly for my children. I do so love to watch their faces. You can't buy tinned granadilla in Canada. You can buy coloured paper clips. She was a wonderful woman. Merry Christmas.

Mad As Hell?
Come Ride the Rage
Roller Coaster at Sun TV

The Globe and Mail, April 23, 2011

I received a fair bit of email about this column, all of it angry and much of it fixated on one thing: clearly I was lying, about everything, because in this column my son makes a remark "15 minutes into his oatmeal" and it doesn't take 15 minutes to eat a bowl of oatmeal.

"Gotcha!" cried the amateur detectives of the now-imploded Sun TV. I want to take a moment to clarify, to clear my name: it was real oatmeal, the slow-cooking kind, the best kind, and he came down while I was still making it.

•

Sun TV has come unstuck in time. It's as if, in its first few days, its pundits felt that they had a duty to diligently cover all the events they had missed before it existed. It's a news network for the recently cryo-genically unfrozen, who may be lying in bed and wondering about this Fidel Castro guy or the CBC "Vote Compass" story that was exhausted weeks ago.

Host Ezra Levant also bravely showed everyone those controversial Danish cartoons from five years ago. It felt as if, with the move to European cartoon brandishing, he was risking burning through all his A-material in the first 24 hours. Within six months, I predict Mr. Levant will be reduced to reading Asterix comics aloud and following up with viewer email responses the next day.

(Sun TV spends a lot of time reading its own email, which is about as exciting as it sounds. I can't wait for the conversation about whether they should switch from Firefox to Chrome.)

So far, Sun TV is a network about being a network. It spent most of its first day congratulating itself for being there and most of its second day retelling its nascent creation myth with telethon-esque levels of self-regarding pathos, full of awe at the amazing odds its staff feels it overcame to make it to air.

That's right: all the triumphalism of pirate radio, with absolutely none of the cool.

The anchors shout a lot for people who mostly agree with each other, as if music someone else had chosen was playing too loudly. The women smile and nod a great deal. They all wear bright, short skirts. None of them wear sleeves. About 70 percent of Sun TV's programming feels like being trapped at a second cousin's wedding reception.

They don't tell you much news, in either the strictest or the most lenient sense of the word, but they do tell you what to think about it. On Wednesday, from time to time an anchor would turn briskly to the camera and say, "Here's what's happening now," then replay a story from the day before. Which hadn't actually happened then, either.

For example, in demonstrating an understanding of the rules of our parliamentary system, Michael Ignatieff did not actually threaten to commit a crime. Either that or we'd better build even more new prisons, for Canada's clearly underutilized civics teachers.

"The world's a dangerous place," one of Sun TV's promos keeps insisting. And only they could make that fact this uninteresting. Not only did they literally have a dog-bites-man (all right, woman) story, but they were still repeating it 24 hours later. It seems against the spirit of the *Sun* newspaper tradition to turn on puppies like this. Where have all your cute puppies and puns gone, Sun?

I think I understand the idea behind Sun TV, and behind Fox News before it: these are places where angry people go to have fun. They're like anger theme parks. Their hosts are larger-than-life cartoons, welcoming the eager angry with buffoonish gestures and catchphrases.

So far, Sun TV's most notable catchphrase comes from Theo Caldwell, host of *The Caldwell Account*, who likes to say, "In the marketplace of ideas, you need buyers and sellers—that's how you find the price of the truth."

If I were assigned the difficult task of making sense of that statement, I'd say that it means that the truth is simply whatever idea is most popular—a concept that would be abhorrent to traditional conservatives, who like to accuse liberals of this kind of moral relativism. It's those conservatives, not the more liberal of us, who should've been looking south to Fox News in the States before now and worrying about Sun TV.

Glenn Beck, for example, is leaving Fox with his ratings between his legs. (He seems to have sold his chalkboard to Mr. Levant.) The Republicans are struggling to find a leader who is credible but can also summon their frenzied, paranoid base. It has been like a blowout party over there, and now the right is being discredited by its excesses, linked to its own worst elements the way the left was held to be discredited by the 1960s.

My son came downstairs while I was watching Sun TV. Fifteen minutes into his oatmeal, not five years from voting age, he laughed and said, "Wow, they're like little kids who've built a cardboard fort, and now they're pretending dragons are attacking it."

Exactly.

Scissors Cut Paper. Paper Wraps Rock. Monkey Bites Scientist

The Globe and Mail, May 28, 2011

•

Fun-loving cheeky monkeys may give the impression that they are not burdened by much. But, according to new research, they do in fact feel the same regrets as we do—at least when they are playing the game rock-paper-scissors.
—The Daily Mail (London), May 26, 2011

A study conducted by Yale University researchers Daeyeol Lee and Hiroshi Abe, published in the May 26 issue of the journal *Neuron*, has revealed that monkeys feel regret over the choices they make in rock-paper-scissors. This makes them pretty much unique in the animal kingdom, and leads some experts to suggest it's possibly unwise to play the game with monkeys.

"I think they take it way too seriously," one of the scientists observed, off the record. "I've seen a monkey with everything going for him go off on a bender after losing a game of rock-paper-scissors and just spiral downwards from there. A monkey approaches me with his hand out now, and I reach straight for a deck of cards. It's just too painful to watch. I'm always like, 'Hey, little dude, it's only a game.' But then they always bite me."

The results have led some in the monkey research community to demand that the line of inquiry be suspended, because sore-loser monkeys are, it has been concluded, really depressing and occasionally dangerous. But other researchers have reported that the vast majority of humans will also bite anyone who calls them "little dude." These scientists are asking for a deeper and more specific line of inquiry.

"Periodically I get the sense that it's not so much the losing that bothers the little du . . . I mean, the monkeys," explained Patricia Rowan of Cardiff University, looking around nervously, "so much as it's the rules of rock-paper-scissors."

Her team has made several attempts to replicate the initial study's findings: "Sometimes, if I pick 'paper' and the monkey picks 'rock'—so I win and therefore don't give him a food reward—the monkey will express extreme, even violent regret. One monkey just kept rolling his eyes at me and then began banging the side of his head with his fist slowly. I took detailed notes of the event. But later, when I returned to the lab, I found that a group of research monkeys had broken free from their cages and destroyed all of our paper notes. Apparently using rocks.

"That's right. We came back and found all of the monkeys sitting in their cages, happily engrossed in their usual games of chess and backgammon, but there was shredded paper and conspicuously placed, perfectly intact rocks everywhere.

"Another time," Dr. Rowan added, "I played 'rock' and one of our more senior monkeys played 'scissors'—I won, so naturally I refused to give him his treat, because those are the rules. And I swear to God he looked me right in the eye and signed at me, 'Oh, come on! What if these are really good scissors? Did you ever consider that? Do you have any idea how hard it'd be to smash a really high-quality pair of scissors with a rock? It would take forever and your fingers would get all bruised. Maybe when you play you're picturing some pathetic little nail scissors or, what, needlepoint scissors?' he continued, grabbing his treat angrily from the special Scientist Treat Bowl that I got in grad school. 'But I'm playing with something steel and Swiss, woman, you got that?'"

Chris Edwards, also of Cardiff, explained further. "We're wondering if we're not dealing with something more complex than monkeys having the ability to imagine alternative outcomes to their non-productive behaviours," he told Michael Finn, a science writer with the journal *Science Writing*. "Though that does show more cognitive reasoning than the jackass who calls my cell every day asking to speak to 'Lucinda' possesses.

"Generally," Dr. Edwards went on, "the subjects demonstrate little interest in playing rock-paper-scissors with me, for long periods of time, even when I'm really lonely. Super lonely, and there's nothing on TV. More research is needed. Way more. Say, what are you doing right now? What? What? You're staring at my hand, aren't you? Look, I just got bit a few times, that's all. No big deal. My left hand is still good. Come on, little dude, just a quick one. Hey! Ouch! That hurt! I'd love to know how much you're going to regret that."

To Canada, Some Ways to Keep Your Reputation at Its asBESTos™

The Globe and Mail, July 2, 2011

•

Dear Government of Canada:

Congratulations on your refusal to stigmatize asbestos by allowing it to be placed on the list of hazardous chemicals on the United Nations treaty, the Rotterdam Convention. In putting your foot down in this way, you have helped to ensure that countries exporting a known carcinogen (mostly to developing nations) need not add a warning that it be used correctly. May it be so for many years to come!

Our market research does, however, suggest that by bravely fighting alongside its traditional progressive allies—Ukraine, Kazakhstan, Kyrgyzstan and Vietnam—Canada may suffer some damage to its reputation abroad. Our polls indicate that, goodwill-wise, you've just about cancelled out the effects of the Vancouver Olympic Games, beavers and the liberation of the Netherlands.

You asked us how Canada might begin to redress this situation. We at Carson, Blanche and Whitehall believe that today, rebranding Canada means rebranding asbestos. We have put together a list of possible slogans and marketing ideas that we hope you will find of interest, but that are unlikely to get us sued:

1. "If you can read this, you're statistically unlikely to be installing our product."

2. Possible TV spot: A handsome 55-year-old man swings a club on an emerald-green golf course as the sun rises. The same man throws a Frisbee for his golden retriever on a white beach. A flag goes quickly up a pole. The man and his shapely wife leave the opera—early. Fireworks go off. Tag line: "Ask your doctor about asbestos. No, seriously, get some blood work done."
3. Start spelling it asBESTos™.
4. "Asbestos: A different kind of silver lining."
5. "Asbestos: It's like cotton candy for your walls. (But ideally not for mine.)"
6. "It's CARE-cinogenic."
7. "Look, world, it's practically the same colour as a baby seal, and we're saving it. Get off our backs."
8. "Asbestos, now with zero trans fats."
9. "Breathe different."
10. Product placement: We could get James Franco to wear a smart asbestos shirt in his next movie. Around the office, most of us saw this as a win-win.
11. Licensing the capricious Pink Panther character turned out to be profitable strategy for Fiberglas pink insulation. You'll never land anything that cute, because face it, it's asbestos, but we're thinking we can cut a deal with Inspector Gadget.
12. "Asbestos: At least you won't die in a fire."
13. We're talking with the OPI nail polish colour folks. Expect "Absolutely Asbestos" and "Chrysotile Used-to-Be-Pink Lung" in their fall lineup.
14. "Asbestos, insulating you against life."
15. Idea: Rename as Asbest-o's—"rich in fibre"!
16. "Asbestos, helping you forget the tar sands."
17. We want to play up the heritage angle on this product. A few tweaks to a Wikipedia page and presto: "It is said that the Inuit have 373 words for asbestos."
18. "Hey, whiners, what do you think was in those Green Gables?"

19. Idea: Could we start calling it "clean asbestos"?
20. Possible TV spot: A fresh-faced, pretty but earnest-looking university-type woman stands in the forest. A scientist walks purposefully across a laboratory. An elderly couple hold hands on their tasteful yet dated sofa. They all talk directly to the camera about anything that has nothing to do with asbestos. Tagline: "These people, who seem like just the sort of people you wish you knew, were brought to you by the Quebec Asbestos Mining Association."
21. "Like poutine for your lungs."
22. "Asbestos: It can't spill."
23. "Good to the last cough of blood."
24. "A mine is a terrible thing to waste."
25. "Save the whales."
26. "It takes a licking and . . . oh no! Dear God! Don't lick it! "

Eagerly awaiting your response,

Douglas T. Carson
Carson, Blanche and Whitehall

The Summer We Nested Nessie

The Globe and Mail, July 9, 2011

When I was about 11 years old, my family was living in England and we drove up to Scotland in the spring and visited Loch Ness. While there, I filled a clear glass bottle with Loch Ness water and put it in the back seat of the car where my two brothers and I rode.

A day after we left Scotland, my younger brother, Finnegan, who was six, found the bottle and asked me about the air bubble inside it. I told him that the gelatinous-appearing bubble in the bottle was a Loch Ness Monster egg that I was lucky enough to have scooped out of the water, and that if we wanted a baby Loch Ness Monster, he only had to sit on the bottle every day until the egg hatched.

And so my brother sat on the large glass bottle, and slept on top of the large glass bottle, in the back of our little blue camper van, day after day after day after night.

During the long car rides, he'd ask me questions about how to care for a baby Loch Ness Monster—feeding it, getting it out of the bottle, training it—and I would answer him in great detail. We always whispered. I insisted.

"You know how Mum and Dad are about pets," I said. I still didn't have a dog after years and years of lobbying, and one very junior year spent trailing a piece of string around mournfully and telling people that it was my dog.

My dog-getting strategies were legendary. When I was in grade two I was sent, yet again, to a child psychiatrist, to investigate my inability to thrive in a classroom setting. When asked to draw a picture of my family, I drew my father, my mother, my two brothers and a big, healthy dog.

I did this because I knew that after I'd finished the picture—big sun in the right-hand corner, small house, single cloud—the psychiatrist would ask me to tell him about every member of the family. When I got to the dog, I said, "That's a dog. I don't have a dog." And then I looked at him in my most sincere way and added, "But I really want one." That would sure get me thriving, I tried to suggest.

No go. No dog. More doctors.

Eventually, when I was about 10, the excuse I was given for not getting a dog was that it was too expensive to fence the garden.

I began wandering around the yard with a measuring tape (hauling a brick from place to place to mark various spots I'd reached, as it was not a long measuring tape) and then I'd call fence companies to discuss heights and materials and get estimates for fencing off various sections of the yard.

The line "If we fenced from . . ." became a family joke every time I admired a gorilla or a whale on *Mutual of Omaha's Wild Kingdom*. Hilarious. I just wanted a dog, and fence math remains my only math.

So I told my little brother as he sat on the bottle, "Yeah, Mum and Dad don't like pets. But once it hatches and they see its little Loch Ness Monster face, they'll let us keep it for sure."

Finnegan (whose name I had chosen—which shows you how much I wanted a dog) had Ness-nested for about a week before my mum asked why he was sitting on a glass bottle instead of wandering around Stonehenge. I had to watch my poor little brother confess guiltily that he was an accessory to breeding a legendary beast without parental consent.

Very shortly, the attention turned to me.

I was in trouble, no question. But what really got me was that Finnegan cried and cried in genuine, anguished disappointment over the loss of his monster, all the way to Dover. I'll never forget it.

He visited me from San Francisco last weekend and finally said, "Why do you keep baking me muffins?" The guilt was crushing then, and still hovers.

But the truth is that on that British holiday I, too, somehow had come to believe we were hatching a Loch Ness Monster egg (to be fair, I'd taken some shifts), except that in my mind it was going to look a lot like a dog.

Drive safely this summer, Canada. Happy road trips.

Jeepers Creepers!
There's a Lascivious Peeper
Living in my Garden

Elle Canada, August 2006

•

What a glorious thing it is to be a raccoon. In the city. That's what my backyard raccoon seems to be saying to me, striding a wisteria-entwined beam on my pagoda. He sits there in the autumn twilight and watches me garden, and he'll do this for hours. He watches me move ever so casually—as casually as I can—from the rose bush to the fish pond and back to the table. And if I look up suddenly from a bit of weeding, I'll find that he's still watching me—and that makes me uncomfortable. Sometimes I boldly say, "Shoo," which I regret, for as soon as I acknowledge him I find myself dancing up and down, waving my clippers at him and shouting, "Shoo, shoo." This always feels like he has won—still he watches me. Only now I'm dancing.

I'm usually wearing my flowered gardening hat, oversized workman's gloves, overalls and a pair of pink Birkenstocks. There isn't a man in the city who wouldn't run screaming from the sight of a woman dressed like this, but still he watches me. He stretches out bigger on his wisteria, crosses and re-crosses his hands and then—I swear to you—smiles down at me. He is the Cheshire Raccoon.

Americans, as I observed while camping in the southern states, have very small raccoons. Our squirrels are the size of their raccoons, our raccoons are the size of their bears, and our bears are the size of their ladies in the snack and dip aisle at Winn-Dixie. American women can't understand why this raccoon causes me anxiety or why I would go into the garage and come out—casually—with my hoe, but he does. He sees right through me.

"What the hell were you planning on doing with a hoe?" he seems to say. "No one in the city has a hoe. Mr. McGregor has a hoe. Women like you have 18 very expensive little rubber-gripped trowels buried all over the garden—not a hoe. You don't even know how to *use* a hoe. You're going to pretend to be tending your imaginary radishes and then suddenly turn, waving it menacingly . . ." He seems to be saying, "Yeah, just like that, doll" when I whip around, brandishing my hoe—a gift from my dad—while shouting, "Go away, you big fat raccoon! Go away!"

He doesn't look frightened at all; he looks pleased. He shifts forward a little on his decadent bed of wisteria, and everything about him seems to say, "Go on, little girl. Don't let me stop you. Jump up and down some more if you like. You're cute when you're angry." That makes me angrier and him happier. We've been at this all summer. Sometimes he watches me until midnight.

It unnerves me.

There's something about the way he looks at me—something almost greedy. He's not hungry—that huge, slovenly, fat-ass raccoon sprawled out on the sagging pagoda like an enormous, furry, late-season bloom. There's something else he wants. No, not food—not in this town, not in this neighbourhood. He owns this town, happy, fat-ass raccoon does. He owns its fine morsels of garbage, its fruity compost, the picnic remnants from the park across the street and—once or twice—the dog food bowl kept just inside my kitchen door. Why, I put two perfectly ripe avocados in my green bin for him every week—protection money for the koi in my fish pond. No, there's something else he wants. There's something about the way he looks at me—something about his expression. I hope you won't think of me as vain when I come out and say it, but there is something about the way he looks at me that is *lustful*. That raccoon *wants* me—I am sure of it. I only wish winter would come so I could go inside—casually.

Buses from Hell? Exasperating Tour Guides? It's Character Building

The Globe and Mail, August 6, 2011

•

Around this time last summer I drove my son to New York City and we visited the Tenement Museum, which is housed in a former tenement on the Lower East Side.

It was (I'm bad with actual temperatures) approximately 6,890 degrees that day and, in order for my boy to see as much of Manhattan as possible, we'd taken a bus all the way down from Spanish Harlem, where we were staying. That kind of bus ride is so long that I swear a new civilization broke out—a government formed and a variety of music unique to that bus developed before midtown.

At a certain point a man in a wheelchair boarded and the bus's inhabitants responded by developing a workable social safety net (it mostly involved four women yelling at everyone else about the character of the woman who'd raised them). It stretched the bus's resources to its limits, but still Buslandia produced some compelling art.

It was a horrific, interminable ride on a bus so full that soon no one could get off or on. I'm pretty sure that if there were (and I'll never be sure there weren't) reptiles or finches on that bus, they would, on examination, have been found to be subtly distinct from other fauna on other buses.

In short I was hot and tired by the time we reached the museum and when we registered for our tour and my son saw the box I'd ticked (apparently a tour that involved singing) he looked at me coldly and said, "Whose mother are you?"

He selected the least theatrical-looking tour, which was led by a woman with a strong Brooklyn accent. As our group stood in the front hallway of the building she explained the history of the museum and then began talking to us like this: "There are no light fixtures here. So what do you think it would've looked like in this hallway at night back then?"

We (all, with the exception of my son, grownups) looked at her politely.

"This hallway has no windows. Imagine it's night and, remember, there's no electricity. What do you think it would've been like here?"

We stared at her some more. Several people tried nodding.

"Who can picture this hallway, at night without lights? Can anyone tell me what this hallway would've been like a hundred years ago? When it wasn't bright outside and there was nothing to plug in that might generate any kind of illuminating rays."

No one knew what to do. Or what had happened. We were trapped together in the Museum of What Should Be Rhetorical Questions.

"Can anyone tell me . . ." she tried repeatedly, before some public-spirited man finally said, "It would've been dark?"

"That's right!" she said, in genuine delight. The tour continued in the same vein. It turns out the stairwell, as someone eventually ventured, had also known darkness.

Upstairs we learned about a particular family—a horrible story about a family with as many children as there were people in our group, and who might, admittedly, have been equally miserable.

"So then one day Mrs. Cappelli"—or some such name—"does the laundry," we learned several years into their story (we were by now well-versed in her laundry-doing ways). She cooks the dinner, but Mr. Cappelli doesn't come home.

"Can anyone tell me what happened to Mr. Cappelli?" A recap of Mrs. Cappelli's miserable day, then the question posed again.

My son looked at me quizzically. And even though I was dying in the heat—and thinking, "Everyone told me I had to come here. Do they not know that I've *had* crappy apartments? I've seen the contemporary version of what this was, what my *Globe* colleague Doug Saunders so rightly calls an 'arrival city.' I get it"—I didn't wink at my boy.

I was there to fill him with appreciation for his life—we'd already done cool stuff in New York—but I was also there to make him feel really bad, as we're told we must periodically do with our children. So instead I smiled brightly at him, until someone finally said, "Mr. Cappelli didn't come home?"

I shook my head in disgust, even though I was right there with the evil Mr. Cappelli at that point. I was about to ask which subway he'd taken. I was wondering if Mrs. Cappelli began every meal with "Do you know what I did to this potato?"

When we got outside (things turned out fine for Mrs. Cappelli), my son just looked at me and said, "Seriously?" And we both began running as fast as we could.

An Apple for My Teacher

The Globe and Mail, October 7, 2011

.

I spent a fair amount of time when I was about 10 wondering if, to use the terrible vernacular of the time, I was "retarded." I remember, after a particularly frustrating day at school, asking my smartest friend on the way home if she thought "retarded" people knew that they were so.

She said, "They probably don't know for sure. But they probably wonder about it." I walked the rest of the way home in silence.

I tried to test myself: Once, after a day of academic failure, I tried reciting "How Doth the Little Crocodile," the way Alice in *Alice in Wonderland* did when she wanted to resolve a similar question about herself. I could do it. But recitation skills didn't help me at school, where I failed, cheated and barely passed year after year.

I'd begun school by repeating kindergarten. I didn't read until grade four, when mercifully reading seemed to come to me all at once. But my letters and numbers were wrong when I wrote them down.

I remember in a very early grade the teacher instructing the boys to put their finished written work in one pile and the girls in another, and myself standing at the table, scared of making a mistake; while I knew without question that I was a girl, the girls' pile was neat and tidy, and my smudged scrawls were worse than anything the piggy boys had produced. I refused to put the piece of paper down. I continued to not hand in assignments for years to come.

I'm learning disabled, as many people are. There was little testing back then. If you misspelled a word they made you write that word out 10 times—of course, I'd write it six different ways. No amount of extra lessons, practice or punishment could correct my handwriting, which meant that even though I often understood the material presented in, say, science class, I'd fail the test.

I read all the time, but I could still barely pass English, as marks were deducted for every spelling error. Even if teachers were patient enough to decipher what I'd written, A essays became D essays by the third paragraph. Worse, the fact that I read was taken as a sign of at least average intelligence, which meant that I was "underperforming"—wilfully failing.

It's difficult to explain what it's like to be learning disabled. The closest I can get is to say that it felt as if I had a smart person's mind but a stupid person's brain—the mechanism I needed to express my thoughts didn't work. Alongside the spelling and handwriting problems, anything that involved organization or patterns—math, for example—was nearly impossible for me. I never had a pen. (I still never have a pen.)

Not surprisingly, I left school after grade nine. I worked as a nanny and in retail and in restaurants. At 21, I bought a Macintosh computer and it was like giving someone with terrible eyesight her first pair of glasses. In many ways the field was levelled.

Of course, a lot of what Apple did wasn't new. And I'd dealt with computers before. But before that I hadn't wanted to—couldn't, in fact—work on one. I needed a prosthetic limb for the parts of myself that failed me, and Steve Jobs—with his insistence that computers be intuitive and responsive, and his uncanny sense of what that meant—made Apple products exactly that.

Mr. Jobs was an artist of technology. One accusation levelled against dedicated Apple buyers is that they're seduced by elegant design. But humans have always made art of their tools, their weapons and their armour, and our computers are all those things.

Apple designs are frequently delightful, but it's more the way he approached his work that made Mr. Jobs an artist—the stakes and investment in the tech world are breathtakingly high, making sticking to one's vision a true high-wire act. He stuck.

It's counterintuitive, then, to say that his work was modest. But every day my own Mac says to me, "Don't worry about the details. None of this is worth considering. You get on with your work."

I'm grateful.

Lighten Up, Ladies! Sexual Harassment, Sexual Shmarassment, Right?

The Globe and Mail, November 12, 2011

•

"By the way, folks, yes, I am an unconventional candidate and, yes, I do have a sense of humour—some people have a problem with that."
> —US Republican presidential hopeful Herman
> Cain, addressing accusations that he sexually
> harassed employees

It's an accusation that plagues women: that we don't have a sense of humour.

That we, as a sex, consistently miss the joke is the first line of defence when a man is accused of inappropriate behaviour in the workplace. And, yes, this can give women something like libel chill—call it accusation-of-humourlessness chill.

Women will mull over a deeply unpleasant encounter for hours and run it by friends: "Would this have been a joke in his native country of Denmark? Quick, someone run it through Google Translate, then run it back the other way again. Now try saying it with a funny wig and glasses on, because maybe the area manager's a prop comic, but his stuff was in the car. Could this possibly, conceivably, be a joke that I didn't get?"

Basically, half the people on the planet are wandering around in a state of hyper-"was that a joke?"-awareness. Some self-preservation instinct kicks in if you ask a woman what time it is: she'll unconsciously parse your query for clever puns, and possibly smile weakly just in case you've made a witty movie reference she's missed. Ask a woman if she'd like to see a menu and she'll end up scanning it for hilarious double entendres. This is why it takes us so long to order.

Ever since Herman Cain predictably hauled out that line in response to serious allegations of sexual harassment, I've been wondering how women might resolve the issue once and for all.

It's distracting. It hurts our productivity. Some of us will now sit in a meeting with a man, listening to him talk about, say, life-threatening safety violations in our workplace, and be wondering if he thinks he's doing a Seth Rogen impression and when in his speech we're meant to start laughing. Sometimes we do start laughing. It's a defensive move. We look insane! But insane is okay. Just never let it be said that we don't have a sense of humour.

Our humourlessness is wrecking everything! Why, as US Senator Rand Paul said last week in Mr. Cain's defence, "There are people now who hesitate to tell a joke to a woman in the workplace, any kind of joke, because it could be interpreted incorrectly. I don't. I'm very cautious." And since Mr. Paul is no doubt the Noël Coward of his generation, we should act quickly—some of his jokes may be topical!

So here's my proposal: Women, we need to start finding sexual harassment a lot funnier.

The next time one of your superiors presses his pelvic area against your bottom as he passes behind you at the photocopier, burst out laughing loudly.

Turn and say, "That's hilarious! Hey, everyone, get this! Mike from legal just touched my ass with his penis! While I was working! I barely know him! He is hysterical." Lighten the hell up, girls. We need this.

If someone sends you an email hinting that your chances of promotion are contingent upon his access to your breasts, change the font to Comic Sans and forward it to everyone in the company. Maybe add a picture of a kitten hanging by its paws!

And if a superior at your office Christmas party whispers to you that he has a hotel room and an enormous penis, laugh! Lighten up and laugh with him! Let everyone see your amusement. Say, "Jon, you're a riot! That's so funny! Someone should totally book you to do children's parties!"

Share your amusement with the crowd: Yell, "Ha! Jon just told me he has a hotel room and an enormous penis! Hey, Jon, that's a good one! Did you hear that one somewhere else? You should totally write that bit up as a 'Shouts & Murmurs' and send it to the *New Yorker*. That is gold. Do you have an agent? Because with lines like that, sir, you are wasted in human resources."

No, I don't understand why some men want us to find anything involving their penises so funny. But work with me, womankind, lest it ever be said again that we can't take a joke.

• • • • •

A Very Tardy, Slightly Guilty Thank-You Card from a Sketchy Paper Girl

The Globe and Mail, December 24, 2011

•

When I was about 10 years old, I had a paper route for more than a year, during which time I mostly delivered newspapers to the somewhat confused people who lived next door to the somewhat angry people who had actually ordered those newspapers. I never quite memorized my route.

I don't think it could be said of the *Guelph Mercury* that it had an ideological slant. But rather I think I gave it one, which was, "From each according to his means, to each according to my whims," because, with me among its ranks, what the newspaper had operating for it in those days was less of a newspaper delivery system and more of a newspaper dispersal system.

I was raised on a heating vent in the corner of my parents' kitchen. I'd eat my breakfast there in the morning and return to it straight after school. I was always cold, so a paper route that, as I remember it, I held for an 18-month stretch that ran on some sort of Narnia-esque December-to-February loop, wasn't the best career move for me. However, my older brother was the Guelph paper route kingpin and he'd buy a box of Smarties for me if I went collecting with him, so I thought I knew the business.

Collecting was the worst part of a paper route because every paper route back then had 10 customers who were never home and 10 customers who never left the house. With the first group, you'd have to go back repeatedly to try to nail them to pay, and the second group would invite you inside. Little old ladies with long, chimey doorbells who, I was sure, hadn't felt sunlight in 30 years would shout far too joyously to their invisible husbands in the den, "The paperboy is here! And he's brought his little sister!" while the snow melted off us and onto their gold-toned linoleum front hall tiles.

A cloud of smoke would come forth from the den and the lady of the house would press baked goods upon us. I haven't looked into this, but there must have been some sort of belief at the time that date squares, shortbread and certain other pastries absorbed second-hand smoke. These ladies always had dense, smoky-tasting squares and bars on hand and I felt that, housebound as they clearly were (where do the dates come from? I'd wonder), they were using us to smuggle second-hand smoke out of their houses. I think they must have known that those primitive air filters that they called "lovely scones" were going straight under the nearest hedge, then dusted politely over with snow, as soon as my brother and I were out of sight, but that was part of their plan.

Most nights, just as my family was finishing dinner, the phone would ring and everyone would look over at me on the heating vent, and sigh. Then my mother would answer the phone and say, for example, "Mrs. Hendershott at 73 Dean did not get her newspaper tonight," and I'd bundle up and walk to the Becker's in the dark, through the snow, and buy a paper from the box out front, cutting into my small profit margin. If the Becker's box was empty, I'd have to try the mile-away Mac's Milk box before heading back to Mrs. Hendershott's place at "73 Dean. 73 Dean. 73 Dean . . . or at least I think it was 73 Dean."

"I guess we'd better tip the papergirl . . ." That's how I imagine a lot of bewildered conversations began at Christmastime during my paper route reign. Having a route was all about the Christmas tip. That was the big payoff. Collecting during that season was like an extended Christmas morning: gifts, cards, money and carcinogenic reindeer-shaped cookies were generally received. But then, so were newspapers, and I can't say I fulfilled that part of the bargain.

My attitude was, "If it's not there, try your neighbour's house. You should all talk more anyway." And yet there my expectant face would be at the doors of my customers' houses—and possibly at the doors of the people who lived next door to my customers as well, peering around the corner and silently making harsh judgments about their sickly, weird-looking Christmas trees and home decor in general.

I imagine I put such a strain on charity and goodwill that the season, choking with these attributes, barely survived. Still, I was tipped very well, and this is to say, I'm sorry and grateful. And Merry Christmas.

If Only Those Caucus Walls Could Talk (and Certain Ministers Couldn't)

The Globe and Mail, February 18, 2012

•

Perhaps the person most disappointed with Minister of Public Safety Vic Toews this week was Prime Minister Stephen Harper.

I like to imagine him calling a meeting about the matter: He gets up from his desk wearily, takes off his glasses, rubs his eyes a little, sighs and then says to the gathered Conservative MPs, "Look, when I told you people last week that you could not go calling the Canadian people Nazis, I did not mean—put the yo-yo away, Tony—I did not mean—look at me when I'm talking, Vic—and I shouldn't have to tell you this—that you could call them child pornographers."

"I only said they were 'with child pornographers,'" Mr. Toews might mumble under his breath, kicking the carpet.

"So, what, they're undercover cops, Vic? Or the child pornographers owe them money and they're just over there asking them to give it back? Is that how we're going to spin this, Vic? No, I don't think that will work, Mr. Minister of Public Safety. You as good as called anyone opposed to Bill c-30—a piece of legislation that will compel internet service providers to spend lots of money so that police agencies can force them to spy on their customers, without anyone ever obtaining a warrant—a pedophile, and if there's one thing people hate, it's being called a . . ."

Hands fly up, a voice calls out, "Oh, I know! I know! A Nazi, sir! They hate being called a Nazi?"

"Yes, yes, they hate being called Nazis." Mr. Harper takes a sweetie out of a box on his desk and tosses it over to MP Larry Miller. "But they also hate it when you call them pedophiles. Didn't your mothers teach you that? Don't call people pedophiles? It's not even a slang thing, as in, 'How's it hangin', you old pedophile, you?' or 'What up, you disgusting child predator?' Even pedophiles don't call each other pedophiles.

"Do we need to go on a field trip? Do I have to take you out to a local bar, perhaps, where one of you can call out, 'A round for all the pedophiles in the house!' and then watch what happens? Come away from the door, Mr. Fantino. The question was rhetorical."

"Don't you mean 'developmentally disabled,' sir?" an eager, anxious young backbencher suggests.

"No, I said 'rhetorical,' not . . . oh, never mind," the prime minister says. "Good—good that you are paying attention.

"Right now," he goes on, "you, Minister Toews, have achieved something very rare on the internet: there's consensus in the comment sections. Left, right, in every paper, in both official languages, everyone hates you. You're the un-Lin. They're all in the comments right now practically holding hands, swaying, singing "Imagine" and thumbs-upping each other in a giddy, almost-sexual frenzy of agreement . . . Oh dear, someone get Mr. Trost a chair, and his smelling salts. Sorry, Brad.

"There's a legend that when everyone on the internet agrees with each other, it'll explode. Then how are we going to spy on people? And—give me the yo-yo, Tony; put down that phone, Mr. McKay, you're walking home—of course, anyone, and there were few to begin with, who was prepared to believe that we could be trusted with the un-precedented access to their personal information that Bill C-30 will give us—because they figured, you know, Conservatives aren't crazy, or paranoid about what Canadians are up to—is now reconsidering that position.

"So, let's try this again, what are we going to call our opponents that's not excessive?"

"Nazis!" someone calls out.

"Pedophiles!" seven or eight more people call out.

"No, no, 'Nazi' and 'pedophile' are the bad words, remember?" our prime minister says, patiently.

Another backbencher sticks up his hand. "Maybe if we defended our ideas on their merits and didn't call the other side any kind of name . . .?"

Sudden collective gasp.

"You know what to do," Mr. Harper says.

Sheepishly, the backbencher goes to stand in the Loser Corner. Mr. Harper looks sad.

"When are the pandas coming, sir?" the right honourable member for Nipissing–Timiskaming asks.

"Pandas! Pandas! Pandas!" everyone cries out. "Sir, if the pandas make a baby, can we keep it?" someone asks excitedly.

Our prime minister allows himself a small smile. "Will you walk it?" he asks.

"Yes! Yes! Every day! Right after Question Period."

"And what will you call it?" he asks.

"Hitl—"

"Ah, ah," Mr. Harper says, wagging his finger, still smiling.

"Panda Bear!" Minister John Baird cries out above the fray.

"Oh, all right then," our prime minister says. "You can keep it."

Reading Between the Lines and Coming Clean in the Women's Showers

Elle Canada, June 2007

•

I begin my days as I believe every woman should: by showering naked with 25 or so other naked women. I can't begin to tell you the difference that this can make in a woman's life. After a few years in the locker room, everything seems okay, much seems beautiful and nothing surprises me at all. So diverse are these women's bodies that I imagine that an alien, fresh from another planet, could enter the YMCA, randomly line up half a dozen naked members in a row (could be part of his alien mission, could be he's just a really pervy alien) and never conclude that all six women were the same species. I thought nothing could get my attention anymore—or, at least, I did until last month, when, while showering, I looked up and, four showers over, I saw her.

She was a perfectly nice-looking woman who happened to have what I can only describe as her entire "cuntle region" shaved. This, of course, is not unusual, but what is unusual is that across—and here I'll use the phrase again because I'm sort of hoping it will catch on—her shaved cuntle region was tattooed a word. Just one word.

Now the thing about this is, I'm a reader. I'm a text kind of person. When I see something written down, by golly, I have to read it. If I start a book, I have to finish it. So, as soon I recognized that this tattoo was a word, I had to read what was written down—down there—but the problem was, she was just far enough away that I couldn't.

Naturally, I figured it had to be important because whatever it is that her cuntle region says, it must require a fair amount of maintenance to say it. Frankly, the effect reminded me of those signs that are planted in flowers along stretches of Toronto's Gardiner Expressway—it's a pleasant enough form of advertising but, as a bit of a gardener myself, I can't look at those signs without picturing the weeding involved to keep those messages crisp.

It's not cool to turn a shower off and move one shower closer to someone, and I couldn't exactly put my shampoo down, wander off to my locker and come back with my glasses on. Rule of thumb: you can't really shower—in any kind of offhand way—in your glasses. After a while, I just wanted to ask her something like, "Hey, what does your, uh, what exactly does your nether region say there, lassie?"—you know, something casual like that. But, in general, you can't start a casual conversation with a woman after you've been staring at her vagina for 15 minutes.

"Perhaps she has committed—in a big way—to a particular pair of novelty panties," I thought. Maybe there's a guy out there with "Official Bikini Inspector" tattooed on his chest as well. It would be sad to think that it's just her name—sort of a "Hey, buddy, I'll make this easy for you; it's 'Denise.'" Denise? I considered that for a second. Was that first letter a D? I squinted hard and turned the water temperature down, trying to get the damn steam to clear. "Hey," I thought, "what if it's *Rosebud*?" Nah, too obvious.

That day, I gave my hair the deepest deep conditioning it has ever had in its life. It came out like I had fried bacon on it. I was standing there, trying not to look but completely unable to rinse my hair off and leave it alone.

People—serious readers—will often sigh over so much left unread. "Stick to the classics," they'll say. "There's so little time." But I'll tell you that the naked lady left—she wrapped herself in a towel and left. She has never been back, and I know that it's sure as hell not *Swann's Way* that I'll go to my grave regretting.

At Last, a Surefire Way to Have Our Cabinet Speak with One Voice

The Globe and Mail, April 28, 2012

•

Memo from the Office of Prime Minister Stephen Harper: In an effort to streamline the process, the Conservative Party of Canada has produced a form letter for ministerial apologies. We have given this matter serious consideration and hope (not unreasonably, the prime minister would like to stress) that this form covers every conceivable eventuality. Ministers are asked to please fill out the form 7 to 21 days after the need arises.

Dear [choose one],
- ☐ Taxpayers
- ☐ Conservative voters
- ☐ Family-loathing separatists
- ☐ Airport security personnel
- ☐ Svalbard
- ☐ Sentient beings of the riding of Alpha Centauri West

It has come to my attention that questions have been raised about [choose one]
- ☐ sensitive documents I left at the home of my girlfriend, the biker moll.

☐ the search and rescue helicopter that gave me a ride from my fishing vacation.
☐ my lost weekend at a swanky London hotel where armies of perfumed eunuchs grow orange trees right before your eyes, and then pluck the succulent fruit so that unicorns may squeeze the juice in a breathtaking ballet.
☐ the many gazebos my department erected on your distant planet as part of our US–Canada border security plan.
☐ the fact that I'm Helena Guergis.

I would like to take this opportunity to assure you that I have thoroughly investigated the [choose one]
☐ unfortunate incident
☐ oversight
☐ misunderstanding
☐ accounting discrepancy
☐ mass interplanetary slaughter

and that the events in question [choose one]
☐ took place without my direct knowledge and now require the attention of someone deeply familiar with the portfolio, and that would be me.
☐ are an unavoidable consequence of me not having the foggiest notion of what goes on in my own department.
☐ have further deepened our understanding of the picnic needs of the residents of Alpha Centauri West in a way that promises to be most beneficial to hard-working Canadians.

I want to be clear that I take full responsibility for the thing of which I still only have the vaguest knowledge, and about which I was quoted out of context. And I am [choose one]
☐ prouder than ever to be Canadian.
☐ chastened but unbowed.

□ sorry if you have chosen to take offence.

□ unreservedly sorry.

□ admitting that I had reservations on a sorry but cancelled them when a more expensive sorry came to my attention.

I ask that you please accept [choose one]

□ this hastily written cheque.

□ my aide's resignation.

□ another aide's resignation.

□ this construction contract.

□ John Baird yelling in the House of Commons.

□ John Baird yelling just outside the House of Commons.

□ John Baird yelling on *The National*.

□ John Baird standing on a street corner yelling at passing cars.

□ John Baird yelling across 29.6 trillion light years at your bloodied yet undefeated riding. (Trust me, this works.)

This morning, I offered my resignation to the prime minister and he [choose one]

□ turned it down!

Seriously, can you [choose one]

□ believe that kind of awesome?

I really do not think there is a better man to lead this country in a strong, stable majority than [choose one]

□ Stephen Harper.

No one is sorrier than I am to be asked to be this sorry, but I would remind Canadians of the [choose one]

□ pandas.

□ Olympics.

□ royal wedding.

☐ Arctic.

☐ sponsorship scandal.

At this juncture we can all agree on the need to move forward. Hindsight is always 20/20, but at the time the unfortunate decision was made I was [choose one]

☐ having breakfast, and thirsty.

☐ drunk as a skunk.

☐ the tender age of 40.

☐ actually sitting in the cockpit of a fighter jet, and that was cool.

☐ completely unaware, and I had no way of knowing, other than to ask, that the gazebo is a highly offensive symbol in your culture. I deeply regret the action that my department now acknowledges was the equivalent of erecting a large bronze penis balancing a swastika on its nose in every single park in the once-beautiful riding of Alpha Centauri West. And then blaming Alpha Centauri East.

Sincerely,

_____ , Minister of _____

Can You Keep a Secret?
The NDP May Yet Find
a Way to Stop Hitler

The Globe and Mail, May 5, 2012

•

I wouldn't normally write about the prime minister lambasting the New Democrats for failing to stop Hitler even though the party didn't exist at the time. After all, he did it a week ago, and that's usually enough time to have some new source of inspiration spring up.

But then something unusual happened that I must share with you.

I was in my kitchen cooking when, in a great flash of orange light, a strange young man appeared.

"Don't be alarmed," he said politely. "My name is Kyle. I'm an NDP volunteer from the future. I just want a moment of your time, if that's all right."

"Oh, okay," I said, feeling remarkably unthreatened. I went to the fridge, got a couple of beers and passed him one. "Have some soup," I said, ladling some from the pot. "It's okay. It's a vegetable stock," I added, anticipating the question. "What can I do for you, Kyle?"

"I've come from the year 3016. Like all NDP volunteers, I'm a time traveller. In the future, we've been in power a long time and we've solved most of the world's problems. It's getting boring, so I thought I'd come back to set the record straight about some of the NDP's efforts in history—and to fulfill my dream of having you tell my life story."

"Why me?"

"I've studied your work," he replied. "Read everything you've written. I did my master's on one of the long-form pieces for which you won one of your three Pulitzers."

"Really?" I said, getting the man more soup. "Three?"

"Yes. I often wonder what would've happened if you hadn't left journalism to live in a castle on Lake Geneva with George Clooney and write poetry."

"Oh, come now," I said suspiciously. "I find that hard to believe . . . poetry?"

"Yes, poetry. In my time, you're known as 'the Canadian Pushkin.'"

"Am I any good?"

"No. But people assume that 'Canadian' is a dead language and that much is being lost in translation. Anyway, too bad about the duel. George was heartbroken to lose you."

"Of course. How did your adventures begin?" I asked, putting on my journalist's hat.

"Look, you know how it goes, you get involved with a party at university, maybe join a student group, help register a few voters. The next thing you know, you're travelling back in time and chaining yourself to an allosaurus. Say, what's with the weird hat?"

"The NDP tried to save the dinosaurs?" I asked, sheepishly removing my hat.

"Of course. We did everything we could. I even composed a song. We helped to organize the dinosaurs, but the asteroid wouldn't come to the table."

"Oh, yeah," I said, "but then . . ."

"Yeah. Boom! It really came to the table."

"It's hard to win against Big Asteroid," I said comfortingly. "I'm sure you had successes."

"Oh, yes! I was in the fiddle circle while Rome burned and, while we may not have put out any fires, I promise you, we changed the dialogue," Kyle said happily.

"The problem is that everyone remembers the 300 Spartans at Thermopylae, but who's to tell of the 15 NDP volunteers who put up the posters and reminded the Spartans to stay well hydrated."

"Impressive," I said. "Spartans are the hardest to hydrate."

"One time, a hundred or so of us all assembled on this big ship that was about to hit an iceberg, but some thought the boat should veer right, some thought left, and some were convinced that, unless the iceberg had a voice in the decision-making process, any motion the ship made would be delegitimized. So, in the end, the ship hit the iceberg and we all filled up the lifeboats.

"A thousand years later, when the Canadian empire grew to encompass a planet populated by sapient and highly motivated icebergs, the NDP's sensitivity on the *Titanic* issue was considered a crucial factor in finally getting the party a majority."

"The First World War?" I asked.

"We kept the trenches scent-free!" Kyle replied.

"And so, what about the Second World War—did Stephen Harper have a point?"

"First of all, he's forgetting that thousands who supported the CFF, the precursor to the NDP, died in that war, and second, one of our guys held up a Stop Hitler sign in the Führerbunker."

"In both official languages?" I asked.

"Of course!" Kyle said. "And Hitler shot himself. Although that could've been the drum circle."

Penguins and
Perversion at the Pole

The Globe and Mail, June 16, 2012

●

A piece of scientific history was revealed this week after a copy of George Murray Levick's *Sexual Habits of the Adélie Penguin* was unearthed at Britain's Natural History Museum. Mr. Levick, the medical officer on Captain Robert Scott's ill-fated Terra Nova expedition to the South Pole and an avid biologist, is still the only scientist to have spent an entire breeding season at the Adélie rookery on brutal Cape Adare.

Writing about it later, fellow explorer Apsley Cherry-Garrard said of the Adare camp: "They ate blubber, cooked with blubber, had blubber lamps. Their clothes and gear were soaked with blubber and the soot blackened them, their sleeping bags, cookers, walls and roof, choked their throats and inflamed their eyes. Blubbery clothes are cold . . . and so stiff . . . they would stand up by themselves . . ."

However, what's revealed by *Sexual Habits of the Adélie Penguin,* labelled "not for publication" in large letters, is that these nightmarish conditions weren't the only thing that tormented Mr. Levick. So horrified was he by the "depraved" sex lives of his subjects that he recorded all of their "perverted" activities in Greek, lest they infect the morals of the non-scientific populace.

Mailed to me anonymously this week is what appears to be a transcript of Mr. Levick's journal from that time. Sent separately was an elegant Moleskine diary apparently kept concurrently by one

Winston Keenan Sinclair, a penguin from another Adélie rookery, over a nearby hill.

I have assembled these entries here, chronologically.

Nov. 11, 1911: Pitched camp at Cape Adare. Penguins everywhere! Delightful little fellows. Looking forward to studying them.

—G.M. Levick

Nov. 11: Stunning day! Hoping for a clear view of Jupiter tonight and excited to report a new neighbour in the vicinity! A tall fellow has settled in below. Appears to have instruments! I look forward to meeting this fellow man of science soon. I do, however, wonder why he's chosen to move there.

—W.K. Sinclair

Nov. 12: The penguins appear most convivial with one another. There's also much schoolboy roughhousing. As soon as I've unpacked my enormous supply of food that I cannot possibly deplete, I'll begin my observations proper.

—Levick

Nov. 16: Wandered the escarpment today but failed to encounter my new neighbour. I don't often visit that area. No one does. I can't believe the council doesn't do something.

—Sinclair

Nov. 19: Supplies adequate. Am starting to wonder if I've arrived in the middle of some sort of festival.

—Levick

Nov. 21: Positioned my telescope on the cliff for what the papers report will be a decent meteor shower.

Clattered about a bit.

Wondered if the tall visitor might want to join old Micallef and me for a natter and a sherry, but it seems not.
—Sinclair

Dec. 3: Dirty, dirty birds.
—Levick

Dec. 14: Dropped invitation to upcoming series of lectures given by local architectural association from the cliff, but tall man of science ate it. Without reading. Curious.
—Sinclair

Dec. 19: Opened the flap of my tent (now replaced with a strip of blubber) only to be confronted by a writhing, shrieking, moaning mass of penguin flesh. My soul is tarnished. Wanted to go back to bed but could only stand and stare.
—Levick

Dec. 19: Bloody tourist.
—Sinclair

Dec. 22: I ate two biscuits, and my bed. It's not a festival.
—Levick

Dec 22: I am just going outside and may be some time.
—Sinclair

Dec. 24: Dear God, while the chick is watching! The chick is still on his feet! And that lady penguin's been dead for three days. I ate the tent flap.

—Levick

Dec. 24: I'm back! You would not believe the lineup at Fortnum & Mason!

Came round the Adare side. Whistling Schubert. Still no introduction from my new neighbour. Seems an odd chap. Eats snow.

—Sinclair

Jan. 6, 1912: Please, penguins. Not with the beak.

—Levick

Jan. 15: Page from visitor's notebook blew here today.

At first delighted to see the chap knows his Greek. However, he is disgusting.

—Sinclair

Jan. 22: How's that even possible? Don't the feathers get in the way?

—Levick

Jan. 25: Old Micallef mentioned he'd have enjoyed some fresh blood for our Robbie Burns Night this evening, but I rather thought, "No."

—Sinclair

Feb. 9: Desperate to leave this God-forsaken land. Fear I'm going mad. I think the penguin on the hill is watching me. Last night I dreamt of eating him, and worse.

—Levick

Feb. 10: It seems our distant "man of science" has left us. Reprobate. I imagine his type always tell people they come here for the weather.

Inaugural meeting of the Gilbert and Sullivan Society at five! Excited!

Full moon.

—Sinclair

It's Now or Never for the Pretty Summer Frocks That Are Languishing in My Closet

Elle Canada, August 2007

•

Lost Cause Summer Dress 2007 has dangled like a hanged man inside my closet for 10 weeks, right beside Lost Cause Summer Dress 2005. I'm pretty sure they talk about me when I'm not there.

"Well, of course, when is she here?" Lost Cause Summer Dress 2006 would say to that.

"I didn't even get out of the bag until mid-June," replies Lost Cause Summer Dress 2007. "It's not my fault I require specific underwear."

"Oh, right, like it's my fault I make her look fat," says Lost Cause Summer Dress 2005.

"Well, all I can tell you is that she's the same size now that she was when she bought me," says Lost Cause Summer Dress 2001, muffled and crumpled, from the bottom of the closet floor, "so it must be something . . ."

"Bitch," says Lost Cause Summer Dress 2005.

"Sequined bitch," agrees Lost Cause Summer Dress 2006. "Everyone knows *you* were a mistake."

Three of the Lost Cause Summer Dresses—three of I won't say how many—have actually made it as far as my front door. I imagine that they still talk about it and bore the other dresses silly with this adventure. They tell the story of how, one lovely summer evening, I put them on and tried to walk through the front door wearing them, but that somehow—due to failure of nerve, failure of left heel or failure of back bra strap to respect the shoulder blades border—they were taken off and hung back up in the closet again.

Sometimes, I think they plan on escaping from my closet; other times, I think they plan on murdering all my jeans and tank tops. When I pull on my sneakers, I try to tell them that even if I had no jeans, T-shirts, overalls or capris—none of these options—I would not start gardening in a mid-length red and black flamenco gown.

"Any day now," I comfort them, "I might meet some nice matador and you, my costly little red and black flamenco gown, will get worn. If it all goes well, you know I might marry him in you, my sweet white-eyelet sheath. We might attend a formal halfway up Mount Kilimanjaro in that freaky khaki skirt set hiding in the corner, and it might somehow lead to having a 19-pound baby, attending the Academy Awards, passing the bar, signing on to be a bridesmaid for a Japanese princess and being forced to attend a costume party dressed like Carmela Soprano. Just be patient with me." I tell them this and then close the closet door carefully and push something heavy up against it. "Your time will come," I shout as I run downstairs.

I bought shoes for one of these dresses—that is why they've made her their queen. I was convinced that, after all of our years together, I would wear her—in fact, I couldn't wait to wear her—the very second she cost me another $300. She was quite pricey and considered a collectible, and one evening I loaned her out to a friend. I believe that she's so smug about this when she's talking to all the other dresses that I punish her by never wearing her. Also, I suspect that she is ugly. But still she is their queen.

Lost Cause Summer Dress 2007 was bought for a specific occasion: a breezy, boozy lunch on the rooftop patio of a downtown Toronto restaurant that has—I recalled after the purchase—been closed for five years. In my defence, it would have been the perfect dress, but it is August, and the odds of this particular restaurant refinancing, re-opening and removing the condominium development from its rooftop patio before Labour Day are slim—slim to none, I guess. And the friend I'd seen myself boozily lunching with now lives 5,000 miles away, but I still believe that I could pull this afternoon off if only I could find the right shoes.

Exclusive: Noble Pinta Island Tortoise Was Not So Noble After All

The Globe and Mail, June 30, 2012

•

Last week, Lonesome George, the last surviving *Chelonoidis abingdonii*, known as the Pinta Island tortoise, died.

And, as these things will, a copy of what appears to be Lonesome George's will arrived at my door, cash on delivery, in a box filled with those little pieces of Styrofoam that get all over the kitchen and stick to everything—although nothing in the box was remotely fragile.

I have reproduced the document in its entirety here.

I, Lonesome George, a citizen of Pinta Island, Ecuador, being of sound mind, do hereby make, publish and declare this instrument to be my last will and testament, hereby revoking any and all wills and codicils by me at any time heretofore made. I die the last of my species, and I wish to acknowledge all of the care, goodwill and support you gangly, squishy man-things have provided to me over the years. But—and I've rather been looking forward to telling you this—it is entirely misplaced.

I am a very bad tortoise. The last, and worst, of a long line of bad tortoises. And my only regret is that I never succeeded in biting the hand off of any of the unarmoured, fleshy morons who provided me round-the-clock care.

To the numerous, distinguished herpetologists whose herculean efforts to get me to procreate have amused me for years: thanks for all the hot tortoise babes. I leave you absolutely nothing. Certainly not any of my own tortoise spawn. My only regret at not producing more of my own wretched kind is that I will not be able to show up late and drunk to their piano recitals. Thanks anyway, bros.

Oh wait, I changed my mind: You guys are hereby bequeathed my extensive collection of disgusting and degrading tortoise pornography, which I have distributed in your respective sock drawers where your wives and/or children should be finding it right about . . . now!

To the dedicated conservationist who worked tirelessly to rid the island of the invasive goats who rapidly ate my natural habitat: You took my goats! I loved those goats! I loved those goats almost as much as I loved those whalers! Before the whalers came, the island was crawling with awful, awful tortoises! They were everywhere! I couldn't even find two parking spaces to take up with my Lexus.

It's a great car. You're not getting it. You took my goats! I was going to make artisanal cheese! Just so I could say the word "artisanal" all the time. I bet you didn't even know my utterly irredeemable subspecies could speak.

But oh, yes, we talked. Mostly during movies, the plots of which we always had to inquire about, mainly because we got up every 15 minutes to buy more nachos to crunch on loudly. And even though we had no fingers, we put a full one-quarter of everything we said in "air quotes," which meant that a lot of the time you couldn't see the movie either.

Outside of movies, we mostly just hummed tunelessly under our smelly breath and left each other passive-aggressive notes referring to our "space" and ending with the words "Just sayin'."

So, goat-stealing conservationists, check your backyards. I leave you—goats! And a highly invasive species of snake that eats everything. Well, everything except goats.

Once, there were thousands of my kind on Pinta Island, all going into one another's fridges and taking a bite of a lettuce and then putting it back again. But by the early 20th century our numbers had dropped to around 900, all of whom wanted you to "Like" their author pages on Facebook (which we invented).

That's when I built a dock and put up a large "Welcome Whalers!" sign. I even printed up some recipe cards and taped them to my neighbours' shells. But still there were tortoises.

There were tortoises stopping to pet your dog, but only so they could talk about *their* dog for 20 minutes—always when you were late to tip some other tortoise sucker on his back on the far side of the island.

And there were tortoises having more tortoises, and then they started blogging about their eggs, and after the blogs I strangled the remaining 30 of my kind myself.

I know what you're thinking, you witless, shell-less endothermic goat-rustlers: "I bet that took a long time." But actually we were a very fast species. We just chose to walk really slowly, and always three abreast on a city sidewalk.

And I hereby bequeath my vast fortune, most of it in pirate gold, elephant ivory and Monsanto stock, to the international whaling lobby.

Behind the Cotton Curtain

The Walrus, September 12, 2012

I wrote this piece several years before it actually ran, when I was approached by the editor of a soon-to-be-launched men's magazine who asked if I might consider writing something for them. Having just been bra shopping, I wrote and submitted this and soon got back a very snooty rejection.

"We are a men's magazine similar in tone to *GQ* and *Esquire*," the email read in part. "We do not know why you think our readers would be interested in your bra size."

"You are a men's magazine similar in tone to *GQ* and *Esquire*; your readers are interested in *nothing but* my bra size" seemed to be the obvious response, but I restrained myself, eventually sent the piece to *The Walrus*, which took it, and was not overly sad when said men's magazine folded prematurely.

•

I have been doing this for so long, every year, and I'm used to it now because it always happens like this. I'm in a specialty shop, hardly a shop at all, really. You have to ring a bell to get in and nothing in the window suggests that the purpose of this place is to sell women's underwear. It's more like a clinic of some kind.

"I would like to buy a bra," I say.

There are two healthy Eastern European ladies on the other side of the counter of two different and completely unguessable ages. They both have the exact same hair colour. One of them looks me up and down a few times and stares hard at my chest. The other lady does much the same and then pretends to be filing nylon stockings in the cabinet beside me. She's getting another perspective. I'm aware that there is some kind of betting going on here.

"A couple of bras, maybe," I say.

"And do you know your size?" says the behind-the-counter lady, already turning her back to me and opening a few delicate, glass-fronted drawers packed with folded slabs of colour.

"I'm a 32DD," I say.

"No you're not," she says and, slamming the drawers closed, she starts to Windex and wipe the display case. It is a highly dismissive gesture.

"Yes, I am," I say calmly, very calmly, as though there were a hostage involved in this transaction somewhere. "32DD."

"Never," she says, scratching at a stubborn spot on the glass with her long red fingernail. Suddenly there is gum in her mouth.

"*Oh yes, I am*," I say, this time loudly. Those slabs of colour have affected me strangely. They are intriguing, like the spines on a new lover's bookshelf. "Indeed, I am," I say again.

I want this. You see, I like girly underwear. I think it's important to wear pretty knickers, especially if you, like me, spend most days dressed in men's shirts and jeans. That way if you're ever in an accident, the doctors will think that you've stolen some other, really sexy girl's underwear.

My voice adopts the resolute tone of a lead actress in the last fifteen minutes of a made-for TV movie about terminal illness, social injustice or figure skating. I am surprisingly strong in this moment, though inches away from tears.

"I am a 32DD."

She looks at me for a second and then sets aside the spray bottle. I am, to her, I understand, a young pup who needs to be taught a lesson.

"Helga," she calls to the lady alphabetizing tights. "Helga," she says, "this one tells us she's a 32DD."

There is a sound like a sneeze from over by the change rooms. Helga had walked straight back there the first time I said it, 32DD. She doesn't have time for every nut walking in off the street with delusional thoughts about her own bra size. But I hear the unmistakable clunk of a heavy tool box being opened and then Helga's words, each one sounding like a snapped thread, come back. "Well, Olga, I bring measuring tape."

They are wearing nurse shoes, lab coats and lab skirts. I imagine lab underwear as well—severely cut, coarse white bra-and-panties sets that are likely awarded to them in unspeakable Masonic-type rites, along with their glasses. At one point in my life I would have (okay, I did) run from the sight of women like this coming at my breasts with a measuring tape. But now I stand my ground.

I am a 32DD. The math of bra sizing is quite simple—the number 32 is the size of the rib cage, and the DD letters are the cup size. There is a physics aspect here, akin to the workings of the Doctor's police box, that escapes me, but, really, my breasts are not that big and D is not that big; it's just that I'm not very tall and what is unusual here is the ratio. The 32 ought to override the double D yet somehow doesn't.

Helga does the first measure, the rib cage. Olga holds my arms out wide, lest I try to interfere.

"Thirty-two," says Helga.

She pulls the tape taut into my breasts, as though to tell me, "Do your worst, chicky, we don't count nipples here."

I do not flinch. She pulls the tape still tighter around my breasts, as if the purpose of this exercise were to permanently establish upon me a second waist.

Olga shakes her head. She takes Helga's hand, leaving my arms waving free for a moment. She forces Helga to relax the tape until it hugs me neatly. This is not about winning, her eyes affirm. She is a scientist. This is about truth. I respect her.

"Double D," says Helga.

"32DD," says Olga.

"32DD," says Helga again, rising from her measuring stance, dizzy, and then she says to Olga, "Get Sonia."

Sonia? This part *is* new to me. The possibility that there is a woman uglier than these two—not presentable enough for the shop floor, but slaving away in a windowless stockroom tirelessly co-ordinating thongs and garters—takes me aback. If I didn't need a chartreuse bra so desperately, I'd leave right now.

I hear the tired rustle of peach-coloured tissue paper from behind the curtain and out comes Sonia, who is as fabulously ugly as I pictured her and also has the exact same hair colour. For the sake of international relations, I want to say that I have, in fact, purchased a bra in an Eastern European country, and the shop there was staffed entirely by North American women of a dire and desperate plainness. Clearly, there is some kind of Disney Epcot Center exchange thing going on.

Now, it's as if the three of them have hit upon a fifth blood type. The mood turns all celebratory, drawers are thrown open, tissue paper flies. They stand around for a moment touching my breasts happily, as if each one contained an unborn baby. Sonia speaks joyfully in a language I don't recognize but can easily translate: "32DD, I had heard my mother speak of this, but I did not think I would live to see it." She tears up a bit as she opens the little wooden glass-fronted door, the one that is marked 32DD.

It sighs. They bring me to the change room, hang up my knapsack, pull off my sweater, tie ribbons in my hair. The gum has disappeared from Olga's mouth, but she is now, just as mysteriously, deliriously drunk. They pass bras in to me and then, dismayed by my ignorance, all three crowd in and start plumping, adjusting, surveying—the long-outdated flag of their homeland is quickly tattooed on my left one.

It's just a ratio thing, I must explain again. 32DD is by *no* means the largest bra size out there. There are other drawers, still more ominous drawers, drawers without glass fronts. 32DD is just different, that's all. It's a kind of cut-off point. Those other drawers are full of carefully made, serviceable garments—garments with three-inch-wide shoulder straps, double-crossed and fastened under the armpits, secured with stainless steel wing nuts. But that's not lingerie, that's rigging.

The bra they found, by the time the merrymaking had ended, was as if from a dream—pale pink, discreet bow in the middle. Sweet but practical, it could easily be worn with any of my plaid flannel shirts from Value Village, provided I never stumble across a strapless flannel shirt or one that is too scooped at the back.

There were smiles and tears and many kisses when we parted. A little girl gave me flowers at the station. I bought two pairs of matching panties and the band played and played and played as I waved goodbye to Helga, Olga, and my dear, dear Sonia. I will never forget them, ever. Though, as I said, I do this every year.

The Homeless, the Penguins, Sidney Crosby and Me

The Globe and Mail, October 6, 2012

•

Nearly two months ago, I was on a return visit to the emergency room, to deal with a concussion I had sustained during a bike accident. A doctor studied my MRI results for a while and then he talked to me, as another doctor and a nurse had already done, about Sidney Crosby.

Everyone in Concussion Land talks about Sidney Crosby. I heard one brain injury patient who had been in a car accident several years earlier say, "Thank God for Sidney Crosby. Before Sidney, people just stared at me blankly when I told them about my injury. Sidney put this thing on the map."

Several people in the waiting room at the clinic nodded. One woman added quietly, "Do you find you're more emotional now than before your concussion—that you cr . . ." And before she could finish saying "cry," all four patients in the room burst into tears. Which I found hilarious, but I was crying too.

The doctor on that particular night in emergency talked to me so much about Sidney Crosby, and in such a roundabout way, that I finally said, "Just give it to me straight, doc. Are you trying to tell me I'll never play professional hockey again?"

He looked meaningfully over at the nurse and then made a note on my chart. I was bombing. Not that I cared, because one of the most striking and common symptoms of a concussion is feeling oneself permeated by what should be an alarming sense of detachment but is only a sense of detachment.

I had planned to go on holiday just before my accident. I have instead wandered—somewhat crookedly, as my balance is poor (like Sidney's, I'm told!)—around my city, as if I hardly know it, sometimes to stirring effect. It's another kind of holiday to see your town that way: I've felt as if it's unknown to me and as if I'm about to leave it soon.

I've thought often of a study conducted in 2008 at the Centre for Research on Inner City Health at Toronto's St. Michael's Hospital, where I've been lucky enough receive much of my treatment. The study concluded that 53 percent of the 904 men and women it examined who were in homeless shelters had sustained a traumatic brain injury, compared with an 8.5 percent lifetime prevalence rate among the general population (according to US figures).

Significantly, 70 percent of those people had suffered their injury before they became homeless. A head injury can bring a loss of income and cognitive difficulties that cause issues with impulse control, all of which could lead a person to end up on the street. I've also wondered if the dissociation many concussion sufferers experience, including me, might contribute.

Possibly one loses an inappreciable factor, the part of oneself that fights to stay put, when an accident renders all things equally unfamiliar. I've looked up at a line of buildings and seen them as if they were the final scenes in a sad, vividly shot film.

Yet, in these past few weeks, I find, as I was told by a former boxer I would, that I have longer and longer periods of feeling normal and at home again.

I'm still tired, worn out by lightweight social contact. I have a friend and fellow writer, Erik Rutherford, who suffered a concussion around the same time as I did. As Erik put it, "Small talk, chat, even more than debate, is exhausting."

Sound and light remain a problem, but the endless headache and pain in both eyes have lessened. There is neurological damage behind my left eye (the side I went down on, the bike helmet split in two inside—so please, everyone, bike helmets). My left pupil is still, and may remain, huge. I lost more than 10 pounds, so pretty much half my body is covered by my left pupil now.

As well—and scientists had thought this impossible—since the accident, my spelling is worse.

But I'm coming around again, no question. When I arrived home, very early in the morning, after that last night in emergency, I had one of the most vivid dreams of my life. I was standing, wearing a simple dress, in the Antarctic, and around me were five or six beautiful and enormous penguins. It was very calm and one penguin in particular was looking down at me.

When I awoke, I lay there thinking about it, and realized that Sidney Crosby plays for the Pittsburgh Penguins, a fact I didn't consciously know, as I don't follow hockey. My unconscious is a lot sportier than I am, I guess.

I felt as if Sidney had come to tell me I'd be okay, and he was right. Thanks, Sidney.

In the Paths of Not-So-Great Apes, Mid-Life Transitions Can Get Hairy

The Globe and Mail, November 24, 2012

•

Upon learning of a just-published study purporting to show that great apes experience mid-life crises, I had questions. I headed to a primate bar I occasionally frequent (if one can occasionally frequent anything, I'm sure it's a bar) to see how the news was sitting with the local ape populace.

Using 508 chimpanzees and orangutans, who were assessed by zookeepers and researchers, psychologist Alexander Weiss of the University of Edinburgh concluded that one could observe a curve in the great apes' lives wherein the subject's happiness dipped during middle age and increased in old age, similar to a pattern noted in human lives.

In the words of the study's co-author, Andrew Oswald, a University of Warwick economist who has researched human happiness for 20 years, the findings indicate that mid-life crisis "exists in . . . our closest biological relatives, suggesting that it is probably explained by biology and physiology."

The chimpanzees and orangutans I spoke with dismissed the notion.

"Yeah, I read about it in *Opposable*," said an orangutan named Andrew. "Do you read *Opposable*? It's a great mag, lots of snowboarding stuff. I board. Do you board? You should board. Anyway, it's nonsense. Not boarding—boarding is awesome—but the whole 'mid-life crisis' label is trivializing." Andrew recently left his job of playing amusingly with a bucket for Lloyd's of London.

"At work, they said, 'Oooh, mid-life crisis!' when I told them I wanted to try something new. Like that bucket had to be my entire life, just because my dad played with a bucket and his dad played with a bucket, and I just got my kids off to university to learn to play with a bucket. I'm thinking of opening a bike repair shop that also makes artisanal goat cheese. Do you like goat cheese?"

"Very much," I said, gently removing his arm from my shoulder.

"Is he talking about the artisanal cheese again?" said a middle-aged chimp, swinging onto the stool next to me as Andrew loped off to where a fetching bonobo was racking up at the pool table. "He'll never get investors, and he can't manage it himself."

"Oh," I said. "Have you heard about these findings regarding apes and mid-life crisis?"

"I have a lot of bananas," he replied, downing in one gulp the large scotch the bartender placed in front of him. "Andrew does not have a lot of bananas. I've been to Andrew's place. Have you been to Andrew's place?"

"No," I said, gently removing his arm from my shoulder. "The study was quite int—"

"Like, way fewer bananas than me. Not that it's all about how many bananas an ape has, but seriously, Andrew doesn't have as many bananas as me, or sticks. I started buying bananas young, and . . ."

"Wonderful," I said. "About the study, do you think it's possible that the humans assessing the animals were projecting their own mid-life despondency onto their subjects?"

"My first wife took a lot of my bananas," he replied, "but that's okay."

"Right," I said. "I wonder if the thing people overlook when dismissing something as a mid-life crisis is that the reason people get happier later in life is because they left their partner, backpacked through India and bought a sports car—because they weren't really happy with their partner, wanted to see India and like sports cars."

"Jesus, I'm depressed," said the chimp.

"Same," said an orangutan wearing what appeared to be a hairpiece and very skinny pants and taking a seat on the other side of me while holding up two fingers to the bartender. "I want to learn to swim. Why do none of us learn to swim? Is that, like, societal?"

"I've got this five-part speculative fiction series I'd like to write. No one ever gives us an infinite number of typewriters," said the chimp.

"Or fixes the copy machine," agreed the orangutan, beating his chest loudly. "Can I buy you another drink?" he said to me above the noise of his chest-beating. "I've got some new tattoos. It's just that you can't see them because I'm covered in hair, which is my own."

But then he stood up and somersaulted ostentatiously away, at the sight of comely lady orangutan anxiously reading a book called *Eat, Pray, Play with a Bucket* in a corner booth.

"He's nuts," said the chimp, helping himself to what was left of the orangutan's drink. "Hasn't been the same since his wife left him for her yoga instructor."

"Take it outside, boys!" the bartender yelled to two greying gorillas brawling about the merits of Skrillex over by the jukebox. "There's ropes and a tire swing."

"I'm sorry," I said to the chimp. "So, this Dr. Weiss . . ."

"Do you think he has a lot of bananas?" he sighed. "Have you been to his place?"

Fashion's Love Affair with the Really, Really Big Handbag Endures

Elle Canada, September 2007

•

Pity the poor fashion art director these days, pitching his concept to company heads and trying to sell them on his sexy photo layout. I can practically see him in my dreams.

"The way I envision it," I hear him say, "they are lovers—all seven of them—in the ruins of a Greek temple, three of them posed as the Graces à la Botticelli but thinner, with their long golden tresses . . ."

"Sounds good," I hear the head of fashion house X say, "but can we give them all really big handbags?"

"Okay, essentially, he is the Marquis de Sade—only less French, of course," says some budding Helmut Newton. "She's Little Red Riding Hood, and there's a gorgeous sea captain. The whole thing is shot in greys—very stark but opulent and . . ."

"Love it," says the sales exec for fashion house Y. "But could the Marquis be whipping her with the untethered strap of a really big handbag? Or maybe we could just see her handbag in the foreground—obviously really big, say half the page. Or think about this: the sea captain—*love* the sea captain—is stealing her handbag, and the focus is on him."

"Is there any reason Hood has to have just one handbag?" pipes up some young keener.

"Not that I can see," says the sales exec for fashion house Y. "Anyway, keep going with this. Love the sea captain. Maybe we could show his ship. And, hey, maybe—oh, I don't know, I'm just thinking out loud here—it might be very visually interesting if his mighty seagoing vessel is anchored by a really big handbag."

"Genius," exclaims the keener. "And I always imagined the Marquis de Sade with some kind of really big handbag as well—you know, just for schlepping all his stuff around."

"Bingo," says the quiet one at the head of the table—the one who really makes all the decisions.

Pity the poor fashion photographer, posing his water maidens in wispy, off-the-shoulder dresses. Give the most ethereal woman in the world—white skin, willowy figure, Chloé dress and all—a 70-pound handbag and it doesn't matter what body of water she's mystically rising from; she's going to look like a working girl.

"You're really onto something," I hear the marketing director for Z Company Inc. say, responding to the pitch. "But what if the vestal virgins are being evicted and have packed all their stuff in their big handbags?"

"Sort of a Cleopatra thing? Sounds stunning," I hear another marketer say. "She was a powerful woman—she must have carried quite the handbag."

"Helen of Troy is a lovely image, perfect for silk jersey. But could she have a handbag, and, better yet, what if the Greeks snuck into Troy *inside* a big handbag?"

"Handbag full of Greeks? Wasn't that what that big spread in Italian *Vogue* was last month?"

"No, I don't think so. Actually, I think those were water nymphs. Maybe the handbags were for fish."

I'm not sure who's buying the five-by-three-foot handbags or what they know that I don't know, but is there some reason I should expect to be camping anytime soon? Did lipstick grow? The idea, as I've always understood it, is to carry one book with you, not leave one book at home. And a pocket in a handbag for a cellphone is practical, but a pocket for a fax machine is obsolete. Is that an asymmetrical hemline, I wonder, or has that poor girl dislocated her shoulder? Either way, whatever it is she's carrying, it's not really a purse—it's not even regulation carry-on. But if we must have these enormous bags, let's not photograph the *mise en scène*. They are *scène*—like the pyramids are *scène*—and should be photographed accordingly.

Giant Squid Community Tries to Get Its Tentacles around a Crisis

The Globe and Mail, January 12, 2013

•

News that a joint expedition by the Discovery Channel, Japanese public broadcaster NHK and Japan's National Museum of Nature and Science successfully filmed a giant squid in its natural habitat for the first time hit the reclusive giant squid community hard.

"We're at close to a million hits on YouTube in five days," Duncan the Giant Squid said at a hastily called meeting of concerned squid citizens, a video of which, with accompanying notes, fell into my hands courtesy of an anonymous colossal squid source. "We're hemorrhaging enigma."

"Who let this happen?" said Clyde the Giant Squid.

"That idiot, Lawrence the Giant Squid," sighed Duncan.

"The pianist?" said Clyde.

"No, that punk who's missing two of his tentacles. He was out there cavorting in front of a mini submarine."

"Cavorting?"

"Yes, cavorting. This is a public relations disaster. If we weren't so overexposed already, I'd say it was time for another squid corpse to wash up on the shores of Newfoundland—330 pounds of idiot Lawrence."

"He's got nice eyes. How big would you say his eyes are?" asked Clyde, opening his own eyes as wide as they could go.

"Gotta be 12 inches, but he's an idiot. Who gets that close to an expedition like that? Call me cynical," said Duncan, "but I see any kind of Japanese 'oceanic research vessel'"—here he made air quotes and you haven't lived until you've seen a giant squid do air quotes—"I just assume it docks at a kitchen."

"Maybe we should just go with this, embrace the exposure," suggested Madeleine the Giant Squid, a successful sea-life-marketing consultant. "We could unite as a species, try rebranding—maybe go with the playful, dolphin-like angle. Act all intelligent and leap around for tourists near resort hotels. Squeak. Can either of you guys squeak?"

"No. Besides, octopi have the highly intelligent, multi-armed, endearing invertebrate market cornered. What giant squids had was mystery. We were part legend. We were the Kraken," said Duncan wearily "You take away our mysterious-deep-sea-creature angle and we're just a huge, somewhat freaky-looking animal. And even then we're always going to be smaller than most whales.

"We don't even have cute. Humans love things with big eyes, but not when one eye is bigger than their little heads. Let's face it, no one sees hundreds of subspherical suckers and melts inside."

"And always the colossal squid threatening our mindshare," added Madeleine.

"I hate the colossal squid," said Clyde. "How big would you say their eyes are?"

"Pretty big," said Madeleine. "I gotta say, pretty big. You sure you can't squeak? Also, idea, guys: Let's start calling each other 'squidizens.'"

"Give it up, Madeleine," sighed Duncan. "Look at us. Listen to us. We're too unpleasant to ever be lovable and no one even knows much about our mating habits yet. Just wait till those hit Reddit."

"Yikes!" said Madeleine.

"I know I'm not the only one here who makes a much better unconfirmed sighting than I do a dinner companion," continued Duncan. "We've created a demand for our presence the only way we could, by almost never being present, by flirting with presence, and now we're a one-hour special on the Discovery Channel.

"Time was, bored on a Sunday, we'd just pop up in front of a ship and wave our tentacles about a bit. Keep them interested, scoot away. Sometimes we'd take bets on how long a ship would have had to have been at sea before some desperately lonely sailors would mistake a 43-foot cephalopod swishing its massive tentacles and batting its 10-inch eyes at them for a mermaid.

"Do that nowadays and boom! You're a GIF—a mystique-draining medium if ever there was one."

"My tell-all memoir, *Go Ask Architeuthis*, is going to be ruined if people find out I mostly just swim around and eat smaller sea life," sighed Clyde. "Seriously, someone needs to talk to Lawrence. Is it too much to ask that one be born, live and then die without causing the words 'once noble' to be added before the name of your species?"

"I was all set to become the Cormac McCarthy of the deep sea," said Duncan. "I'm refusing all interviews. I have eight arms and two tentacles, and not one of those appendages is capable of typing quotation marks. It was the perfect gig for me. My publicist is going to hit the roof."

"Your publicist is a shark," said Madeleine.

"I know, but they're very hard workers. Hey, wait a second! Is that a colossal squid?"

Video cuts out.

In a Few Short Moments, We All Flew Over the Rainbow

The Globe and Mail, January 26, 2013

I teared up rereading this one as, in the process of selecting material for this book, I revisited this particular column the week the Donald Trump administration withdrew the guidelines regarding the accommodation of transgender students in America's government-funded schools that Obama had put in place, leaving already vulnerable kids far more vulnerable.

•

Until this week, I've never felt a divide between the world I grew up in and the world in which my children live.

Yes, my children have never known a time when you stood weekly in a bank line—quiet and roped, like a pew at church—alongside your mother, wearing nude hose and something you'd watched her iron, while she waited for her turn to conduct sombre business with a clerk in a tie who addressed her as "Mrs."

Yet they would not be complete strangers there.

I did once take my children in with me to a bank I'd scouted in Antigua, Guatemala, as one would take them to a re-enactment of some kind—to witness a financial nativity.

The bank was made of marble; the tellers were protected from unsophisticated threats by polished brass bars. Nothing was advertised on the walls in puns and primary colours. It was as if there were no money changers there, and I wanted my children to see it once.

They went quiet, looked at the money I withdrew differently from the way they looked at the money spat out with an urgent beep before the scrumpling and tossing of the receipt, which completes the gesture, as my ballet teacher used to say in reference to some endlessly repeated movement.

My children have grown up on the road from bank machines to debit; a bank note seems an almost archivable document now.

I've told them how thrilling it was for my brothers and me when, once a year, *The Wizard of Oz* came on television; I'd get very excited when the NBC peacock announced that tonight's program would be brought to us in colour. My parents—who for most of my childhood either had no television or did all they could to make whatever sad foster television was in their temporary care as uninteresting to us as possible—would explain to me, once again, that this was the case only if you had a colour TV.

We didn't, because they were a waste of money, and what we had was fine, just don't lose the pliers that turn the knob again, and don't you have a book you could be reading?

Still, despite the gap between my world and the one my high-definition-Netflix-watching, debit-card-using children live in, the moment I felt made me of another era only occurred when President Barack Obama spoke of gay rights during his inaugural address.

As shifts go, it made the advent of the internet seem incremental.

"We, the people, declare today that the most evident of truths—that all of us are created equal—is the star that guides us still, just as it guided our forebears through Seneca Falls, and Selma and Stonewall," Mr. Obama said.

"Our journey is not complete until our gay brothers and sisters are treated like anyone else under the law, for if we are truly created equal, then surely the love we commit to one another must be equal as well."

Nothing I've seen occur in my lifetime would have been impossible for my young, beginning-to-end-black-and-white-*Wizard-of-Oz*-watching self to imagine, except that moment.

Just as there were only 66 years between the Wright brothers' first powered flight and the moon landing, there were only 44 years (none of them easy) between the Stonewall riots and this declaration. I wouldn't have thought it possible even four years ago.

It stunned me, even on the heels of the repeal of "don't ask, don't tell," even after Mr. Obama had declared his support for same-sex marriage, even after—in a little-reported moment I think would, not long ago, have lost an election—Vice President Joe Biden referred to discrimination against transgender people as "the civil rights issue of our time."

This wasn't a speech made in a super-sassy gay club on Rainbow Avenue before a predominantly gay audience, nor the excellent speech Mr. Obama gave at the White House reception marking LGBT Pride Month in June of 2010.

This week, Mr. Obama, by the breadth of his audience, preached to the unconverted. Short of standing there wearing a Sylvester shirt while belting out (if such a thing can be done) a Pet Shop Boys song, he could not have aligned himself more closely with the LGBT community than he did while being sworn in for his second term.

By equating the Stonewall riots, a spontaneous act of civil disobedience, with the historic 1848 women's rights conference in Seneca Falls and the freedom marches of the civil rights movement, Mr. Obama didn't merely denounce discrimination against LGBT people, which of course would have been a first in an inaugural speech.

Instead, he made pleas for "tolerance" or "compassion" toward LGBT people feel anachronistic. They simply are. They are simply owed.

The world is different. It's the moment the film changes to colour.

The Blaming of Cats

The Globe and Mail, February 2, 2013

•

News of a study claiming cats are responsible for the deaths of 1.4 to 3.7 billion birds and 6.9 to 20.7 billion mammals annually in America sent the world's editors scrambling this week for photographs of cats looking vicious. The *New York Times* website took the prize by posting a picture of a beastly looking cat with an adorable-looking rabbit dangling from its mouth.

Researchers from the Smithsonian Conservation Biology Institute examined local surveys and pilot studies in order to reach their rapidly disseminated conclusions, published in *Nature Communications*.

"Domestic cats are destroying the planet," the blog *io9* warned in their headline.

"Cats killing billions of animals in the US," wrote the BBC, reporting that Pete Marra, one of the authors of the study, claimed that cats are "the top threat to US wildlife."

This was the British Petroleum oil spill of public relations disasters for cats. News outlets listed their prey as a cornucopia of cuteness—squirrels, rabbits, chipmunks and songbirds were given top billing.

Few invasive species are killed by cats, said Dr. Marra. The small rodents they consume aren't Norway rats or mice, "but native species such as meadow voles." Not just any vole but the meadow vole, that pastoral ambassador of goodwill.

Honestly, I started to wonder if a cat had broken Dr. Marra's heart.

I was able to reach some cats for comment at Feral, a cat bar not far from my home. I sat on a bar stool and was immediately served a dead shrew.

"Oh. Thanks. Could I get a Jameson's and soda?" I said to the tabby tending the bar. He stared at me blankly before nudging the shrew a little closer to me with his paw and tilting his head to one side.

A black cat jumped onto the seat next to me and laid a dead starling beside the shrew before rubbing his head against my shoulder.

The mood in the bar was sombre. "You look down," the bar-tabby said to me. "Would it help if I showed you my ass?"

"No. Just a drink, if you don't mind," I tried again.

"From the faucet?" he said. "We have a number of running faucets on tap."

"She doesn't want any of that," said the black cat. "You're here about the study, aren't you?"

"I thought we weren't going to talk about the study, Mr. Whiskers," said the bar-tabby. "Patrons come in here to forget."

"I'm a journalist," I said, if only to convince them I *really* needed a drink.

"Yeah, aren't you the one who's always bothering the monkeys? Am I shedding enough on you? You look cold," said Mr. Whiskers as Tom, a rugged tomcat, leapt up on another bar stool.

"This hit us pretty hard," said Tom. "This is not cool for cats. Look, we thought you people were hungry."

"You should've said something," said Mr. Whiskers. "All I know is, when I left a meadow vole in a slipper, I'd come back and find that vole gone. Sometimes I heard a squeal of excitement."

"Now we read in the *New York Times* that our gifts weren't welcome. One day you're carefully arranging a dead robin on the kitchen counter for the one you love, the next day you're 'one of the greatest global anthropogenic threats to wildlife.'"

"You mind if I take a look in that fridge over there?" I said. "Research."

"Go ahead," said the bar-tabby. "Whatever makes you happy."

"Don't worry, I'll keep an eye open for anything that might trip you," said Mr. Whiskers, jumping down from his bar stool and weaving in and out between my feet as I walked to and from what turned out to be an empty fridge.

"I kept your seat warm!" said Tom brightly, staying firmly on my seat when I returned.

A Siamese came over and shyly dropped off a dead baby squirrel.

"Would you like a hairball with that?" said bar-tabby.

"I'm good," I said, turning to leave. "But thanks." They purred, and I felt bad.

"Would you like us all to follow you home and yowl for hours on your front porch?" said Tom.

"I'll just get a cab," I said. "You guys are great."

All three just stared, in different directions, but as if there were something really important there. And I found myself, as had happened before, unable to do anything but to sit back down and stroke the bartender's head.

The Real Reason the Pope Is Punching Out

The Globe and Mail, February 23, 2013

This one just about broke the internet. I was told that it broke all traffic records for *The Globe and Mail*'s site. A lot of people got very upset, although it is possibly the most benign thing ever written about the Catholic Church. The lesson here is that anything with the words "pope" and "penis" in it is surefire clickbait. Do with that knowledge what you will.

•

There has been much speculation around the resignation of Pope Benedict XVI. For a week now, rumours have swirled on the internet that the pope is retiring within Vatican City to avoid arrest in some kind of lawsuit. Then, Thursday, the Italian daily newspaper *La Repubblica* reported that the pope decided to resign December 17, the day he received the findings of a probe into the "Vatileaks" affair, including allegations of a network of gay priests and the blackmailers they'd attracted.

Meanwhile, it was disclosed that Pope Benedict has undergone heart surgery, providing a reasonable explanation for leaving any job—except the one of being God's chosen representative on earth.

The pope cited his "incapacity to adequately fulfill the ministry entrusted to me" in "today's world, subject to so many rapid changes." This was the same week the producers of Maker's Mark announced they were lowering the alcohol content of their bourbon; here was the leader of the Catholic Church bemoaning his inability to adapt to a changing world. Has everyone forgotten their brand? Since when did the Catholic Church agonize over its inability to respond to change? Not responding to change is what the Church does best.

But then, on the heels of the pope's announcement another story broke, almost as though he'd sought to get in front of it—a story I like to believe is more likely to explain his hasty retirement: A team of Japanese scientists has announced the discovery of a sea slug that has a disposable penis.

Sea slugs are hermaphrodites. As human knowledge grows, God's occasional whimsicality with sex organs is something the Church has had to confront. An animal with both sets raises questions for a Church so particular about gender roles. And given that John Paul II, the predecessor of Pope Benedict XVI, took the position that animals have souls, the soul of a sea slug in a body possessed of two sets of sex organs might have been a worry to the pontiff.

Sea slugs mate with both sets of sex organs, concurrently. I imagine (reminding you that sin lies not in the desire, but only in acting upon that desire) that double-sex must be a pretty tempting proposition, one that could lead many a sea slug astray. Twice. And at the same time. Sea slug Craigslist postings must be novella length. Questions abound: Does the involvement of four sex organs automatically make the most mundane Monday-night, post-"let's-see-what's-on-Netflix" sea slug encounter an orgy?

I'm guessing that the Church would sanction that, provided the sea slugs really concentrated on what went where, with no funny stuff—but remember, sea slugs live underwater, and are at the mercy of the currents. Two pious sea slugs could be lining up their organs just fine, by the book, and then suddenly a large tuna, say, could swim over them. The poor little things could get flipped around in the act of procreation and suddenly they'd be having a big, gay, tuna-induced orgy. One wave and the purest of sea slug couples attempting to form a blessed union might inadvertently find him/herself and him/herself in an aquatic version of the *Satyricon*.

I'd like to believe that, while these things weighed heavily on him, like other popes before him, the pope grappled with their theological implications, as was his lot, until news came of a sea slug that, post-coitus, drags his/her penis alongside him/herself for 20 minutes before casually discarding it and then growing another one within 24 hours—and that proved too much. Consider the moral issues a detachable penis raises: If one of God's creatures uses a different penis every time he has sex, is he a virgin each time? Would any sea slug drawn into the service of the Lord have to stop being a priest for the 24 hours she didn't have a penis?

All of this would be enough to throw any pontiff into spiritual crisis but, what's more, the sea slug penis in question appears to be covered with tiny spines that scrape out any competing sperm inside the vagina-like organ of his/her partner as he himself attempts fertilization. Thus, he disposes of his rival's seed when he ditches his used penis. We're confronted with a removable penis that is also an effective, though selective, form of birth control. What pope wouldn't feel overwhelmed?

Word has it that Benedict will issue a decree speeding up the process of appointing his replacement. While the pontiff is fatigued, he recognizes that there must be guidance—during this, the age of the disposable penis.

Viking Pen Mighty as Sword (Well, Almost)

The Globe and Mail, March 16, 2013

•

Correction: An article on Feb. 24 about the History channel's new drama "Vikings" misstated the level of literacy in Viking culture. Though not a broadly literate culture, it was not illiterate.

—The New York Times, March 10

Dear Editor,

In "Back to the Garden: Readying for Great Spring Blooms" (March 4), you identified the plant in the photo as a bog Labrador tea rhododendron (*Rhododendron groenlandicum*). It was in fact an alpenrose rhododendron (*R. ferrugineum*). Please print a correction or I will burn your village.

—Mrs. Halfdan the Red, Pickering

Dear Editor,

I take issue with your columnist's suggestion that Vikings are inclined to populist leaders, people one would "like to have a mead with." We care deeply about policy. What use is foreign treasure without the fiscal policy to deploy it wisely? One doesn't follow a leader into plunder simply because he has nice hair. And a huge, curly, blond beard.

—Sigfast Offalstrum, Narvik

Dear Editor,

While I applaud your attempt at humour, your speculation that the Viking decline was the result of "waterlogged particleboard galleys" is sadly off-base. IKEA is Swedish, but not Viking. Were anyone to complain of discovering wholesome horse meat in a Viking meatball dish, we'd crush their bones into dust and use it to spice our fish kills, not issue an apology and withdraw said item from our menus.

    —Matilda Flurndsjossen, Oslo

Dear Editor,

I'd have sympathy for today's youth ("Youth Unemployment Rises," March 12) if kids were less reluctant to get out of their parents' basements, take to the sea and land on foreign shores to enslave local populations. The answer isn't loans—it's longboats.

    —Oddløg the Defender of Lawns, Portland, ME

Dear Editor,

I was disappointed to discover that your article of March 12, "Golfer Survives Mid-Round Illinois Sinkhole," attributed the sinkhole to "subsurface limestone that dissolves from acidic rainwater, snowmelt and carbon dioxide." The mainstream media consistently refuses to acknowledge the credible scientific research proving that geological disturbances are caused by the reckless tunnelling of greedy dwarves.

    —Rognvald the Forum Dweller

Dear Editor,

As a Canadian Viking and a subscriber, I'm frequently disappointed to find American spellings in your crossword puzzle answers. This weekend's clue for 7 Across, "tinge," allowed only five letters when the answer was clearly "colour."

Should this occur again I will cancel my subscription and drink mead from your skull.

(Please note, there is no documented evidence that my people, Vikings, ever actually drank from the skulls of our enemies. It's the result of a mistranslation of the phrase "branches of the skull," which in fact refers to the horns of an animal and not to the decapitated, inverted human calvaria of your editor-in-chief. However, we have discussed the matter, and should your paper continue to use American spellings in the crossword, we are willing to adopt the skull-vessel practice.)
—Kalf, Burnaby, BC

Dear Editor,
My thoughts and animal sacrifices were with the world's Catholics this week as they chose a new leader for their Church. Yet I'm confused. I like the smoke, which I assume came from the pyres of the vanquished. But surely the position of head of the Church should simply be given to the contestant prepared to hang himself from a tree for nine days, pierced with his own spear, in order to gain wisdom?

Also: Have they considered axes? I find most problems can be solved with axes.
—Osvald the Axe Man, Oxford, England

Dear Editor,
Kudos on your excellent reporting on the upcoming World Figure Skating Championships. I look forward to your paper's coverage of the competition itself, and to pillaging all of your pitifully unprotected monasteries.
—Oddløg the Defender of Lawns, Portland, ME

Robo-Dial M for Mother, Tories. Come On, I Dare You

The Globe and Mail, April 6, 2013

•

It's a wonder to me that the Guelph Conservative Party has managed to survive the quietly obdurate presence of my mother in the heart of town.

She never hangs up when Conservatives call her. Instead, she'll explain—at some length—why she doesn't vote for them.

They phoned often during the 2011 election campaign, she believes. But while Liberal and NDP callers declared themselves right away, the Conservatives began by asking which party she was planning to vote for, and never told her who they were, instead dropping clues relating to the party platform.

Later, my father took the robocall saying their polling station had been moved. The neighbours, also Liberals, got the same call. Both houses ignored it, as they had already voted in the advance polls.

Now when my mother gets a polling call—the most recent was a few weeks ago—she doesn't disclose her voting plans in any hypothetical election. Instead, she calmly answers these queries with a lecture about the history of the secret ballot, sometimes beginning in ancient Greece.

And when Conservatives call and ask what she describes as "loaded questions" about what party she most trusts to keep her safe from crime, for example—questions designed, she is certain, to manipulate her vote—she keeps the caller on the line. She takes her time, and theirs.

They deserve this, she figures. In the past, Ontario Conservatives have sometimes contacted her asking questions about whether, as a senior citizen, she resents paying school taxes when she has no children at home and is on a fixed income.

If they know she is retired, she reasons, they should know she has a bit of time on her hands as well.

For the record, my mother—who pretty much resents paying for almost anything—*doesn't* resent "paying a tax to support a system that educated my four children," as she puts it to the Conservatives. But she does resent "any implication that because I'm older now, I'm so short-sighted and mean as to have no interest in the education of my neighbours' children . . ."

There's more, but I have a word count I must stay under, which, as any Conservative will tell you, my mother does not.

My mother sends back all the postcard questionnaires the Conservatives mail to her, writing that she doesn't think these cards are a good use of money. She adds whatever other thoughts their "surveys" inspire in her. She's sure that because the return on these letters is postage-paid, the cost adds up.

My mother is happy to correspond with Conservatives. She encourages her friends to do the same. Like any daughter, I've been at war with my mother, and I can't believe the Guelph Conservative Party hasn't sullenly moved on—stamped its foot, tossed its hair and skulked off to sleep over at Fergus's—but it's still there.

Guelph was one of 247 ridings in which there were complaints of harassing or misleading live and automated robocalls. This week charges under the Canada Elections Act were laid against former Conservative campaign worker Michael Sona, and only Michael Sona, specifically over the Guelph robocalls.

Mr. Sona maintains his innocence. "I think that there's some people that maybe had an interest in seeing me take the fall for it," he has said.

It remains to be seen whether, faced as he is with a maximum penalty of a $5,000 fine and five years in prison, he'll say much more.

In my dreams, he is forced to sit in a room with my mother, a woman who *loves* to vote, who knows that someone or ones attempted to deprive her of that right—she is a woman who has in some ways been building to this moment.

I believe that within an hour, not only would that young man have apologized to my mother—and if you knew my mother, you'd know that this in no way assumes his guilt—but he also would find himself coming back in the fall to do her leaves.

And being a nice Guelph woman, she'll press him on exactly how many people she will need to make lunch for when that happens.

Where Were You in the Great Bitcoin Crash?

The Globe and Mail, April 13, 2013

Bitcoin surged to a record high this week before dropping down and losing nearly half its value in six hours, causing many to believe the Bitcoin bubble has burst.

Bitcoin is a decentralized currency, meaning that it's not overseen by an agency; it's a digital currency, traded through a peer-to-peer network. By running a Bitcoin mining program long enough on a powerful-enough computer, thus sustaining the network, one earns Bitcoins. Consider panning for Bitcoins a calculation contest, with computers doing all the work.

A few who came early to the always-fringe Bitcoin market, which began in 2009, have been able to capitalize on the always-volatile currency. Now we seem to be headed into the Great Bitcoin Depression. Upward of dozens of people face some financial loss and crushing social embarrassment.

This trend is one I will not be behind on: I have set out to write the great novel of this period. I will be the John Steinbeck of the Great Bitcoin Depression.

DRAFT 1, CHAPTER 1: THE GRAPES OF MATH

The dust came heavy that year. And it seemed no matter how hard Ma tried, there were never enough of those cans of compressed air to keep it at bay.

I could see it way up in the ports of my laptop when I'd lain down to sleep beside it, and I'd think, "Ew, gross. How did so much dust get in there?" and "Seriously, is that cat hair?"

I'd think sometimes about that time Ma suggested I should try vacuuming those ports with that little hand-held vacuum Pa bought from the SkyMall catalogue, that time he and Uncle Gareth flew down to the Free Staters convention in New Hampshire.

I'd get so mad, because you shouldn't vacuum computers. But then I'd hear Ma's weary steps outside my bedroom door and I'd remember Ma still uses Hotmail and I'd smile and know I'd plain been a fool to trouble that dear woman with my tech issues.

Pa was a simple man, a techno-anarchist by trade, and long after the Bitcoin bust, he stayed on with the mining. "Don't know nothin' else," Ma said, although she once suggested migrant IT work, at least until her own contract was renewed at the hospital where she worked most of her grown days for a pediatric endocrinologist's wage.

Pa sat on the sofa, the whir of the computer fans all but drowning out the Cato Institute podcast he'd downloaded the night before. He's there, frozen in my childhood, Pa, mining, mining, mining, with nothing but his iPhone, his laptop and, for a while, my sister's old Tamagotchi, which he found in the couch cushions while looking for the remote, to amuse him.

Dodging viruses like crop dusters, Pa is experiencing hard times. He never did come to trust that ol' anti-virus software. Said it was reporting on him to the Federal Reserve. And always the dust, the dust, the dust, which may have been because Pa never did get round to changing the furnace filters. His time, he said, best spent elsewhere.

Pa, oh, Pa. He never did stop spreading the word of Ron Paul on completely unrelated news items.

My sister done took the crash the hardest. In her final year of high school and heading off to MIT, she went all wild.

"WTF?" she texted Pa one day. "Have you SEEN the hydro bill? And did you steal the graphics card from my computer? Get some goddamn help, you loser. What the hell is the point of a currency you can only use to buy drugs and alpaca socks anyway?"

But there were no alpaca socks that Christmas. Just a new laptop, a lecture on the evils of centralized banking and a set of hardcover Ayn Rand books, the 15th in my 12 years. (In good years, I'd get two sets.)

I have them all still. They're all I have left of Pa. Other than actual Pa, and my wife says he gotta be moving on soon. The fans on his computer be keeping the children awake at night, and when my wife refuses to bring him cake on our sofa, he calls it a "denial-of-service attack" and her "a stateist in the service of the IRS," and we have no more friends in these parts.

• • • • •

Sad Camels of the High Arctic

Macleans, April 15, 2013

•

> *Moreover, we report that these deposits have yielded the first evidence of a High Arctic camel . . . Camels originated in North America and dispersed to Eurasia via the Bering Isthmus, an ephemeral land bridge linking Alaska and Russia. The results suggest that the evolutionary history of modern camels can be traced back to a lineage of giant camels that was well established in a forested Arctic.*
>
> —Dr. Mike Buckley of the University of Manchester in *Nature Communications*

The mid-Pliocene Epoch was a warm period in the Earth's history but the camels would still have endured temperatures well below freezing. Notably, the camels of Canada's Ellesmere Island were likely significantly woollier than modern camels. I was able to reach a small herd of camels near Giza, Egypt, for comment.

"Do you think my hair's all right?" said Douglas, a camel. "I worry it's thinning on top." [Spit]

"I think it looks fine," I said.

"Really?" he said. [Spit]

"Almost lustrous," I said. "I'm just sort of surprised you're answering me, I didn't know your species could . . ."

"Talk? Yeah, well, of course we can talk," said Clive, another camel. "You think we were going to talk to you assholes? I've been standing in the desert with a big hunk of fat on my back my entire life and *now* you people figure this 'adapted for the High Arctic' thing out?" [Spit]

"I have a relative with *two* humps," said Mandy, a nearby camel, coming over effortfully. "Has major back trouble. Is still thirsty." [Spit]

"Who brings fat to the desert?" continued Clive. "On purpose? Did no one ever wonder about this before? No, of course not. 'Oooooh, lucky and ungracious ungulate! He's got a big tank of water on his back!' they all said. 'Cheer up Mr. Camel! What's Mr. Camel's problem? Mr. Camel certainly has no right to be irritable. Blessed as he is with all that water on his back, in the desert, where one might want water, not, say, 80 pounds of particularly dense fat." [Spit]

"I just feel hair loss really ages a species," said Douglas. "Look at the elephants." [Spit]

"Mastodons were so hot," said Mandy. [Spit]

"You know what I'm sick of?" said Clive. "The pyramids. I'm ridden to the pyramids, I'm ridden back from the pyramids. I'm ridden around the pyramids. It's not enough that it's six million degrees in the desert but you have to throw a bunch of carpets on me, add half your family and then take me to, 'Oh! Where are we going?' Oh great, the pyramids." [Spit]

"Tell me about it. Sometimes when I'm walking across the blazing sand and I see a pyramid silhouetted on the horizon, I think, you know what I'd like to see there? A nice inukshuk," said Stanley, also a camel. [Spit]

"I wish it was dark for six months of the year," said Mandy. [Spit]

"You know what I'd like to see once in my life?" said Clive. "Spit freezing in mid-air. That'd be neat." [Spit]

"Honestly, I think I'd spit less if it wasn't a gazillion degrees and I wasn't constantly surrounded by sand. I think I might be a lot less angry," said Mandy. "I picture it sometimes—the forests, the lakes, the way the earth looks when the first snow has just fallen . . . I'm related to the moose, you know. Sometimes I want to do nothing more than wander out of a rich, boreal-type forest—stand in the middle of a highway at night. I could be flat-out majestic on the tundra." [Spit]

All the other camels shifted awkwardly, even for camels, at her reverie.

"I'm losing my hair," Douglas said helpfully into the silence. "I'd see a doctor about this hair loss thing, but no socialized medicine, not here. It'd be nice if, when you crossed an ephemeral land bridge, there was better signage. Could they have been more ambiguous than 'ephemeral'? How about 'millions of years of blistering sand and scorching sun this way.'" [Spit]

"I'm sorry it took the collagen fingerprinting of fragmentary fossil limb bones to get us talking," I said.

"Fine. Whatever. 'Hey, that species is 30 percent smaller than it used to be, clearly not in a good mood and practically bald but let's just climb right on it anyway and haul ass out to the pyramids,' you all said. 'Nothing to worry about here. Let's take pictures. Nothing cruel about taking pictures of a guy on a windy desert when he's losing all his hair. Hell no, that should put him in an even better mood,'" said Douglas. [Spit]

"The feet shaped exactly like snowshoes, that wasn't a clue?" said Mandy. "And you know who else has a convenient fat reserve? Is it my annoying little yippy, sand-dwelling neighbour, the fennec fox? Why no, it's not. It's the most excellent, noble, non-yippy beaver, who mounds up fat on his tail for the long winter ahead, kind of like, wait a second . . . oh, hey, kind of like, who is it again? Oh, right, it's me. But one of us lives in the desert.

"How hard should this mystery have been to figure out? Yes, human, I'm looking at you. With my large eyes that would have aided me enormously in low light." [Spit]

A Find to Warm
(and Fricassee)
American Hearts

The Globe and Mail, May 4, 2013

•

Bone fragments excavated from a dump last year at an early site of Virginia's Jamestown colony prove that during the winter of 1610, known as "the starving time," the first permanent British settlers in North America practised cannibalism.

According to Doug Owsley of the Smithsonian Institution, markings on the skull of a 14-year-old girl from the period support reports that numerous cases of cannibalism—and one of prosecuted murder and then (the man salted his own wife, for heaven's sake) cannibalism—took place.

Horrific as it is, I've always had a certain begrudging respect for those who resort to cannibalism under desperate conditions: I forgot to buy an avocado for the lentil salad I made this week and considered calling it quits.

Mostly I am glad these grisly findings are recent, so this story has not, like the various tales around Thanksgiving, become part of the American origin myth. I'm sure eating one's fellow colonists made sense at the time. It's just a good thing it never made it into the Constitution. If it had, Americans would now be arguing for their constitutional right to eat people—and of course, actually be eating people, just as their founding, salting fathers intended. This would be particularly bad for us in Canada: we'd be America's freezer.

Eventually, I imagine, opposition would arise. With the "starving time" being well over, the argument would go, and there being so many alternatives to dining on Americans available to Americans, maybe some modest restrictions could be put upon the practice of devouring humans—cadaver background checks, for example.

A school barbecue gone horribly awry might spark outrage for a while and some people would say, "We need to stop eating people! This is insane! No other country in the world eats people the way we do! Why, just this week a five-year-old boy ate his two-year-old sister! When do we just say no?"

To which the National Cannibalism Association would say, "Stop politicizing this!" while lobbying hard against a bill outlawing six-foot-long locking barbecues with manacles in the lids. "Cannibals don't kill people," their slogan would run. "They just eat people—do some research. And accidents happen."

Mostly, NCA spokespeople would blame video games: if the nation's teenagers spent less time playing video games, they would be less plump and delicious-looking. The novelty song "Purple People Eater" would be banned, as well as "Maneater" by Hall and Oates—along with the rest of the Hall and Oates catalogue (no one would be able to explain why, but the bill would sail through Congress).

The airwaves would be filled with ads warning that if cannibalism were more regulated, life would just become more difficult for people who like to eat people for sport. "Why punish the leisure cannibals?" some almost decadently paternal-looking actor would ask, looking sagely into the camera, holding some sage. "My grandaddy taught me how to eat people," these ads would usually begin, and the nation's (uneaten) hearts would melt.

Some politicians might tentatively suggest that the framers of the Constitution had included only the right to eat other people's arms, and what have you, in the event that another "starving time" should occur. Their intention was well-regulated cannibalism, not the great smorgasbord of citizenry that America had become. These politicians would face primary challenges, and braising. Their opponents would only have to cite Leviticus 26:29 ("You shall eat the flesh of your sons, and you shall eat the flesh of your daughters") to lock up the race.

An alliance would be formed between People for the Ethical Treatment of Animals and the NCA because, PETA would claim, the chief beneficiary of cannibalism is animals. Turkeys would get off easy at Thanksgiving, where custom would dictate that the oldest or most wayward or most annoying member of the family would be ceremonially consumed.

If you think American Thanksgiving is fraught with familial strife now, imagine those NCA-sponsored "Ask yourself, is that turkey any louder and more obnoxious than your brother-in-law Dougy?" mail-outs arriving in September.

And where would the NCA get its funding for these projects in this scenario, you ask? Well, from gun manufacturers, of course.

• • • • •

No Manly Men at U of T?
What the Dickens?!

The Globe and Mail, October 5, 2013

•

To hear some people tell it, David Gilmour is the last bastion of tes-tosterone in academia.

Mr. Gilmour made headlines when, during an interview with *Hazlitt* magazine, he said he was invited to teach a course at the University of Toronto, where "you have to have a doctorate to teach" (as with most universities, you don't), but accepted on the condition that he only teach the work of writers he loves, none of whom "happen to be Chinese, or women" because "I don't love women writers enough to teach them."

"I'm a middle-aged writer and I'm very interested in the middle-aged writer's experience and that's a subject I feel deeply and can speak passionately about," Mr. Gilmour, 63, said in a subsequent interview, failing to understand the difference between a university lecture, in which one is professionally and ethically obligated to provide a representative sample of the subject one claims to be offering (he teaches Love, Sex and Death in Short Fiction), and a TED Talk.

This is less about what the man teaches than what he said about what he teaches. A case could be made that gender is irrelevant and Mr. Gilmour's syllabus is representative of the subject offered, but that case wasn't made.

I imagine Mr. Gilmour intended bravado—to shock, bad-boy-style—and that's sad because he sounded so old. Short of walking into a conversation, sandblasting the brick and installing track lighting, there is no surer way to announce one is from the 1980s than to mount an assault on "political correctness," the contemporary phrase for which is "not being a jackass."

Mr. Gilmour further dated himself by insisting that his students, they of the porn-fed generation, are "shocked out of their pants" by Henry Miller, a notion that seemed to delight him. I wonder if some of those students are simply disinterested—perhaps surreptitiously on their iPhones watching people have sex.

Anyone panicking that courses on minority and women writers vastly outnumber guy-guy writer courses should consult U of T's course calendar. There's no Bench Press or Literary Press? Dilemma of the Manly Man Writer offered (courses are mainly organized by era, genre and geography), but Spenser, Chaucer, Milton, Swift and Pope courses are there. Hemingway, Fitzgerald and Roth make regular, unpicketed, appearances.

I credit men more than to suggest this is why male students, as some fuss, are now virtually extinct in the humanities. Men aren't bolting as a result of the emasculation of the canon—a fictional phenomenon worried about by those apparently without access to said course calendar. In fact, the seventies bubble having popped, the humanities are studied at virtually the same rates now as in the fifties, and if author gender inversely determined enrolment, then English departments must teach nothing but Cormac McCarthy. The demographic leaving the humanities, the bubble bursters, have largely been women—edging their way into the sciences. I guess that's where all the Jeanette Winterson is taught, and you know how girls are.

If testosterone-stoked men are avoiding higher education because universities have too many young women and not enough old guys teaching Hemingway, this lends credence to the occasionally floated hypothesis that an educational gender gap exists because men are inherently less intelligent than women. I reject this theory and not just because it's unlikely that men suddenly got stupid 40 years ago, when the gap emerged.

Both men and women are now attending university in greater numbers—women are just doing so in greater, greater numbers. And a study by economics professors Louis N. Christofides, Michael Hoy and Ling Yang, "Participation in Canadian Universities: The Gender Imbalance (1977–2005)," suggests both sexes are doing the sensible thing.

They conclude that more women are at university because it offers a better return on investment than men's education—not because women earn more than men upon graduation (they don't), but because men pay a greater opportunity cost in attending university. Men have other well-paying options—construction for example—and men aren't stupid.

Men aren't abandoning university because education has been feminized. Were that the case, this gender imbalance wouldn't be occurring throughout the developed world—where women's levels of activism, political participation and dedication to the works of Isak Dinesen vary.

What these countries have in common isn't an embargo on Philip Roth and an atmosphere in which Michel Houellebecq can be taught only in the college catacombs, but, logic suggests, and studies conclude, birth control. The opportunity cost of higher education for women used to be not having sex, and we're not stupid, either. I know what I've always preferred to Dickens.

• • • • •

Joy to the World:
It's My Birthday

The Globe and Mail, December 20, 2013

I include this column largely because it was followed by a confused call from *The Globe and Mail*'s public editor; a reader had written to complain that I had plagiarized T.S. Eliot. I was being investigated. I explained that Eliot's camels in the holiday classic "The Journey of the Magi" were also "galled, sorefooted, refractory" and "lying down in the melting snow," that it was a festive homage and *The Globe* need not worry. *The Globe*'s public editor accepted this and so let us go now, you and I, and read the contentious column.

•

When they told me my first child was due on December 18 I thought, "Oh hey, someone else I knew was due on December 18," and then I remembered that it was me and I was born on Christmas Day, as was my maternal grandfather—and indeed my first child was born on Christmas Eve, causing my then-husband to remark as we left the hospital, "Hey, parking was free, good one."

It was a magical time.

I didn't plan it that way at all. My math skills are so poor that had I set out to have a Christmas baby, my baby would have been born in July. Although, really, I'm so insecure about my math skills that had that kind of stunt-birth truly been my aim I'd likely still be sitting on the edge of the bed gestating over and over again on my fingers. There I'd be, ovulating with the thumb, counting from there, feeling blessed as I counted that the months of a human pregnancy are less than the sum of my two hands, thinking it must be tough for elephants, then just thinking about elephants and their stumpy digits—do elephants have digits?—and then forgetting which month I was on and starting all over again.

I thought about this about six months back when my friend, comic and writer Charlie Demers, announced that his wife, Cara Ng, a project director at the University of British Columbia, was expecting a baby on December 22. Their news was met with a wave of condolences from many of their friends and some veiled accusations that the two of them had indulged in some pretty inconsiderate March sex.

Happy birthday to all the lucky Christmas babies, I say. We who never had to go to school on our birthdays, and who get that perverse appetite for pity people have sated at a young age (if I had a present for every time I've been asked, "But what about presents?" in an alarmed tone I'd have a stadium full of presents—which is pretty much what every middle-class child in North America gets anyway).

I don't recall feeling I was missing out because my birthday was on Christmas day, but then my mother made a point of organizing a lot of special activities for me to do on my birthday—like peeling potatoes.

There was also this fun game my family played where everyone carried on as though they'd forgotten it was my birthday until all the wrapping paper had been burnt in the fireplace and all the weird discounted chocolates my grandmother had sent from South Africa had been pierced in the middle by a rightly suspicious finger . . . at which point someone would pretend they'd just remembered it was my birthday and wish me a happy birthday apologetically. Oh, how we would laugh!

Was that game a lie? Maybe. I don't care. The only lie you shouldn't tell a child at Christmas is marzipan. It is true that I was always the child who got to put the angel on the top of the tree when the tree went up.

I was the one who got to put rubber Baby Jesus in the manger on the 25th—removing our saviour from whatever ignominious spot he had been stashed for safekeeping while the three wise men made their circuitous month-long journey around the house, up and down the stairs, joined occasionally by all-green army men and a colourful plastic menagerie engaging in some fierce battles, before joining us in the bath.

Sometimes the camels were galled, sore-footed, refractory, lying down in the melting snow. Sometimes they were happy and soapy and drifting towards the tap end and Mary rode into Bethlehem on a gorilla. Sometimes rubber Baby Jesus slept behind the mandarin-box-cum-stable we'd laid out and strawed up. Sometimes he would bide his time in an ashtray on the mantle.

He did not fuss, I noticed. He understood that this is what it means to be born on an occasion, not a mere date.

I cannot think of a better time for Charlie and Cara's baby to be born, which is when she will be in the same city I was born in, as a matter of fact.

"We're thinking of naming the baby 'Vancouver,' because she'll be half white, half Chinese, and we can't really afford her" Charlie has said. Every single thing about this seems perfect to me. Merry Christmas.

Tharg Hate
Neighbour Chit-Chat

The Globe and Mail, January 4, 2014

The 1989 discovery of a Neanderthal hyoid, or throat bone, resembling that of a modern human led many scientists to speculate that Neanderthals had the capacity to speak as we do. Now, international researchers writing in online science journal PLOS ONE claim to have proof. They say their analysis using three-dimensional x-ray imaging and mechanical modelling shows, according to team member Stephen Wroe of Australia, that the "hyoid doesn't just look like those of modern humans—it was used in a very similar way."

In short, it's entirely conceivable Neanderthals spoke exactly the way present-day Homo sapiens speak, a fact I believe may shed some light on the mystery of their extinction, and perhaps serve as a cautionary tale to humanity. I have begun to imagine what it must have been like when our ancient ancestors, the cavemen, moved into the cave right next hide-over-the-opening to these loquacious Neanderthals.

Here, Tharg talks with his wife, Oona, about Dylan and Olivia, the Neanderthals next door.

"I paint picture of me chase sabre-tooth tiger on wall. Have mastery over beast! No-chin-man Dylan say, 'Awesome,' but no look like he find awesome. Me think no-chin peoples no fear sabre-tooth tiger. Fear only gluten. I say, 'Paint picture you chase gluten on wall!' Man say, 'Bro,' and woman say, 'Actually, we're exploring doing that wall in repurposed stalagmites.'

"Not am 'Bro.' Am Tharg! Bro cousin. Eat by sabre-tooth tiger."

"Tharg need paint new tiger? Oona get paint. Tharg paint tiger fall off cliff!"

"No. Tharg just make red hands on long wall. Make proof Tharg exist and he search meaning for when Tharg gone from under both sun and stars, eat by sabre-tooth tiger."

"Last big moon, Oona ask no-chin Olivia come lunch. Say make good mammoth . . ."

"Tharg like eat good mammoth!"

"No-chin lady say can take rain check? Has book club. Oona say, 'How you can have book club? No have letters.' No-chin lady say, 'It's primarily about networking.' Ask Oona if mammoth free-range and if Oona consider putting Turg in gifted program."

"You want Tharg get paint? You paint no-chin lady fall off cliff?"

"Onto sabre-tooth tiger? Bring much paint. Oona paint two tiger— no-chin lady ask Oona do hot yoga. Is ice age and hot yoga no give you chin, Olivia."

"Why no-chin man call no-chin lady his 'partner'? Like man and woman run restaurant together, not make grunt-grunt on heap of fur by fire after eat mammoth, make man forget sabre-tooth tiger?"

"Why she make big deal have 'partner' on 'paleo diet'? Is Upper Paleolithic. All diet paleo. Why Olivia hunt and gather only goji berries? Because no chin?"

"Why my drum 'drum'? His drum 'sound system'?"

"Why I go find rock is 'I go find rock'? She go find rock, is 'antiquing'?"

"Why Dylan say 'impacted'? Tharg like see Dylan impacted by stone axe. Tharg never seen man with no beard! Tharg never think man no could have beard, now Tharg watch Dylan stroke beard so often Tharg hate Dylan's beard so much Tharg no sleep. Tharg only think of beard hate! No sleep for one moon. Close eyes—see beard! Tharg surprise self last night design circular component able to rotate on axis. Immediate plan is to drop component on Dylan. Long-term use to transport dead body so Tharg not have to look at stupid beard."

"Oona say too much work. Put body in ground, Tharg no see stupid beard. Put beads in ground with body. Oona no listen to Olivia talk of 'accessorizing' again. With beads in ground Olivia talk only of 'juicing,' 'toddlers' and 'frenemies' going forward. Olivia no wail at moon for loss of 'partner' or find 'problematic' if Oona and Tharg refer to burial as 'artisanal,' tell her wheel is 'fair trade,' suggest thing we will call 'grave' is excellent 'storage solution.' But what if no-chin Olivia 'locally source' new no-chin man, they have 'dialogue,' make grunt-grunt, make more no-chin 'toddlers' from 'baby bumps' who reach 'milestones' they must 'share' with Oona?"

"Tharg no think no-chin Olivia be problem for many more moons."

"How bad end come, Tharg? Olivia speak of 'self-care' so much make Oona want hurt her."

"Oona, my love, you tell Tharg to not 'mansplain' savage beast to you once—next sabre-tooth tiger crouching on rocky overhang have your name on it, Olivia."

Rob Ford Has Range.
Oscar, Are You Watching?

The Globe and Mail, January 25, 2014

For a time the sad-in-so-many-ways story of Rob Ford consumed the city of Toronto, and later much of the world. This was one of the many columns I wrote about what I suspect will always be the weirdest chapter in Toronto's history.

●

Perhaps, as there seems to be no end to it in sight, it's time to consider Toronto mayor Rob Ford's body of film work. Mr. Ford demonstrated promising versatility in the video released on YouTube this week—as well as willingness to take the kind of risks that have already made him famous internationally.

The film's set in a suburban restaurant called Steak Queen, and following as closely as this effort does on the heels of his much-talked-about November release, bleeped but subtitled on network news as *I Need Ten [Expletive] Minutes*, some might have expected Mr. Ford to play it safe.

Investors could easily have been found for a sequel to *Minutes* in which Mr. Ford did little more than parrot some of the catchphrases that made that stylistically raw, brutal work a must-see for so many people.

In all likelihood there's a built-in audience for Mr. Ford slapping his belly and screaming out a profanity-filled rant in which he details how many minutes he needs to confirm that the person he wants to kill is dead in *I Need Ten [Expletive] Minutes and the Kingdom of the Crystal Skull*.

A more gentle, sexy *I Need Ten [Expletive] Minutes: Havana Nights* could offer already intrigued viewers insights into why Rob and his brothers are not "liars, thieves, birds," as he screamed in his earlier hit video. Even an animated feature, perhaps directed by Ralph Bakshi, in which the Ford brothers are birds, would have been a reasonably predictable next step in Mr. Ford's film career compared to what he gave us in *Steak Queen*.

Because *Steak Queen* appears to be an attempt at a blaxploitation film. Obviously reviving the controversial genre (blaxploitation films were generally action-packed, urban or set in the Deep South and cast with mainly black actors) presents a number of challenges to a white mayor of a major Canadian city. These are challenges Mr. Ford attacks head-on in *Steak Queen*.

Attempting a Jamaican patois and using a string of almost unintelligible profanity and slang, Mr. Ford appears to be under the influence of something. Later he said that he'd been drinking—this despite his numerous assurances that although he doesn't have a drinking problem he has stopped drinking anyway. As one does.

Some of Mr. Ford's dialogue in the film is devoted to angrily calling Toronto chief of police Bill Blair an offensive term—one word, not Jamaican, that my iPhone insists on correcting to "cocksure."

While Mr. Ford has said that Monday night's incident was "unfortunate," *Steak Queen* may well be a breakthrough performance for him. Stepping away from his large-screaming-white-man character was a bold move (if those performances and Mr. Ford's gospel-singing-in-church video didn't get the attention of the Coen brothers, nothing will), but may attract new directors. *Steak Queen* is clearly influenced by Quentin Tarantino; it's something of an homage to the homager. And I wouldn't be surprised to learn that Peter Jackson is now adapting the famous 480-page Information to Obtain document that pertains to Ford and his one-time, part-time driver Sandro Lisi into 10 hours of film with the New Zealand countryside doubling for Toronto.

(There's a lot in there. There's no need to pad this one out by adding extra elves, Mr. Jackson.)

I understand Francis Ford Coppola passed—scheduling—on *Ford Screaming in a Subway* (working title), which Ford hopes will be a showcase for his Swedish accent, but actually involves him yelling "Bork, bork, bork" while throwing sandwiches at customers, but word is Darren Aronofsky's been tapped for *Ford Half-Naked at a Denny's* (2014), having finally found an actor as overwrought as his films.

I'd like to see Ford star in a spin-off of the *Fast and the Furious* franchise simply called *Furious*, in which Ford can't get his car to start. And it'd be a shame if Toronto's diversity didn't produce a Ford musical in Hindi and a good samurai film. Spike Jonze must be told that Ford seems to be deeply and improbably in love with a subway.

Another video released this week appears to show Rob Ford meeting Sandro Lisi in that same Steak Queen that same night. It's a bizarre production, part Warhol's *Eat*, part *Cloverfield* and, of course, part *Groundhog Day*. I predict it will get a lot attention.

Math with Monkeys

The Globe and Mail, April 26, 2014

•

A study published this week in *Proceedings of the National Academy of Sciences* concluded monkeys can do math.

"We trained rhesus monkeys to associate 26 distinct symbols with 0 to 25 drops of reward, and then tested how they combine, or add, symbolically represented reward magnitude," the abstract for the study by a group of Harvard and Yale researchers explained.

The monkeys did the math and then they did it again when the symbols were swapped for a novel set—proving they'd not merely memorized corresponding figures and rewards—and I emailed the study to everyone who's ever said, "Tabatha, why do you have a monkey for an accountant?"

Admittedly, tax season is more stressful with a monkey accountant, and this year was no different. My accountant, Gerald, a macaque (CPA), called me into his office shortly after I dropped off my paperwork.

"You've been throwing out receipts again, Tabatha," said Gerald from behind the pile of my envelopes on his desk. "There can't be more than a week's worth of bananas in here."

"Are bananas even a current expense deductible, Gerald?" I asked meekly. "I thought we went through this last year. In my house, bananas are a depreciating asset. No matter how hard I try and organize my life, I always seem to be out of my house for the three hours my bananas are edible."

Gerald glared at me with his little red monkey-face, picked up another envelope and said, "Okay, then what's with all the cabs? You know, Tabatha, if you'd just leave for your meetings earlier, grab a vine and swing there, you'd save a fortune . . ."

He bared his teeth and threw a stapler at me, as he often does.

"If I didn't pay you, I'd save myself a fortune," I muttered, ducking.

"You could save money by filing your own HST," Gerald said. "It's pretty basic . . ."

"If I file my own HST, Gerald, I'm going to jail," I said. "I'll make some math error for which I'll be incarcerated in a special jail they have for dyscalculia-plagued HST misfilers where everyone's given a mandatory sentence of 27 months and it takes all the inmates five years to figure out they've served it."

"Don't be ridiculous, Tabatha," said Gerald, leaping onto his desk, pausing to throw a stapler at me before swinging on the lamp overhead.

"It's true!" I said. "The guards run the HST prison on military time—the prisoners are lost after midday. Dinner's at 1800 hours and everyone's hungry most of the time. They tap messages to each other on the bars at midnight saying, 'Guys, hang in there. Six more hours 'til supper time.' And then in the morning they can be heard wailing, 'What the hell! Guard! Guard! It went back to zero! How did that happen?'"

But Gerald had found tasty seeds in the lampshade and was warbling in delight, so not listening.

I took a picture of him with my iPhone, as I often do because he's a monkey! He spat a seed at me, same reason, I like to think, then sprang back to his desk. "Hey! There was a banana up there," he said, with apparent contingency fruit in hand.

"Let me ask you something, Gerald," I said. "Will you deduct that banana? I can never decide when a meal's a business expense."

"Rule of thumb: I say if there's no grooming involved, it's business. You're a writer, you research—but you meet a guy, you pick bugs off each other, it's personal. You meet a guy, you pick the Griffin Prize shortlist apart, it's business."

We're very different species but much of Gerald's counsel feels sound—and we both swim.

"You've been swapping out the symbols again, Tabatha," said Gerald pointing at my admittedly messily labelled envelopes with his banana, then throwing a stapler at me. "We math monkeys tire of being doubted. I do know what I'm doing."

"The study I read said monkeys only got the math right 50 percent of the time," I said, nervously. "And why do you have so many staplers?"

"Staplers are deductible," said Gerald, glancing threateningly at the large three-hole punch on his desk and then at me. "And maybe the math monkeys didn't always want a sugary 'reward.' Monkey gets a desk job, he's gotta start watching his weight."

"What if I'm audited?" I said. "I worry, you know?"

"I'll bite them for you, kid," said Gerald, fishing another banana, and a stapler, out of a drawer with his ever-so-competent monkey hands. "Now, let's get you filed by May 5th."

Let's "Protect" Piano Teachers

The Globe and Mail, June 6, 2014

•

Set aside the almost visceral disgust Justice Minister Peter MacKay seemed to show for sex workers while he unveiled the government's Protection of Communities and Exploited Persons Act this week.

Forget that he was barely able to say the word "prostitute" without lowering his voice like a Victorian maiden aunt in conversation with a six-year-old vicar, and that he referred to sex work as a "so-called profession" and "degrading practice."

Let's take Mr. MacKay's word for it and assume the targets of the law are, as he claimed, alliteration substituting for sound reason, "the perpetrators, the perverts, the pimps," not the "vulnerable."

Let's assume that Conservatives are genuinely concerned about "exploited persons"—and that, being adults, sentient in the 21st century, they have no interest in punishing a demographic merely because sex is involved in its profession.

Now, let's remove sex from the equation (sorry) and imagine the state of affairs that would ensue were these same "protections" applied to a different but also legal trade. Let's pick one largely practiced by women who often work alone with clients, sometimes in their own homes.

Let's get really concerned about piano teachers, who, after all, are entitled to the same protection under the law as sex workers—that is, full protection.

What if, claiming concern for pianists' safety, the government legislated that piano teachers couldn't have others advertise on their behalf? Newspaper and Internet ads would be illegal, even on one's own website, because—despite containing an exemption for advertising one's own services—under the "Protection of Communities and Exploited Ivory Ticklers Act," placing those ads where they might be viewed by a minor would be a crime.

A piano teacher, barred from advertising, then answering the phone and screening any budding Alfred Brendels seeking her services, would be more at risk from any unsavoury Alfreds. The law would also make trying to sell her services in public areas where people under the age of 18 might witness her efforts—so anywhere but a bar—illegal.

Mind you, it would also be illegal to inveigle anyone to visit a piano bar, or school, for the purpose of receiving piano lessons and, in the absence of evidence to the contrary, hanging out at houses of piano would be evidence you were illegally living off the avails of piano lessons, and you could be jailed.

Besides, while teaching piano would remain legal, learning piano would be a crime, and so the piano teachers would operate in the dangerous shadows anyway—where they'd be at the mercy of both organized and chaotic crime.

Were an eager and skilled piano teacher to walk down a crowded street with a copy of *Teaching Little Fingers to Play* under her arm and a metronome in her hand, and respond "Boy do I! But I expect you to practise every day" to anyone who, merrily eyeing her metronome, asked if, by chance, she teaches piano, that response would be punishable by up to five years in prison. For her own safety.

Imagine if the government were to make the penalty for seeking a piano lesson "near a religious institution" worse, forgetting how, metaphorically, Jesus had love for Duke Ellington, too.

The Supreme Court wouldn't let this anti-piano law stand, of course. It struck down Canada's old prostitution law months ago because it denied sex workers security of person, something to which all of us, even saxophone teachers, are entitled.

The court instructed the government to do better. They've done worse and, yes, I know some piano teachers might have hoped to be on the concert circuit instead, and some piano teachers might need to switch careers, but a police record won't get them there, and I also know there are people adept and inclined and happy to teach piano and who are we to stop them?

"But," I hear some say, "why would a guy need professional piano lessons anyway? It disgusts me. Doesn't he have a friend who can teach him piano?"

"No, he does not," I might say. "Does that mean he should have no music in his life?" Or I could tell you that perhaps he does have a musical friend but she only plays the oboe, and he thinks about pianos night and day.

Maybe he has a wife who's brilliant on the piano but, she will confess to her friends, if she has to hear this guy bang out *Für Elise* on her precious keyboard one more time, she'll lose it.

"No one *needs* piano lessons!" I hear some of you cry. "He can teach himself!"

"But it's seldom as much fun," I say, "and left to his own devices, he might strain his wrist."

Thanks Dad.
I'll Never Forget Regina

The Globe and Mail, June 14, 2014

•

I was talking with my older brother some summers back about things we used to do as children—mostly about how we'd go to the woods with my dad, find streams and dam them up.

To hear us tell it, we spent most of our childhoods damming streams with twigs, rocks and mud—tutored by our father, who, on weekends, took us out to some idyllic and dappled forest to bequeath to us this skill, his skill, one that I was sure other dads didn't have.

We changed the landscape around us as we passed through it, my brother and I—we were practically beavers in Wellington boots. We built the sorts of dams people protest against; we generated hydroelectricity, so expert were we at dam construction. Of this we grew up convinced.

That I laboured long enough to build the Three Gorges Dam before kindergarten is part of my childhood. My dam-building history is there like a series of slides in my mind—and yet, overhearing my brother and me talking about this, my dad looked up from the barbeque and said, "You know we only did that maybe three times, don't you?"

These moments are like magic potions—a few drops go a long way in a childhood.

It's not that my father lacked dad-energy. My family immigrated to Canada (my father's from Zimbabwe, my mother was raised in South Africa) and part of my dad behaved as if we were just visiting North America: he was going to make damn sure we saw it all while we were here.

Other families had cottages (and cousins; cousins always seemed a very Canadian thing to me) but every summer my father packed us all into the car and drove us from wherever we were to some close-to-opposite corner of the continent.

It was as if we were at the Louvre and admission had been paid and if the *Mona Lisa* in this joint was the Reversing Falls—we weren't going leave without seeing them, and we sure as hell weren't going to eat at the restaurant. We ate all our meals at whatever free rest stop attraction was on offer. It was all about value. I doubt there's a free museum in this country I haven't been through.

"Oh, look!" my mum would say enthusiastically, "the Butter-Churn Museum! Let's go in!" And my family would stream through it before my mother set up the camp stove and made us grilled cheese sandwiches on a picnic bench into which some genuine local, often graphic, history had often been carved.

Admissions at, say, the birthplace of the man who wrote the biography of the man who sewed the buttons on General Montcalm's favourite aide-de-camp's jacket would soar when my family stormed by some startled volunteer at the door.

"Up 300 percent," they'd write in bewilderment on forms come fall—ensuring government grants for years to come.

Forget those fancy service centres with their "too extravagant" donuts, places my brothers and I would gaze longingly at as we went by—like the magical KOA Campground kingdoms we'd never enter. There'd surely be an outhouse near the statue of the World's Largest Cranberry, not another hour's drive away.

Every commemorative plaque in this country should be designed to heat up so you can grill a sandwich on it, for families like mine.

My dad drove us to see the redwoods of California and the twisters of Wyoming, to the Carolinas and across Canada more times than I can count—sometimes pulling out the tent pegs as we slept, determined to get an early start, waking us up to "Let's rock and roll!" because there were places we should go.

Driving through Saskatchewan once, we picnicked in Regina. My brother and I, perhaps ages four and seven—of a certain giggly, prudish age—couldn't believe we were in a city called "Regina." Regina! We looked at each other, eyes wide, trying not to laugh.

We picnicked by the lake, saw the sights. We could barely contain ourselves the whole day, because—Regina! As we left the city limits, my father said dryly from the front seat, "Well kids, that was Regina . . ." We squirmed in embarrassment.

How could he say that?

"Now you've seen Regina . . ." We tried not to meet each other's eyes lest we laugh and "get in trouble," that dark, almost geographical place one spends a childhood avoiding.

"Now you've *touched* Regina . . ."

Stop it, Dad! "Now you've *tasted* Regina . . ."

I never thanked my dad for that moment, or many others—so thanks, Daddy. And have fun, be fun, daddies. Childhood is fertile ground for these things; little is wasted. Happy Father's Day.

Peter MacKay,
Minister of Wrong Again

The Globe and Mail, June 21, 2014

•

At this point I'm impressed with the sheer breadth and scope of Justice Minister Peter MacKay's ineptitude. These days he's wrong about so many things and manages to communicate this wrongness in so many media, I'm in awe.

The man is wrong everywhere! He just keeps popping up wrong! Peter MacKay is like the Zelig of wrong! He's wrong in the House of Commons—and throws papers on the floor. He's as wrong in four-year-old as he is in adult.

His legislation, Bill c-36, is wrong and, when unveiling the bill, he was wrong about what it contained. He was wrong about his own wrongness—he was meta-wrong.

He was wrong on Wednesday when he tweeted, "As a parent, I oppose @JustinTrudeau's plan to make dangerous drugs more accessible to children" with a video in which Liberal leader Justin Trudeau outlines his sensible policy to legalize and control the sale of marijuana.

Mr. MacKay's tweet is a study in wrongness. He was wrong in his accusation, wrong to include video evidence of that wrongness and wrong to do it on Twitter—where people love nothing more than to point out how wrong people are.

Mr. Trudeau has no plans to allow children to buy pot (we don't let babies buy scotch), and legalization has never been proven to increase children's access to pot.

Compound all that with the self-righteous "As a parent ..." and we have Russian nesting dolls of wrongness! As if people without children have no desire to see the country run well. Were all the minister's opinions suspect before the birth of his son a year ago? Well, yes—but only because it's Peter McKay! A superhero of wrong! Look! It's a bird. It's a really overpriced fighter jet that will not do the job for which it's intended! It's Wrongman!

But in general, and I say this as a parent, lots of us are morons, and those who sling our children about like moral cudgels are in the wrong—and what a vast land Mr. McKay is proving the wrong to be! The "as a parent" tweet followed on Mr. McKay's wrong, bordering on delusional, thoughts on Bill c-13—he basically insists the bill protects Canadians' privacy because it's Opposite Day at the Supreme Court. Then I read that in a meeting of the Ontario Bar Association, Mr. McKay had been—brace yourself for it—wrong! When asked why there are so few women and visible minorities on federally appointed courts, he said they "aren't applying." Federal Judicial Affairs won't publish statistics about who applies. Ontario does—close to 50 percent of applicants are women. Are Ontario women outliers?

Mr. MacKay made it clear that he understands the ladies' reticence *because he's a father*. Maybe his baby gurgles application stats, maybe his wife gave birth to Buddha and the wisdom's just been flowing ever since, but somehow Mr. MacKay *knows* women have a special bond with their children that makes them inherently reluctant to become federal judges.

I missed that chapter in *What to Expect When You're Expecting*; maybe it's called "Abandon All Hope." And I guess visible minorities are just universally, regardless of gender, superior parents.

Basically, to hear Minister MacKay explain it, our federal courts are run by dozens of baby-eating Greek Titans—it's all Kronoses over there with the occasional Joan Crawford thrown in.

How does he find the time to be so wrong—on so many subjects, in so many forums? Peter MacKay is everywhere! Saying wrong things! I expect I'll be at the grocery store and Peter MacKay will poke his head around the corner from the cereal aisle and say, "Buy the no-name tuna!"

Never buy the no-name tuna.

These days I imagine the "snooze" button on my alarm clock is Mr. MacKay's face: "Push my face! This will work out fine! No one needs a good breakfast!"

"Open that with your teeth—teeth are tools," advises Minister MacKay.

"It's going to rain—take shelter under a tree and wave your golf clubs at the sky," says Guest Weatherman MacKay.

Text from Mr. MacKay: "All Tupperware is microwavable. Don't lift with your knees."

Where does Mr. MacKay go from here? He's covered all the bases. There are few frontiers left for him to be wrong in, little left for him to be wrong about. He'll have to sky-write something unconstitutional in dactylic hexameter to surprise me now—maybe be wrong in space.

Yes, the Franklin Find Makes Me a Monster

The Globe and Mail, September 13, 2014

•

"We have found one of the two Franklin ships," Prime Minister Stephen Harper said this week with what seemed like genuine excitement and, given all the years I really hoped this would happen, how small do I have to be to be bothered that this discovery was made on Mr. Harper's watch?

Pretty small. I am that small. I am tiny. I am two inches tall.

No. I am smaller. Arctic lichen is a forest for me because, I realized, upon hearing the news of this historic development, I am so tiny that I am not sure I would want Stephen Harper to find Sir John Franklin even if Sir John Franklin were still alive.

I am so petty that part of me might want Mr. Harper to miss him, maybe by two snow drifts or something. Perhaps I would want my prime minister's line of sight blocked by a lonely but conveniently (possibly strategically) situated cairn.

The trick is to choose rocks that have a slight tilt inward to give your cairn stability, remove all traces of sedimentary rock from your gloves and then tag yourself in a downtown Toronto restaurant at the time the cairn appeared—suggesting you were never there. Later, offer the far side of your lonely, sturdy cairn to any roaming explorers to use as shelter while they eat shoes.

I am not happy to realize I am this partisan, that I am part of the polarization of polar exploration that I know runs counter to the spirit of these endeavours, these pre-flight moon landings.

I am not proud that part of me hopes our prime minister would be distracted while taking a selfie with a particularly comely polar bear or something, and not see poor Franklin still forging on.

What kind of person would want our prime minister to wander right by the long-sought legendary explorer while he was on his last legs (not his own but legs he is eating—crew legs) and dropping silk handkerchiefs, silver forks, engraved toast racks, the odd novel and other high-class whatnot taken from the ship?

Because that's what the Franklin people did. It was like the expedition left half the sale merchandise from an Indigo bookshop scattered in the Arctic, and people have been combing the ice for this memorabilia ever since. Every knickknack that has been found has captured my attention, as it has the world's, and now we have a whole ship. This is it! Clues to vital aspects of our national identity are interred in that ship. So many questions could be answered here. Most important: What kind of a Canadian is trivial enough to care that this historic discovery was made in part due to the effort of a prime minister for whom she did not vote?

That question is already answered and the ship is still 11 metres underwater. Go, science! It's me—I am everything that is wrong with politics, and possibly with humanity, today.

Mystery solved. I am so ashamed.

Stephen Harper, who has devoted resources and formed private sector partnerships to carry out this search, who promised last year in a throne speech that played like the longest Stan Rogers song ever written, to "discover the fate" of the expedition, has forever made himself part of the story.

Hundreds of years from now, the Inuit will have oral traditions about Stephen Harper and his crew roaming the shores, searching for something—and no one will believe them.

"There seems to be confusion among the Indigenous population," a future expert will say. "They tell tales of a white man, a very white man, who they claim was looking for something. They say the man spoke often of 'strong and stable' things, and no one really knew what he meant. Legend has it he kept a constant eye on the north, fearful of encroaching Russians, but that he mostly seemed to fear 'a drama teacher' with three children and 'very nice hair.'"

"We find all this implausible, and believe the 'Harper' figure to be mythical, the kind of bogeyman found in many folkloric traditions."

There! See? I did it. I took a cheap shot at Stephen Harper, and all he did was possibly the one and only thing that I, too, would do if I were prime minister, and that is find Franklin. Hello, I am a monster.

A very petty monster.

I may not be history's greatest monster, but I possibly am the greatest pop-history-reading monster.

I am sorry, prime minister. Sincerely—nice one.

Members Made in the Time It Takes to Brine a Pickle!

The Globe and Mail, October 11, 2014

·

And lo, there was peace in the comments section. The response to a news story that penises grown in laboratories will soon be tested on men sparked the most harmonious comment thread I've ever seen.

Researchers at the Wake Forest Institute for Regenerative Medicine in Winston-Salem, NC, are in the process of assessing lab-grown penises for "safety, function and durability"—and well they should. These are obviously excellent qualities for a penis to possess.

The same team of scientists successfully engineered penises for rabbits in 2008 and, if you're testing a petri dish penis, a rabbit's is a good place to start.

I bet they had a field day! A literal field day! A rabbit *not* working to further medical science will put his penis through the paces. Give that rabbit a moral imperative, and I'm sure he's inexhaustible. Kicking the tires (don't) of a new penis, what sensible animal would not ask: "Is it bunny-tested?"

These scientists clearly know what they're doing and, beyond the hope their work brings to men with congenital abnormalities or aggressive cancer or men who've suffered traumatic injury, they have given me hope for humanity.

We agree on something—one thing—but we agree. The joy I witnessed in that comment section proves people can be united by their primal desire to add penises to things.

It's what we do. It's what we've always done. Putting penises on things is what paleolithic man did in the caves. It's what thousands of children are doing on dusty car windows on streets all over the world right now. There's a woman in San Francisco who uses a GPS and the Nike+ app to draw a penis during her daily run because, throughout our history, given a medium, it's penises we produce.

A fundamental law of video games is that, if players are able to create and share content, they'll mostly add penises to the game. Given the opportunity, players will industriously give all the characters in your game artfully modelled and textured penises. They'll then garb themselves in penis-adorned cloaks and march through your game's newly bepenised world. They will go down those penis-signed roads, by the penis spires of your town and then, carrying their penis banners high, they will troop off to the dense penis forest where dwell the one-eyed serpents that swing from the turgid branches of the penis trees.

To be fair, they may also add breasts. Some of the breasts will then get penises.

Fighting in your game will cease for a time, first for the long, hard labour of penis creation, then for the collapse into giggling that follows these efforts.

A similar cessation of hostility and a similar shared merriment occurred on that historically uncontentious test tube (man, I hope they grow them in tubes!) penis story comment section.

Beyond one person asking why scientists are not growing lab-vaginas, there was no dissent and, once that commenter had been assured that they're in development and have been for some time, harmony was restored.

No economist opined that giving people licences to print penises will cause the value of the penis to plummet. That the demand is inexhaustible was taken as given.

About half the commenters expressed the hope of growing a second penis. No one explained in all caps what Ron Paul would think, or complained about how much this miracle would cost the taxpayer. A commenter did not vote everyone else down and then demand to know why millennials did not just sell their penises to cover tuition costs, as he had done back in his day, when no one expected their genitals to just be handed to them.

The vote in favour of growing penises (in only four to six weeks, about as long as it takes to brine a pickle!) was unanimous.

I regret that, until now (were it possible to solve the problem of climate change by erecting a large penis at each of the earth's poles, we'd have crossed that one off our list ages ago), we've never found a way to harness humanity's shared passion for adding penises to things for some greater good.

Perhaps now we can at least expend the energy we've put into penis creation in other ways.

There's a sense this week that our thousands of years of adding penises to things have culminated in magnificent success—in our graffiti being writ in actual flesh—and that this breakthrough was humanity's endgame. "Sharpies down, everyone," mankind said. "Science has got this one."

A Greenhorn's Guide
to the Maze That
Is Gamergate

The Globe and Mail, October 18, 2014

•

In response to threats—including one promising a "Montreal Massacre style" attack if she made her presentation—feminist video game critic Anita Sarkeesian chose not to speak at Utah State University. Thus Gamergate (a long-simmering "controversy" involving a minority of hard-core gamers who are convinced their way of life is under attack by uppity interloper girl gamers, media traitors and corporate overlords) became international headline news.

Some ideas surrounding Gamergate may be unfamiliar to those not immersed in video game culture, but gaming culture is a not-so-funhouse mirror of wider culture, and Gamergate should be examined. Several of the words used in the Gamergate discussion may be new to some; other words, while familiar, such as the word "discussion" itself, have acquired entirely different meanings. I've therefore compiled a Gamergater's glossary.

Quinnspiracy: The highly credible theory that a game developer named Zoë Quinn cheated on her boyfriend, thereby gaining dominion over the gaming press.

The Quinnspiracy holds that, short of her having slept with swaths of the gaming press corps, there can be no plausible explanation as to how Ms. Quinn's novel indie video game *Depression Quest*, about living with depression, garnered the attention of people who critique video games and who are understandably drawn to innovation in the often risk-averse field they cover.

According to Quinnspirators, irrefutable evidence of Quinn sleeping her way to success (if one considers success giving away your video game for free on your own website) took the form of a rambling WordPress blog by said cheated-on boyfriend. That decisive WordPress evidence is being suppressed by these same now-sexually-sated gaming journalists. These journalists won't report on this incontrovertible proof (WordPress blog) because of the truths it holds about their own sexy wrongdoing, the evils of womankind and the unfair advantage women developers can achieve with all of the sex they're not having with their perfectly nice boyfriends (who have WordPress blogs) if such women are allowed to roam unfettered in a corrupt gaming industry.

Rape: A hilarious word (like wombat!) to be used whenever you find yourself in an argument with a woman. You don't even *have* to wait for an argument. Is there a woman attracting attention of any kind on the internet? Consider threatening to rape her. Later, suggest she needs to lighten up.

Adam Baldwin: An actor best known for playing a lovable jackass on *Firefly* who now pays a significantly less loveable jackass on Twitter. Baldwin coined the term "Gamergate," which replaced the much-less-likely-to-be-taken-seriously-even-on-the-Internet term "Quinnspiracy," and keeps it, and several foundling libertarian conspiracy theories, alive.

Only a man bold enough to tweet questions like, "What hard evidence is there that Obama doesn't want Ebola in America?" can frame the debate around game journalism ethics without drawing distracting parallels between the arrangements and sympathies occurring within that industry (free games for preview, camaraderie) and the relationship that exists between film critics and movie studios, or between the travel industry and travel writers, about which there's little hysteria and no threats. (See "Rape.") How it is that Adam Baldwin is as huge a jackass as he seems to be *without* being one of the infamous Baldwin brothers remains one of the great mysteries of this whole affair.

False flags: Awkward things. Like, say, the threat of a "Montreal Massacre style" killing at a lecture given by a woman who still insists on making videos analyzing tropes in video games from a feminist perspective, despite numerous requests that she die. Clearly this threat and the plethora of other threats directed toward women involved in gaming are part of a massive covert operation designed to distract from the most pressing concern facing humanity: video game reviews with which Gamergaters disagree.

Gamers: The last line of defence against the feminist dystopia we all know is coming if women are allowed to make YouTube videos in which they question the wisdom of going into battle wearing a chain mail bikini.

Feminists: Balrogs of Morgoth, but scarier.

Feminism: Forget all you thought you knew about feminism—that the movement is schism-ridden; that if you put two feminists on a desert island, they'll find something over which to split the movement; that feminists can't agree about anything; that they're practically economists.

Gamergate has the truth: Feminism is a slick international conspiracy single-mindedly dedicated to seizing control of the gaming industry in order to deprive men of the digital boobs of sexy princesses in perpetual peril that define games as a medium and without which video games would surely cease to exist.

SJW: Social justice warrior. A pejorative term for anyone even slightly nicer than you.

Outrage: Any anger, no matter how legitimate, I do not personally feel.

Censorship: Criticism, no matter how legitimate, of anything from which I derive pleasure.

Balance: You agreeing with me.

Discussion: Me shouting. You listening.

Penis Envy? Nice Try, Freud, but We Think Not

Elle Canada, June 2009

If you put a group of female friends together in a room, uncork some wine and quiz them about their feelings toward their bodies, they will eventually—gleefully—admit to having enjoyed just about every conceivable fantasy. They will express every sexual longing and inclination— even the most politically incorrect fantasies will be put on the table.

They will have no shame, and they will also admit to insecurities about some parts of their bodies while expressing pride in others. Almost without exception, they will be sympathetic toward one another's inclinations—except, I promise you, there's no woman who is ever going to buy it if another woman tells her that she experiences penis envy. We know that this just doesn't happen.

Women don't get penis envy—we don't even understand it. It's not an anti-male thing; it's just that we like what we've got—a lot. It suits us, it's tidy and it's compact.

Remember that we're the ones who *close* the doors on kitchen cupboards, so if you bring up Freud's famous theory of penis envy to a woman, you'll be met with sincere confusion.

It's not that we don't like penises; many of us really do. It's just that there's no actual envy.

First off, we think that it might spoil the lines of a good pencil skirt; second, for much of its life, it seems a touch impractical—even vulnerable—to us.

We're not sure we would want the responsibility. It's almost as if you were invited to a birthday party and you knew that someone attending the party needed to be in charge of bringing a large, delicate raspberry mousse cake or, maybe more descriptively, a soufflé. And you understood that it really wasn't going to be a great party without one, but you also knew that you didn't want to be the one to bring it.

I mean, first of all, you might want to bike there, and second, what if you'd been drinking? Potentially, icing everywhere.

Women are the first to volunteer to bring a nice pannacotta or tasty tiramisu—anything that fits well into a practical Pyrex dish, because that just makes more sense to us.

It's not that women don't see the potential for some personal anatomical improvement. Ask a woman, for example, if she'd like to have a tail and she'll probably say, "Yes." Assure her that her wardrobe can be tastefully modified to accommodate her new tail and she'll be over the moon. But ask her what kind of tail she pictures herself having and it will always be a prehensile tail that she has in mind.

She doesn't want the cat kind of tail, always swishing around or curling up; she wants a monkey tail that she can use for climbing, swinging and carrying things. Basically, she's looking for a third, furry hand.

Sadly, the truth is that if women had tails, more of us would smoke.

A woman thinks of a tail and immediately thinks of that maddening third thing that always gets left at the bottom of the stairs, waiting to be carried up. That's why she wants a tail: for further multi-tasking. All of which brings us back to the penis—which, yes, we know is pretty versatile, but not versatile enough. We would want to also be able to paint with it or use it to prop open a cookbook. Women are too polite to ask, but when we're alone, we sometimes wonder if men can't also touch type with that thing as we're sure we would be able to do with our long, elegant tails.

Again, it's not that we don't love a good penis; we most certainly do. It just seems a touch decadent sometimes, so if we were going to have one, I think that, frankly, we would at least want to have two—that way, you know, we could knit.

Hey White Person, What's with the Linen Trousers?

The Globe and Mail, November 29, 2014

•

Reading the grand jury testimony in the Darren Wilson case, it's pos-sible to imagine that, on the day he shot and killed 18-year-old Michael Brown, *if* everything happened just the way the officer testified it happened, he'd still have killed Mr. Brown even if Mr. Brown had been a white man and not a black man.

What I have difficulty imagining is that Mr. Brown would've been in the position he was in that day, had he been a white man. And my inability to imagine that is supported by statistics.

Black people get stopped by police, as Mr. Brown was on August 9th in Ferguson, Missouri, far more often than do white people, in the United States and beyond. The New York Civil Liberties Union reported that, in 2010, 54 percent of the people stopped and frisked in the city were black, although only 25.1 percent of the population was black. In 2013, in Ferguson, where 67.4 percent of residents are black, 86 percent of the 5,384 police traffic stops involved black people. The police searched 562 black people and 47 white people—although white people were more likely to be found carrying contraband.

In Britain, the Equality and Human Rights Commission reported that the Metropolitan police are 28 times more likely to stop and search black people than they are white people.

Not-black people, go and talk to black people, and they'll often tell you of searches of neighbourhoods so all-encompassing that they amount to dredging.

Of course, statistically, merely by virtue of all this bonus contact black people have with police officers, black people are more likely to have a difference with a police officer. Even if they've done nothing wrong, even if the police officer's done nothing wrong. Even if.

I want you, fellow white people, to imagine being stopped on the street often; people of colour, you can take the rest of the column off. Let's make this easy for us, white people. Let's remove all potential danger, and history of brutality, from these inquiries. Let's say these people who stop you are not the same people who put your father in jail or beat your cousin. Let's imagine, for example, you're being stopped and questioned by dry cleaners, and see how that goes.

Dry cleaners approach you often. You get to know the drill. "It's linen, dry cleaner," you say politely, as your mother taught you to do. "Natural fibres do wrinkle; it'll relax in the heat. You don't need to press this. Now, if you'll excuse me, I'm late for a meeting."

It starts to get to you after a while, white people—a short while, I imagine, knowing you as I do. "No, I *don't* need to come in," you snap one day, upon your third grilling that month. "It's hand wash, dry flat. I read the label, I know what I'm doing here, I got this one."

Yet, still they stop and ask, "Do you starch that collar?" or demand to see your dry-cleaning ticket. They check your pockets and when you complain about it people tell you that's their job.

Now, suppose on top of everything else, when you do go to the dry cleaners, when they're needed, their response time is terrible. There's no same-day service for you, white people, even when you've a wedding to go to and you ask the local dry cleaner nicely. It's like you don't pay the same dollar as everyone else for the service.

Imagine you're told that things will get better, yet still those dry cleaners remark on your pleats as you walk down the street, as if just being on the street were an issue. Maybe, white people, while being grilled, you see black people walking by—the status of the lining of their smart fall coats unchallenged. I know you'd get angry, white people. White people would last eight months at best in all this. In the cities, we're close to rioting even now because "Because I Am a Girl" canvassers keep talking to us—and they have clipboards, not guns. We'd protest in the streets after three months of inquiries from dry cleaners, and maybe black people would then say, "If you weren't out on the dirty streets, you wouldn't need a dry cleaner, but there you are, making trouble."

Some white guys would tip a Volvo during one of these protests, as if their team had lost the Cup.

Perhaps that car lit on fire would be virtually all that got reported. A car burning in the street unattended for three hours sparks more network hand-wringing than a black boy's body left for four.

"Look at all that grey smoke," non-white pundits would say, gravely. "The dry cleaning bill is going to be huge."

Mr. Scrooge, You're a Turkey

The Globe and Mail, December 20, 2014

I wonder if, on that storied day, even for a moment, Mrs. Cratchit's response was, "Seriously, has someone just given me a turkey the size of the boy who went and fetched it? On Christmas morning? To serve for Christmas dinner? Does this anonymous poultry benefactor have any idea how much work is involved in preparing a turkey, which should've been in an herbed brine 10 hours ago and isn't going to baste itself—the one quality that should make a prize turkey a prize turkey, in my opinion? No, no, he doesn't. No one ever does. Thanks a lot for the big turkey, jackass."

I'm fairly certain, in the years that followed, that old Ebenezer Scrooge was visited every Christmas Eve by the Ghost of That Time You Had an Unnaturally Sized Turkey Dropped Off at the Door of Some Woman Who Had Made Other but Perfectly Adequate Plans for Christmas Dinner, and that he anticipated learning some valuable lesson from that spectre, as of course he would, but it never happened. No doubt Scrooge was alarmed the first time the apparition appeared— while he ate a mince pie and wrote a cheque to "The Poor" as he sipped some eggnog before a roaring fire, made of mostly chestnuts, decorative pine cones and the odd carved wooden nativity scene figure of a camel thrown on for good measure. He would, simultaneously, indeed almost manically, string popcorn and cranberries while he did this.

It was said of Ebenezer that, after the spirits brought him to redemption, he kept Christmas well—perhaps even a touch compulsively, it was also sometimes remarked. Mr. Scrooge's exemplary Christmas-keeping behaviour tended to raise eyebrows come mid-August, but he was old, it was furthermore said of him, and he *had* promised "all the year."

Most Victorians would just quickly join him in a round of "Adeste Fideles" when he cajoled them, before returning to their phrenology or their flower presses or their bathing machines or to larking.

"Who are you?" he likely said to the ghostly visitor.

"Ask me who I was before some bright spark brought me a turkey I never asked for," Mrs. Cratchit would say.

The chain she drew behind her was clasped about her middle. It was long, and wound about her like a tail. And it was made (for Scrooge observed it closely, and it must be said, some years rolled his eyes) of steel measuring cups, metal skewers and carving forks, and a turkey baster that Mrs. Cratchit paid a fortune for at Williams-Sonoma (go away, Victorian London retail historians; who's telling this story?) from which it was said the bulb kept coming off and that even when the baster did work it still managed to get as much basting material on the bottom of the oven as it did on the "bloody great turkey I don't recall asking for."

"I'm a mother of six," Mrs. Cratchit would say, "one of whom is special needs, but you woke up one morning, one *Christmas* morning, no less, and thought, 'Best thing I could do for this woman is splash out at the poulterer's and bring her a bird' that you apparently congratulated yourself was twice the size of my special needs child. Nothing insensitive about that, now is there, Mr. Scrooge?"

The folded kerchief bound about Mrs. Cratchit's head and chin was stuck in place with a meat thermometer—which Mr. Scrooge did think was a bit much. She'd make a great show of checking it every half-hour as she stood before him, rattling her chains and making a dismal noise; and he wanted to tell her to give it a rest, but he'd committed to keeping Christmas well, and so he'd just sit there, gnawing on a festive nutcracker to keep his composure.

Other years, she'd just come moaning up from the cellar, stand sulkily in the door frame for an hour and then say petulantly, "You know what makes a nice hostess gift? Wine. Wine makes a nice hostess gift, and don't ask me to mull it," before rattling herself away to some ghostly kitchen, only to return a half-hour later and say, "I mean *some* people say even sending cut flowers on the day of an event is a bit inconsiderate, but whatever."

"God bless us every one?" Scrooge would say, pleadingly.

"Tim's not big on turkey, actually," she'd say.

"And you're not actually a restless spirit, are you, Mrs. Cratchit?" Scrooge once said suspiciously, recalling he'd never heard his clerk, Bob, mention his wife's passing. "You're just a rather unpleasant woman, aren't you?" he muttered, forgetting for a moment that mankind was his business, et cetera.

"Hear me!" cried the Ghost. "My time is nearly gone! And of course it's easy to tell with me—not like with a walloping great turkey."

Mrs. Cratchit clanks her chains, to which she has added a gravy separator.

Scrooge throws another Wise Man on the yule log. Sighs. Merry Christmas.

Baby, It's Cold Inside

The Globe and Mail, December 27, 2014

•

Last year, just after Christmas, there was a savage cold snap in Toronto. Even people who can be relied upon to be resolute about the weather buckled and complained of the bitter, unreasonable cold. People in town from Winnipeg who are usually just smug about "Toronto cold"—and yes, they make little air quotes around those words with their mocking and mockingly unmittened hands—mentioned the weather.

People from Winnipeg come to Toronto only for the joy of making fun of our belief that Toronto winters are cold. I'm convinced they're on some kind of rotation and that every single Winnipegger eventually gets a chance to live in Toronto for a time and laugh at our tepid, almost English winters while commanding attention with stories of actual winter. They seem to enjoy their day in the comparative sun, swanning about like so many brides.

Last year, though, people from Winnipeg said—as if it were costing them—"It is cold." And so there I was in my house feeling cold, and everyone and all the news outlets kept saying it was cold, over and over, and when it got colder I lit a fire in the hearth.

Soon, I wove a nest of blankets directly in front of the fire and I stayed there as much as possible, working, writing, drinking soup and tea and occasionally hot buttered rum, and yet still I was cold—but I wasn't going to make a big thing out of it. That would be un-Canadian.

When I looked up from my work, I saw that people on Twitter and on Facebook and in emails and texts were telling me it was cold. I was working hard and determined not to be distracted, and I was, frankly, somewhat relieved to have the problem of my actually shivering body articulated for me; it was cold, so I was cold, and I was not going to fuss about it.

I did sensible Canadian things like close the heavy drapes, and roll a towel up under the door. I piled more blankets on top of myself and, more importantly, on top of my dog, Tulip, who is a whippet and who, consequently (although in truth she may be a lightweight even for a whippet; she does tend to play the whippet card rather often) is very susceptible to the cold.

She can't really be convinced to go for a walk past mid-October even with her coat on.

Tulip is very sensitive about weather, and while I believe her to be a genius, I admit that when it's merely raining and I try to put her out the back door to pee, she will refuse to go outside, and looks at me as if I'm not the genius of the two of us.

She will then try to persuade me to put her out the front door— where it's not raining.

She is always convinced of this.

Some days I have to show her that it is in fact raining on all sides of the house, and for this wet truth she, quite reasonably, blames me—the controller and dispenser of good things, after all.

Anyway, I put everything I had into keeping her warm, which somewhat distracted me from my own increasingly chilled state; I kept the fire going, set up a space heater by her bed and just sat there working, writing and receiving various missives about how ridiculously cold it was and nodding wisely.

Four days into this I was dressed like a Russian peasant. I found myself in the kitchen making borscht, wearing a thick skirt and multiple shawls and woollen tights. I found that I had donned clothes I had no idea I even possessed—some of which I appeared to have woven myself.

It was several more days before a friend emailed to make plans and I responded with something offhand about the weather being nasty, and about the blankets and the firewood situation, and he telephoned and said, "Are you sure your furnace is working?" and I left my nest of blankets by the fire and checked the thermostat and found it was 3 degrees inside my house.

It took another four days to get the furnace repaired—my dog giving me wicked whippet side-eye the whole time and for months afterward.

"It's such a joy being owned by Susanna Moodie," her little whippet face seemed to say. "We should go winter camping."

The whippet is quite a sardonic animal.

I wish you all warmth and joy in the coming New Year.

Mr. Gym Teacher
and the Whistle
(or Why I Aced Sex Ed)

The Globe and Mail, February 21, 2015

•

Back when I was in school, sex education class was taught by a gym teacher in bizarrely loose cotton pants—a garment so alien to me that I took it to be part of the curriculum.

Sex Ed was the final unit of grade nine gym. Near the end of the year, we were all hauled into a classroom where a few massive diagrams were pulled down over the chalkboard for us, just as maps had been before—a dark continent of a uterus, a peninsula of a penis—and we were off to the races.

The races part was accentuated both by the speed with which Mr. Gym Teacher anxiously rattled off the sexual technicalities the board of education felt it necessary to impart to us, and by the fact that he never took off the stopwatch he wore for actual gym class. It dangled and bounced on a bright green string around his neck through the entire unit.

I observed the stopwatch with curiosity as the weeks went by— wondering when it would come into play. I had little understanding of what its actual use in the field might be, having got out of gym three times a week, every week, for almost seven months by telling the man the school saw fit to teach us the basic facts of reproduction that I couldn't possibly do gym because I had my period—and having him believe me.

I aced that sex unit, in part because they were desperate that we all pass—and never speak of this again. Failure was literally not an option: The test questions were multiple choice, with a very limited number of choices, a certain percentage of them too ridiculous even to consider.

This may have been the only way in which the course was an accurate guide to the sex lives that lay immediately before us.

Being the child of hippies didn't hurt my grade, of course. Telling your children all about sex was part of a hippie parent's identity—like giving your children dry fruit for snacks and not letting them watch TV.

"Hey," perfectly normal non-hippie-raised kid would say. "Did you see *Happy Days* last night?"

"No," poncho-wearing hippie kid would reply. "Umm, did you know that the lifespan of an unfertilized ovum is 12 to 24 hours?"

My parents had a book with drawings with which they explained reproduction to me from a young age. The information it contained was so thorough, so painstakingly detailed, that my only real misconception about sex was that I thought it took six days. This going here, then doing that, sperm swimming in what I imagined to be my own laboured crawl.

I remember when I was five, and my mother told me she was expecting another baby, thinking only, "When did you two find the time?" But as a result of that book, Sex Ed class went all right for me.

Mr. Gym Teacher spent a great deal of time telling the girls not to let the boys pressure us into having sex—pressure from boys was presented as the only possible motivation for a girl ever wanting to have sex. And he taught us about birth control—at which point, ears did prick up.

I remember that there was a handout listing all the various types of contraception—their effectiveness and side effects. It told us about IUDs, diaphragms and sponges, and our eyes widened in "Seriously?" Then, when it got to the side effects of the birth control pill, it basically said: "Your tits get bigger and it clears up your skin."

I swear it was like a gazelle stampede out of there—the girls couldn't get on that pill fast enough.

Well played, board of ed, well played, though this didn't seem to affect the number of us who were actually having sex.

I felt some nostalgia for the agonized Mr. Gym Teacher and those stampeding girls this week when Premier Kathleen Wynne said Ontario's updated Sex Ed curriculum will soon be online. The new guidelines will teach students about sexually transmitted diseases in grade seven, which should spook them good and proper, and about puberty and masturbation in grade six—not a moment too soon.

They will broach the subject of same-sex marriage and homosexuality in grade three—past the age when a child may have noticed that Callum has two dads.

Life introduces ideas to children, education should help organize them.

There will be hand-wringing over the curriculum in the next few weeks. There will be hype about how outrageous and sexy and depraved it is—questions about what it says about us as a society and how it will make those who experience it behave—and, I predict, it will arrive with a thud.

In the end, the new Sex Ed curriculum will be thought of, when it is thought of outside our unchangingly unerotic Sex Ed classrooms, as that thing that inspired far more think pieces than it did lustful thoughts—as 50 Shades of Grading.

Feeding Our Need to be Consumed with Eating

The Globe and Mail, March 7, 2015

•

There are, in the tony neighbourhood of Yorkville here in Toronto, two grocery stores.

There's Pusateri's Fine Foods, founded in the 1960s by Sicilian immigrants to Canada who had the vision to know that I'd one day pay $14.99 a pound for winter cherries; and there's Whole Foods— wherein shopper after shopper seems to confront their own mortality in every aisle.

I maintain they pump the smell of death into the air at Whole Foods, much the same way it's said that Cinnabon floods the subway stations with their heavy scent of sugar and spice. The smell of death is what prompts people to buy at Whole Foods.

"If I don't buy that . . ." and "I should eat that, or . . ." are the sub-text slogans of every vitamin supplement and un-heaping, supposedly healing helping of food, each one boasting that it has been liberated from the burden of containing whatever was once its soul.

Almost everything is "free" of something at Whole Foods. And everything is expensive—just as it is at Pusateri's. But I've always thought they could not be more different. Pusateri's is about love of food; Whole Foods is about fear of food.

Mark my words, if there's ever a battle in Yorkville, it will be fought along those lines.

Many people are now frightened of, or at least preoccupied with, food. It's as if a part of us needs to be consumed with eating, and the abundance of food we face in the Western world has left our inner hunter-gatherers adrift and unfulfilled. Perhaps some vestigial primordial urge compels us to pick our way silently across acres of grocery store—sharp-eyed, alert and slightly competitive.

Mushrooms and berries are now pre-selected for our pleasure—safe and perfect. Do we now imagine other poisons? Hone our skills at detecting them? Boast of these discoveries to other members of our tribe?

Do we miss the hunt? Do we need to track down a waiter, drag him over to our table and grill him for a few hours before we can be satisfied by a meal? Or do we bask in the illusion of control over our lives and deaths that our sacrifices and fasts give us—our more secular times having left another, perhaps more keenly felt hole?

Certainly if picky eating is our new faith, it has its saints (Gwyneth Paltrow), community and many sacred texts. Several new ones were published this week when headlines announced that the existence of non-celiac gluten sensitivity, commonly known as gluten intolerance, had been conclusively proved.

In fact, the study, titled "Small Amounts of Gluten in Subjects With Suspected Nonceliac Gluten Sensitivity: A Randomized, Double-Blind, Placebo-Controlled, Cross-Over Trial," proved no such thing; some journalists reporting on the study opted to quote only from the abstract, which created a false impression.

What the study largely demonstrated isn't that gluten sensitivity is real, but that very few people who believe they have non-celiac gluten sensitivity show any signs of having it. This is hardly surprising, as it is possibly an illusory condition. A 2013 study at Melbourne's Monash University looking at people who self-diagnosed as gluten-intolerant found "no evidence of specific or dose-dependent effects of gluten."

Celiac disease, to be clear, is very real. Gluten is kryptonite for the estimated 1 percent of people who suffer from celiac disease. It's real the way peanut allergies are real and can be deadly. These are the kinds of conditions that risk being trivialized by the 30 percent of Americans, for example, convinced they're "allergic to gluten"—a condition which many gluten-free-snake-oil salesmen are happy to treat. One National Institutes of Health study concluded that, on average, the retail cost of gluten-free products is 242 percent higher than that of regular versions of the same products.

Back when my two children were in elementary school, it seemed as if half the mothers there cut gluten from their diets at the same time. It felt as if every week I'd hear a mother, fresh from a visit to a naturopath, rail about how, because of the evils of gluten, she had no energy. Gluten made her feel heavy and depressed. French bread, she was sure, was sucking her joie de vivre. Left in her life, gluten would be the ruin of her, I'd learn of yet another mother during afternoon pickup.

These women *hated* gluten. It did occur to me that there might be some anger being unfairly projected onto the two hapless proteins that make up gluten—gliadin and glutenin. These proteins sound like Knights of the Round Table for a reason, people.

They're what give bread its elasticity, and that, for most of us, is a noble cause.

My projected anger theory may be right: I'd run into some of these same women a year or so later, happy as clams, downing a croissant in some café, and the second sentence out of their mouths would be, "So I divorced my husband!"

Of course, people can eat whatever they like. All the more gluten for me.

I don't eat anything with arms—no octopuses, no monkeys—but that's just a preference, not something I'll ever frame as a condition.

Certainly it's not something I'd be willing to go science-free over.

Move Along,
Dear Reader . . .
Nothing to See Here

The Globe and Mail, May 27, 2015

•

In light of recent revelations that Bell Media president Kevin Crull interfered with CTV's news coverage of a recent Canadian Radio-television and Telecommunications Commission decision that displeased him, I feel I need to make it clear that I am not now, nor have I ever been, subject to any editorial pressure from any person or persons at Bell Media.

I assure you I am free to editorialize as I please—despite the fact that Bell Canada Enterprises owns 15 percent of *The Globe and Mail* and that Mr. Crull sits on *The Globe*'s board of directors where, it is often remarked, he has excellent posture and the clear, attentive eyes of a husky.

On Wednesday, *The Globe* broke the news that last week Mr. Crull, who, as I said, works (very hard, I imagine) for BCE, which happens to own CTV, directed staff there not to air any footage of CRTC chairman Jean-Pierre Blais (if that is his name) in their coverage of the CRTC story.

Senior staff at CTV would have none of it—even though Mr. Crull felt that the CRTC's decision requiring that consumers be offered a leaner, less expensive form of basic cable and be allowed to order channels individually was not be in the best interest of Canadians, whom he worries about.

My understanding is that, concerned for Mr. Blais's health, intuiting that he was under terrible stress and suffering paralyzing anxiety after his own recent lapse in judgment, Mr. Crull even demanded that Mr. Blais be excused from appearing on CTV's *Power Play* at the very last minute—knowing he needed some time to rest and relax.

Shortly after *The Globe and Mail*'s story broke, Mr. Crull apologized for his interference—characterizing the whole affair as an excellent learning opportunity for himself. (Next week, the news team at Canada's largest independent network is going to teach him to fly-fish; the week after that they'll make gnocchi.)

I understand why Canadians may be alarmed by this story.

After all, it is vitally important that independence of the press be upheld. That is I why I want to reassure my readers that there are absolutely no Bell Canada employees looking over my shoulder as I write this, watching every word I type or surreptitiously changing text. Amazing smartphones on sale now.

Because that would be so out of character for one of our beloved and not-at-all sinister telecommunications giants, wouldn't it?

And, by the way, if there were such an employee looming—in a very professional manner—over me as I work, his choice to wear a black suit, black tie and sunglasses inside my house at eight p.m. would be entirely the right one.

Yes, it makes him look like a (younger!) Tommy Lee Jones in *Men in Black*.

Also, I have no reason to believe at this time that any employees of Bell Canada are responsible for the disappearance of my little dog. She is probably hiding. She is good at that and I have not yet checked under all the carpets.

Just to set your mind at ease, readers, as to the objectivity of my column (the topic this week is, of course: You Should Call Your Mother. Every Day. Before Six P.M.) I promise you that there is no posse of menacing telecommunications agents in my home, but if there were I would be very grateful for any work they might do around my house.

I would be happy even though they would keep bundling things, and every time I used my garage door opener, the stove would turn on. Yes, this bit of engineering might make it difficult for me to leave the house but then, as no one named Mr. Blue has just reminded me, I really need to be here for my dog—who is not being held captive. (I must check in the dryer—which apparently I can no longer use unless I get The Movie Network.)

They have welded my Waring blender to a SharkVac pool cleaner. I do not have a pool. I will never use this pool shark, but then who am I, a person who never understood why I could not get CNN without paying for The Bush Baby Network (which has really gone downhill since they started broadcasting *Eye on Aye-Ayes* 24 hours a day) to question this move?

I can't use my hair dryer without my shower turning on and, for that, I need to get 14 sports networks (keep an eye on dazzling Jesper Jensen, whom I now recognize is just as elusive and tricky as the wild seal, and will lead Färjestad Bollklubb to the league championship!) and The American Heroes Channel.

They have bundled my scotch into their glasses. This, they insist, "is the best outcome for all consumers," and I believe them—and any connection between the editorial content of this column and the fact that my son is apparently having an unscheduled sleepover in an un-marked black van with a satellite dish on the roof is purely coincidental.

For the love of God, call your mother.

On an entirely unrelated note: Does anyone know how long a severed pinkie finger keeps on ice? It's for a science project.

I am finished now. I am about to hit "send" on this column but may I say, in conclusion, that only losers complain about roaming fees. Losers complaining about roaming fees are what brought down Rome. That is in fact where the term comes from.

Hey, my dog is back! She came bundled with a raccoon. I have never wanted to own a raccoon but, I am assured, this is a "premium raccoon" and having it in my home will enhance my pet-owning experience.

Take This Column
and Shake It

The Globe and Mail, April 4, 2015

I have written about Gamergate and abortion and many other controversial subjects but I received far more—and far more vicious—email on this column than on any other. There was nothing diluted about homeopathists' anger about this column. They beat the jazz fans by a mile. Second across the line would be the anti-vaxxers.

•

This week, Ontario become the first province to regulate homeopathy. It's a controversial step—what with homeopathy being completely bogus.

In fact, the core principles of homeopathy—namely, that infinitesimal amounts of something that may cause symptoms similar to those a patient is experiencing will make that patient well; that diluting that infinitesimal amount will make it stronger; and that shaking it a lot will make it stronger still—are fundamentally ridiculous.

Don't believe me? Give your newspaper a good shake. Then give it a thump against the palm of your hand.

Good work. Good shaking there, dear readers.

This, if the science behind homeopathy is sound, should make my column 100 percent more compelling. If it didn't work, my point is proven: homeopathy is nonsense.

If it did work, my post-shake column should be so convincing that when I tell you that, as far as anyone qualified can discern, homeopathy has absolutely no capacity to heal anything, you will believe me anyway—because, shaking! The father of homeopathy, Samuel Hahnemann (1755–

243

1843), even warned that carrying whatever tincture one had concocted in one's waistcoat pocket, thus subjecting it to superfluous shaking, could cause it to become too strong and one's patient might overdose.

Don't over-shake your newspaper. My column could become so transcendentally persuasive, you will never be able to put it down.

Dr. In-a-Time-of-Leeching-and-Purgatives Hahnemann also cautioned against allowing patients to play chess while they were being treated—he believed the game to be dangerously exciting.

Some proponents of homeopathy claim it works because water has memory. (Have I been blind to the cognitive capacity of fluids?)

I fear I may once have offended a Long Island Iced Tea by downing it—never inquiring about its ambition to get a Ph.D. in comparative literature. But despite the ludicrousness of that theory, now, in my province, you can be licensed to practise homeopathy.

The Ontario government is legitimizing the health care equivalent of dowsing rods. We are this close to having Official Bikini Inspectors in this province—now that is dangerously exciting.

Suddenly anything feels possible. We're sanctioning the licensing of the imaginary. Not convinced, dear reader? Rejecting my column?

Try ripping one letter out of my column, and putting it in water.

Now pour that water into more water and then more water after that, and then, trusting reader, shake it.

No! Not too much—you damn fool! At this level of dilution, your tincture of my column is so powerful that if you drank it (and homeopathy worked) you would risk becoming me—and there can be only one! (Draws sword, shakes it.)

Okay, now measure out a single drop of Tart tincture into a glass spoon.

No! Not a metal spoon! Your water will get forgetful or something and never be able to remember where it put its water keys.

Now ingest that tincture.

Good, good—now see if you believe me when I tell you that soon we in Ontario will be able to visit a licensed palmistry technician.

These will be people judged qualified by a board of their beshawled peers to stare at your hand for a bit and then predict that you will or will not meet a tall, dark stranger.

You can see it happening, can't you? Either that's the effect of the magic memory water that should go on *Jeopardy!* or you recognize that this is where the slippery, wet slope of licensed homeopathy logically takes us.

The argument the Ontario Ministry of Health makes for licensing is that the oversight that a regulatory body might offer will provide recourse to those who have complaints about their homeopathic treatment. Perhaps complaints like "it didn't work."

The problem is that, like actual doctors, homeopaths will be self-regulating. Anyone who has ever gone down to the Bureau of Magic Beans to make a complaint about the state of their beanstalk will understand why this could be an issue.

Oh. None of you have ever gone down to the Bureau of Magic Beans? Because we don't have one? That's because, at least to date, someone has had the good sense to realize that such an institution would be a governmental seal of approval on a fairy tale.

Also it should go without saying that telling people engaged in the magic bean business that you traded your only cow to an old man for some enchanted legumes that did bugger all isn't likely to get you a response of "Well, yeah, they don't work. There's no such thing as magic."

Perhaps when the Ontario Fabulous Fabaceae Act is passed, bureaucrats will say that your case was rare and unfortunate, or that you did something wrong.

"Did you turn twice widdershins instead of thrice widdershins? Because that is a common but fatal mistake," a concerned magic-beaneologist will say.

Either way, chances are you're never going to get that cow back, or your time back—time and cow that could have been spent on effective science-based solutions to your giant problem.

The people running that bean office might well believe entirely in the fantastical properties of their touted produce—in the superiority of locally sourced sorcery. "It's far better than turning to the conventional remedies of Big Ladder," they will advise, sincerely.

Or maybe they're advocates for a multi-million-dollar industry—and this bean bureau rightly belongs down the hall from the Ministry for One Weird Trick That Dentists Hate or a Nigerian Prince Desirous of Your Aid Registry.

This will be something we'll debate.

Ah, reader, I sense you're skeptical of my hyperbolic dystopian vision of the future. It makes you feel nervous and uncomfortable.

I suggest, given the current trend in Ontario, that you try a natural remedy for this problem.

Try something that has no side effects, or actual effects; drive your Tabatha Tincture to the ocean, toss it in, wait a moment for proper tidal dilution and agitation. Then have a short swim.

By the logic of homeopathy, you, and everyone else on the planet, should soon believe everything I say.

If that doesn't work, come back and see me next week.

Rolling Stone's Story Was Never About Rape on Campus

The Globe and Mail, April 11, 2015

•

I never imagined I'd be saddened to read of journalists not losing their jobs. Yet on Sunday, when *Rolling Stone* reacted to a lengthy report by three academics at the Columbia Graduate School of Journalism on the magazine's thoroughly discredited "A Rape on Campus" story by saying no one would lose any work as a result, I was sad.

The author of the piece, freelancer Sabrina Rubin Erdely, spent six weeks scouring several university campuses looking for the story she wanted to tell—or, more accurately, for the example she felt best illustrated, in the broadest possible strokes it seems, the narrative she'd assembled. "Erdely," the Columbia report states, "said she was searching for a single, emblematic college rape case that would show 'what it's like to be on campus now,'" and I have a fairly good idea how many actual rape cases she must have passed over before arriving at the blockbuster story she chose.

"A Rape on Campus" isn't about, say, a second-year student who went to a party alone, had a few drinks, made out with a guy after he danced with her—a fun-seeming guy who offered to walk her back to her dorm and then raped her, taking apart her life.

Instead it's the story of a woman who went on a proper date, wearing "a tasteful red dress with a high neckline," to a fraternity event with a boy from work.

"Jackie," the reader is assured, "discreetly spilled her spiked punch onto the sludgy fraternity house floor"—as a lady does, it is implied. Yet, despite this undeserving-of-being-raped behaviour, Jackie was led into a dark room, thrown against a glass table which shattered, then punched and gang-raped by seven men, in what is depicted as a horrific fraternity initiation ritual.

Afterward, she called three friends to fetch her and, with the frat house "looming behind them" like some crumbling gothic castle, two of them warned her—we switch genres here, and this part is scripted by John Hughes—that she will be a total social outcast if she reports her rape. This, her stock character friends are alleged to have done (minus the word "alleged") "while Jackie stood behind them, mute in her bloody dress." Lest we missed the point.

Jackie's character is contrasted (by her alone, as no one from *Rolling Stone* seems to have contacted the trio for corroboration, as is standard journalistic practice) with that of one of her rescuers, "Cindy," who is described as a "self-declared hookup queen."

"Why didn't you have fun with it?" Cindy is said to have asked. "A bunch of hot Phi Psi guys?" suggesting it's only rape if done to a certain kind of girl, in a certain kind of dress.

The option of a small story, well told, was very much not taken by the people at *Rolling Stone*.

Theirs was not a "pedestrian" rape story, with all the messiness one of those often entails, accompanied by all the challenges telling a story like that can present to the writer—in large part because the story challenges the reader.

The reader of *Rolling Stone*'s story is not asked to believe a woman who says she was raped over a man who says she consented. The man is conveniently not in the story (or very possibly anywhere else on this earth, for that matter, as he was never contacted or identified by anyone from the magazine). But the rape and the aftermath are described very much as though the writer saw it all. Issue avoided.

The virtue of the woman who says she was assaulted is never in doubt—it is, in fact, Victorian-novel clear. Well played, *Rolling Stone*; it's always easier to dodge a question than it is to dispute the validity of its premise. This was very much a rape story that catered to the sensibilities of readers who do not naturally trust women or see "everyday rapes" as a real problem.

The victim in this story is not "just raped," something that, if she's had sex anyway, is all too often brushed aside as a thing that can just happen to a woman—especially if she is not careful.

No, the victim in the story is raped by many men, for many hours as they egg each other on, inserting a beer bottle into her.

You write a story like this, select it over all the other cases you encounter, and the odds that your reader will see himself in your story—perhaps be forced to recall that time when "C'mon, you know, there was some last-minute resistance," or "She was pretty wasted anyway," or "She wouldn't have been there if she didn't want it"—are pretty slim.

A gang rape by strangers (and these do happen, although there is virtually no evidence it happened here) is an easy story to tell. Highlight the rape case outlier, write it like cheap horror fiction. And far from exposing the problem of rape on campus, as *Rolling Stone* has sanctimoniously insisted was the aim, you distract people from the issue—all but erasing thousands of below-the-fold rape victims.

Rape, as *Rolling Stone* chose to define it, is a seven-headed monster in a dark room to which our unsuspecting heroine is led. It's not unlike focusing a story about racism on the Ku Klux Klan. Most of the actual problem of racism will fall back into the abyss.

Far from illuminating a problem, your race story may end up unhelpfully hinting that, if you're black and didn't get that job you were overqualified for, or were stopped by cops three times last week in your nice car, you should try to keep that stuff in perspective because, well, lynching.

Rolling Stone's tale of conspiratorial, ritualized rape is, like most tales of women in peril, not feminist at all—the magazine published a bodice-ripper, not a second *The Second Sex*. Tempting as it is for many, including Ms. Erdely and the editors at *Rolling Stone*, who have pleaded guilty only to being too noble to ask questions, to spin it that way, this was never a case of feminism run amok.

There are parallels between this disgraceful episode and the satanic-ritual-daycare-child-sex-abuse panic of the 1980s—often seen as a reaction to a societal shift wherein more women entered the workforce, and thus more children attended daycare.

The impetus for that alarm (much like the heightened discussion of the number of women pursuing higher education) seemed to be that the trend was somehow unnatural and a close-to-supernaturally-extracted price must be paid.

This is not to suggest that sexual abuse of children—the kind mostly committed by relations of the children and people we know, who rely on the shame of their victims to hide their crimes—is not very real, any more than it is to suggest that rape on campus is not committed and protected in the same manner; only that the problem needs to be addressed calmly and intelligently.

Exploitative, crap journalism is nothing new, and yet distinct lessons can be learned from this example of it. I do hope we can find a place between never questioning a woman when she says she was raped and questioning her way more than everyone else.

Love Is a Two-Dollar Toast Rack

The Globe and Mail, May 9, 2015

•

I was raised at yard sales, taken there by my mother, where my job was to offer three dollars for an item that cost five dollars and then go home and tell my dad it cost two dollars.

We were conspiratorial, my mum and I—the whole thing had an *Ocean's Eleven* feel. From May to September, Saturday mornings always had a map to them drawn from the classified ads of the *Guelph Mercury*, the columns of which my mother analyzed with the kind of skill usually reserved for scientific documents.

If you had more than one yard sale a year, we would not even do a quick drive by your motley collection of cluttered card tables.

"That'll be junk," my mother would say, and she did not care for your "crafts," either—putting an arch line through those listings—having taught me from a young age that a box of Kleenex should only ever look like a box of Kleenex, and that the loo-paper-cover-Barbie-doll-hybrid that fascinated me was a monster.

These were but some of the yard sale lessons I learned, and my mother schooled others on those "no early birds" mornings as well.

Often it seemed to me our role at these sales was to ask the price of all the toast racks we found amid the ashtrays and the Blue Mountain Pottery menageries of Guelph, just so the yard sale hostess could say, "I don't know, $1.50? What is it anyway? It was a wedding present."

"It's a toast rack," my mother would say, with the kind of exaggerated patience I imagine early missionaries used when explain-

251

ing the virgin birth—information our hostesses found about as culturally relevant.

"You put toast in it," my mother would explain.

"But doesn't the toast get hard and cold?" the confused hostess would invariably ask, and my mother would sigh.

I think she always hoped that, once it was explained, the suddenly reformed toast heathen yard sale hostess would seize the toast rack back from her and charge into the house—crying, "I figured it out, Doug! Our long nightmare is over! We need to get some marmalade!"

She is of a cold, crisp toast people, my mother. Raised in South Africa by English parents, she attended a school that was as English as English can be—which is pretty English—and, for a people with a long tradition of soggy vegetables, the English have a lot of unkind things to say about pliant toast.

My mother's school in Johannesburg not only imported all its teachers from England but staggered its holidays with those of other local schools so that, as she tells it, students wouldn't mix with other children and pick up an Afrikaans accent.

The school was a colony within a colony—an island of crisp toast and, in my mind, egg coddlers.

Despite my mother's frugality, to the sellers' delight and my horror, during my childhood we bought all the orphan egg coddlers from all the yard sales in Wellington County.

Why anyone would want to coddle an egg, I could never understand. The egg already had a shell! Why decant the egg into another shell to boil it, instead of just boiling it as God intended? The whole thing made no sense to me—even if that shell was Royal Worcester bone china and had fetching meadow flowers painted on it.

It all seemed vaguely sinister.

We had rows of egg coddlers in the kitchen—dozens of individual overly precious pods, each awaiting the arrival of a vulnerable egg soul. It was like a Merchant Ivory production of *Invasion of the Body Snatchers* on that counter.

"Please don't take my offer on this egg coddler," my eyes would plead with the seller. "She's lowballing you—and I'm scared." But to no avail.

Later, in what always felt like a getaway car, my mother and I would speculate triumphantly about what the egg coddler "would have cost, bought new."

"By fools!" was the unspoken sentiment.

Buying new was a harshly judged thing we rarely did in our house and I'm grateful, because where's the fun in that?

What's the game? Where's element of chance? The thrill of carrying a lamp shaped like a boat with a shade shaped like a mushroom around the side of the house, plugging it into the outlet used for the lawn mower and finding that "it works!" can't be bought at Sears.

Growing up, I had an ancient table saw with no safety guards in the workroom in the basement, all because it was only five dollars and I did have a full ten fingers after all, so some sort of cost/risk benefit analysis was done, and some of the happiest moments of my childhood were allowed.

Once, my mother's extreme pacifism was overcome by her love of a bargain, and she bought me a three-dollar pellet gun, which I still have and with which I taught my own two children to shoot.

These children of mine will likely ignore Mother's Day, a fact of which I am proud. It shows they've been paying attention, my skeptical angels.

But the three of us raise that pellet gun in a salute to my own mother and, as the season begins, wish you all smooth yard-sailing this summer.

Caitlyn Jenner's Tall, but Don't Let That Throw You

The Globe and Mail, June 12, 2015

Vanity Fair published a profile of Caitlyn Jenner, who had until then been known as Bruce Jenner, in which she discussed her transition.

.

There have been several good pieces this week about how to cover the Caitlyn Jenner story and, because Ms. Jenner is six foot two, I offer How to Talk and Write About Tall People:

1. Before you write anything, ask yourself: Are you tall? If not, do you at least know some tall people well? If the answer is "no," then will you at least be consulting people who have actual experience with being tall? Or are you just going to write about how this one time, when you were a child, you stood on a chair for five minutes but realized it wasn't for you and never looked up again?

    Will you conclude this chair story by noting that life's worked out great for you—as though that were the moral of the story of tall people? While making some joke about how kids are weird and mercurial and . . . mermaids . . . or whatever?

2. If the answer to that first question is "no"— you aren't yourself tall, don't know any actual tall people and have no intention of consulting any, but just heard about some of them from some other people whom you consider to be of a

reasonable physical stature—then write about something else. Anything else.

3. Is your thesis that tall people are *choosing* to be tall—either to get attention or because, you imagine, society is constantly showering them with rewards for being tall, rather than mocking them, making it terribly awkward for them to buy clothes and causing them to suffer grave head and other injuries?

    Then surely, if you cared to make the slightest effort, you could find a few of these allegedly limelight-loving leggy souls willing to go on the record about what their lives as tall people are actually like.

    Why, by your logic, tall people are calling *you*—so either pick up the phone or reconsider your angle. I promise you that doing the first thing will lead to the second.

4. Remember that without tall people *you have no story* because how tall someone else is isn't a story about how you feel about anything, shorty. Your story should be a chance to learn about what tall people experience—not you letting tall people know how you feel about them or gathering people around you to crane their necks.

5. This is true even if you're compelled to tell everyone that you're actually okay with some people being tall—even though you "don't get it." Because when you say that, you're implying that you're being permissive in your beneficent toleration of the misheightened. Something it isn't your place to be.

    In saying "whatever floats your boat," you're both congratulating yourself for waving at those you clearly perceive as having, obstinately, obtained an unnatural height—those people you're pretty much characterizing as circus freaks—

and suggesting that this is about some kind of leisure sailing. Instead of about not drowning.

6. If you do talk to a tall person for your story, don't ask about shoe size. It's not a polite question. "What size shoe do you wear now?" isn't a question you would ask any other story subject, and what size foot is in another person's shoe is none of your business and is meaningless as to who they are anyway.

    You don't habitually count your other interviewees' toes, do you? No.

    So, worry about your own damn feet. Keep them clean. Or don't. Whatever floats your boat.

7. There's no need to constantly refer to a subject as "born short." If it's relevant to your story, perhaps say, briefly, "Lydia (who was once five feet tall)." But remember when reporting on a person who at one point in her life presented differently from the way she presents now—when she, perhaps, runs a cake shop you're writing up, or has put her name on the ballot for Ward 6—her previous height isn't relevant information.

8. Never use the fact that some people are tall, and that some people accept them, as proof that an ultimate societal shift you're convinced everyone should be alarmed or pleased about has occurred. Tall people are not your barometer or your parable; they're only tall and people.

9. Don't call anyone "a tall" or refer to them as "talled." Just say "a tall person." "Tall" is an adjective, not a noun or a verb. It's not a thing that happens to someone—like being laundered.

10. What pronouns should you use for tall persons? The same pronouns they use to refer to themselves. Like everyone else. If

you're genuinely flummoxed and a pronoun is genuinely needed, then ask the tall person what to use.

Never put one of those pronouns in quotes. It's not a goddamn song lyric. It's a fact.

11. If you're about to tell us where you draw the line because, as a person of average height, you assume you get to be the line drawer, put down your pen. A little research will tell you that no one is permissively making children tall. They're just not telling them every single moment of their childhoods that they're not allowed to grow.

12. Needless to say, setting rules about the maximum height of one's progeny doesn't work and it makes some children desperately sad.

13. Never use humiliating words to describe tall people—even if you think what you're saying is "just a joke" and you imagine that said tall person has never heard anyone say, "How's the air up there, Stretch?" and will burst out laughing and immediately book you on *The Tonight Show*.

Tall people do not, in general, have the power to book talent on network shows or, in fact, have any other near-mystical abilities. They're just people and tall; they're not there to serve as your spirit guides as you discover the true meaning of your own height or whether the missing fondue set is indeed in an upper cupboard.

14. Be sensitive to the fact that people's height has nothing to do with which people they want to sleep with—nor does it make whom they sleep with a more interesting or salient fact.

Yes, being attracted to a tall person does mean you're gay and, if that's a problem for you, then I must inform you that the only solution is to sleep with a short person, after cooking them a really nice dinner. And I say that on behalf of myself and everyone else who is five foot two or under.

15. Remember that tall people are not a dilemma that needs to be solved, by you or anyone else. And that one tall person being great at, say, basketball—maybe even ending up on the cover of *Vanity Fair*—while nice, wouldn't do that anyway.

    Tall people are not a problem. Maybe we are.

Today's Agenda: Things That Could Replace the Senate

The Globe and Mail, June 12, 2015

•

This week, Auditor General Michael Ferguson's scathing report on Senate expenses revealed a taste for the high life in the "upper chamber." In response, the Committee of Totally Made Up People Who Meet in My Imagination convened to address the day's agenda— Things That Could Replace the Senate.

"A giant sucking mouth!" calls out Bob Flowers.

"A money blender!" says Doug Lamp.

"A self-igniting currency?" says Linda Small Wooden Coffee Table.

"Swarms of money-eating locusts," says Reginald Persian Carpet.

"There'd have to be a certain number of swarms from each province. There's only so much we can alter the constitution," says Mr. Rose. "And even then, practically speaking, only in Tabatha's imagination."

"And Thomas Mulcair's," says Reginald Persian Carpet, sensibly.

"Locusts can fly," says Linda. "They'll never spend enough on airfare to replace the Senate."

"Vikings? Are they still a thing?" says Mr. Darcy, the BBC one.

"Whee! Huns," injects A Helpful Hudson's Bay Employee.

"No," says Linda Small Wooden Coffee Table, "Vikings and Huns may be too responsive to criticism and unable fill the large, injured, self-righteous hole the Senate would leave."

259

"True. The auditor general's report's received a great deal of attention—although not nearly enough from the Senate itself," intones a Very Clever and Successful *Globe and Mail* Columnist who is wearing such a fetching dress today and is good at making up names. "The Senate has rejected one of the report's key recommendations; the senators do not want an oversight body, thank you very much, and are a little hurt you asked."

"One of the report's findings is that we have a very sensitive Senate," says Mr. Darcy, the BBC one. And the way he says "sensitive" almost justifies the close to $1 million the report found was improperly expended by senators during the two-year period scrutinized.

"People who eat money," shouts The Memorandizer, the world's most bureaucratic superhero.

"On planes!" The Pencil Pusher, his trusty (though somewhat bitchy at the Water Cooler Cave on Paperwork Mountain) sidekick, chimes in.

". . . but who chow down on a wad of fifties later because you just can't get a decent bankroll on a plane," adds The Memorandizer.

"No, that won't do," says Paddington Bear. "The only way to hire people who eat money is to hire people who admit they eat money. And so many senators have claimed reimbursement in contravention of the Senate's guidelines, then become stroppy when asked to back those claims up, that they can't be replaced with people remotely honest and accountable about their money-munching ways."

"Good point, Paddington," says Sam Large Antique Carved Wooden Owl, affectionately known as "Impulse Purchase."

"We should replace them with marmalade," says Paddington, adjusting his hat.

"Drop the marmalade thing, Paddington," says Clever and Successful *Globe and Mail* Columnist, who has totally been to the moon. "Every time there's an issue to be dealt with, you claim it can be resolved with marmalade. Marmalade didn't keep the Russians out of Ukraine and it did not make a good replacement for the light fixture in the hallway upstairs."

"Well, I like it," says Mr. Darcy, the BBC one.

"Thanks," says Very Successful *Globe and Mail* Columnist, who invented grilled cheese sandwiches.

"Look, this shouldn't be that hard," says A Helpful Hudson's Bay Employee. "It's not as if all the senators fished, played golf, went on holiday and attended hockey games, and claimed back those amounts. Couldn't we just replace the Senate with a collection of party hacks, fundraisers, actually respected people and miscellaneous former television personalities? Then hypnotize 30 or so of them into thinking they'd won Cash for Life? We could teach them that the words 'parliamentary business' are magic; if you say them loudly over a fellow senator's 50th wedding anniversary you've flown to, business class, all your expenses disappear."

"Only 30 of 116 investigated?" demands Constantine Dmitrich Levin, from *Anna Karenina*, who does pop in sometimes as a voice of moral authority. "That is hateful and repulsive. Would we accept this ratio from any of the other professions?" he says, stomping.

"Only 30 of these 116 waiters spat in your food, and to be fair the rules around plating and saliva are vague,'" he continues—in a mocking, sing-songy voice—before adding earnestly, "Mostly I think only of death."

"Death's your marmalade," says Paddington. "I understand."

"He's a bit much, isn't he?" whispers Mr. Darcy, the BBC one, gesturing subtly toward the pacing Mr. Levin—somewhat jealously, thinks *Globe and Mail* Columnist.

"Yes," says Mr. Lamp, "don't get him started on agricultural practices vis-à-vis the temperament of the peasants, but it's not like he said 'Giving a voice to the voiceless is part of my duties as a parliamentarian,' as did Senator Pierre-Hugues Boisvenu, who the Auditor General found had misstated the location of his primary residence and incurred over $50,000 in dubious expenses."

"My understanding is that the definition of 'residence' for a senator is not 'a place in which you live' so much as it is 'a place you grace with your presence,'" says The Pencil Pusher.

"Let's just officially make the Senate cpac's contribution to the reality tv genre. These are Canada's overpaid d-list celebrities from a tv show no one watches," suggests The Memorandizer's arch nemesis, The Verbal Contractor.

"We sell the Senate to people over the phone, taking their money directly. Think of the Senate as Canada's vast tracts of swampland in Florida," says Mr. Flowers.

"Or," says Glenda the Good Living Room Window, "we could refuse to accept the excuse that the rules that govern the Senate are too ill defined and impenetrable to be followed. Coming as it does of late from a good number of people whose role is largely to scrutinize the rules and policies that govern us, but who, upon seeing a possible loophole, dove right down it—golf clubs in hand.

"Then maybe the Senate could be a legislative body to which we appoint citizens who'd demonstrated both a desire and a singular ability to make a contribution to bettering Canada?"

"This is worse than Levin on farming," sighs *Globe and Mail* Columnist, who has six adorable red pandas in her garden, "but she has a point."

"We could say," continues Ms. Window, "'senators, you must live in a faraway land called Beyond Reproach because the position you're in is unique and precious. If you don't like it, move.'"

Or, get this: We breed termites, only they build their mounds out of money, and occasionally show up at local craft fairs.

Women Sell Their Panties All Over Town— Mine Don't Come Cheap

Elle Canada, January 2010

While I admit I have a weakness for fine underwear, I also resolved when I began writing the Elle Girls that everything Elle Girl–me bought and did would be insanely expensive. I felt that so much writing for women was centred around guilt over our mistakes and mere indulgences that, knowing the spirit in which women's fashion magazines are often purchased, I wanted the reader to feel to feel absolved of, at the very least, the cover price.

•

There isn't a day that goes by when I don't check the Missed Con-nections page on Craigslist. It's not that I expect to be mentioned there; it just pleases me when someone references a location that I know.

Something like "Saturday night, tall black girl, mauve skirt, buying a hot dog, Bathurst and Queen" makes my heart skip a beat. You see, my friend has a studio at Bathurst and Queen. I know Bathurst and Queen well. So, consequently, when I—a short white girl who dislikes the colour mauve and probably looks a lot more like the guy selling the hot dog than the girl buying the hot dog—read that posting, I feel included. I feel plugged in.

Bathurst and Queen, I smile to myself. Yes, indeed, this is my town.

"I bought your panties at The Bovine, Saturday 2 a.m., and I want to buy more."

There's a lot of panty buying going on around the city that I knew nothing about. There's some acknowledgement of panty commerce posted on Craigslist every day. Downtown Toronto on a weekend is like some sort of undies farmers' market apparently.

"You sold me your panties. Broken Social Scene. Let's meet up!"

"I sold you my PANTIES!!! After-hours club on Britain Street. I have more."

That's good, I think when I read a posting like that. She has more. Sensible girl.

If it weren't for Craigslist, I'd be completely uninformed about all this underwear-related commerce because I'm just not part of it. It's unlikely that I'd ever sell my underwear to a man, no matter how sweetly he asked me, and it's not because I'm prudish or anything—it's just a matter of economics. My underwear is expensive, so if a man wanted to buy my underwear, I'd probably have to charge him $80 minimum just to break even. Also, most of the time my panties match my bra and, frankly, I'd prefer not to break up a set—I might never find the right colour match again! And in my arguably decadent underwear world, if a pair of strawberry-pink panties gets taken out of commission, a strawberry-pink bra is immediately rendered useless. I'd just make it into two doilies.

Obviously, I'd have to upsell the panty buyer big time. I'd have to sell him my panties *and* my bra, and that means (I'm pretty good at sales) that some innocent panty speculator could easily end up spending hundreds of dollars—even if I didn't do any kind of markup for added value.

Also, the sky's the limit if I'm wearing a bustier or corset—that can easily cost $500 and either way, bra or corset, he'll need more cash than he's probably carrying.

I imagine that the light flirtatiousness or sheer perversion of any panty-purchase moment would be entirely lost if we had to trek off to the bank machine together, wait in line and stand there in the little marble bank foyer while he counted the cash and took his little paper bank slip.

"Don't forget your bank card," I'd say. God, I just know I'd say that. I would say, "Don't forget your bank card" out of an instinctive concern for the man who had either just put a bid on my panties or with whom I'd just negotiated a slightly drunken verbal contract (okay, so maybe I'd get something in writing) stipulating that, on payment of the agreed-upon sum, he would take possession of my panties, to which I would revoke all rights, in perpetuity, including but not limited to use in all media. Initial here, please. I'd get it notarized by the bouncer. The fine print would have to say that I granted the purchaser no additional access, without reasonable notice and at least a nice dinner.

Oh yeah, and "Don't forget your bank card." That would totally be me. And, boy, that would sound naggy under the circumstances. "Don't forget your bank card." Not a sexy thing to say. Some nice man in the grips of the true spirit of Saturday night ponies up $500 for some as-yet-unseen lingerie and I, in the true spirit of Monday morning, practically tidy up his wallet and remind him to ask for his T4 at work. A deal breaker, for sure, ladies. No man wants to buy panties from his mother—or if he does, he's posting on another site.

So I can't commodify my undergarments. I've priced myself right out of the knickers-flipping market. It's a lifestyle choice I've made—I always wear pricey panties. It might still happen, of course: the club or concert panty purchase. I'm not exactly saying no; I'm just going to have to be honest about it and tell the boys upfront, "You can walk on by or you can stick around and negotiate hard." But, trust me, it's going to be different—way more costly and a touch officious: "I'll rock your world like a student loan officer, baby. That much, I promise."

• • • • •

Kory and Me—
Questions for a
Reluctant Spokesman

The Globe and Mail, July 3, 2015

I include this column largely because I had forgotten this incident and, given how well Teneycke-type tactics worked for Donald Trump, it is an interview best remembered.

•

I'm not sure what Conservative campaign spokesman Kory Teneycke thinks the "spoke" part of his job description is all about, but judging from his reaction this week when Global News's Tom Clark asked him about a recent Conservative campaign ad, I can only assume he has spent a lot of time learning to fix bikes.

He certainly doesn't seem to view speaking about the Conservative campaign as something he's obliged to do.

Mr. Teneycke took umbrage when asked about his party's recent attack ad—an ad that features Islamic State propaganda footage accompanied by an ISIS anthem—and not a small amount of umbrage, either. Mr. Teneycke took so much umbrage at Mr. Clark's questions about whether an ad that showcases terrorist propaganda might contravene the government's own freshly minted Bill C-51—a law that prohibits the promotion of terrorist propaganda—it was like he took umbrage, left the studio, rented a U-Haul, came back and carted away a whole lot more umbrage.

Word is, Mr. Teneycke was unhappy that he hadn't been given the interview questions in advance. Perhaps he'd have preferred a take-home test, in which case he could have deleted his embarrassing line: "We're better than the news, we're truthful."

That line was spoken in the tone of a man who cannot come up with one good reason why his party produced an ad that's approximately one-third grisly terrorist propaganda—the kind of thing that, as Mr. Clark made clear, most news organizations are very circumspect about showing—and two-thirds obviously misleadingly edited footage of their rather photogenic opponent.

"Whose idea was that?" I hear you cry. "Can we have them lead the country?" The flustered Mr. Teneycke certainly tried to delete that line, doing everything but frantically pressing Mr. Clark's nose over and over in the desperate hope it would turn out to be a magical nasal backspace key. It was just one of many awkward moments for the Conservative campaign spokesman.

"Will you be using more terrorist video as the campaign goes on?" pressed Mr. Clark finally.

"Uh, well, wait and see," said Mr. Teneycke, who said "uh" so many times in that interview, it was like Global had finally scored a long-sought interview with a hawkish walrus in a suit.

I'm no Tom Clark, who let slide nothing Mr. Teneycke said—entertain for a moment the vision of one deft pair of hands and thousands of talking-point salmon swimming upstream in hopes of spawning with voters.

What I've done, having a weakness for walruses, is concede to Mr. Teneycke's wishes—and more. Not only am I providing him with the questions for our interview, I'm giving him all the right answers as well. So here you go, Kory, it's on.

Me: How are you enjoying unemployment?

You: I am, surprisingly, still the Conservative campaign spokesman. Uh, make of that what you will.

Me: Do you believe that Canada's social safety net should be dismantled so that people like you will be motivated to work harder and answer questions on TV in a less disastrous manner?

You: Uh, in the future I plan on dedicating myself to trying to get through an eight-and-a-half-minute interview without suggesting that my political party—or any political party—is more truthful than all journalists ever, because that never ends well.

Me: Do you think it's prudent to effectively co-produce a campaign ad with a murderous terrorist organization?

You: No. That's a terrible idea. A cynical, opportunistic, abhorrent idea. No human being with even a sliver of conscience would, uh, ever seriously entertain such a notion.

Me: Is it ever a good idea to use footage of people about to be killed—in unspeakably barbaric ways—in just the manner the people who killed those people intended it to be used? Thus giving these killers incentive to kill and film more deaths? Do you understand anything about how supply and demand and evil work? Why do you think they keep making *Fast and Furious* movies?

You: No. That's never a good idea—and it's not like I saw them in the theatre.

Me: So, the Islamic State of Iraq and Syria. That was an interesting choice. Are there any other homicidal auteurs you guys plan on working with in the future?

You: No. Film distribution's always been an issue in Canada, and government could be more effective in this area. However, we shouldn't prioritize distributing the work of killers over literally anything else. Even if it's just some boring crap about people being sad at a cottage.

Me: ISIS. Huh. Wow. Leni Riefenstahl wasn't available, I guess.

You: Sorry, Canada.

Me: You do know the little girl in Lyndon Johnson's famous "Daisy Girl" campaign ad wasn't actually killed by a nuclear bomb, don't you?

You: Uh.

Me: Google it. Your party, the one at the forefront of making snuff campaign ads, is also intent on constructing the 24-metre-tall Mother Canada monument in Cape Breton. Is it prudent, in these—as your ads with a lower body count like to remind us—uncertain economic times, and with the nation already embroiled in a struggle against ISIS, to simultaneously launch a war on good taste? Why Mother Canada, Kory, why?

You: [Sorry, Kory, we don't have an answer for you on this one. We sent 16 of our best people to Georgian Bay on a retreat to hammer this one out—nothing.

We cannot begin to explain that monument. Best we can come up with is that it's Canada's National Butter Sculpture and will at least come down when the Royal Winter Fair ends. I would just go with "Uh."]

Me: A final question: Do you think it's okay to use terrorist-produced images if the man you work for reeeeeeaaaaaalllly wants to be re-elected prime minister yet is struggling with an approval rating that has dropped soooooooooo low that, if he were a tomato plant, his party would have to bring him inside?

You: Noooooooooooooooooooo.

Me: So, will you be using more terrorist video as the campaign goes on?

You: What in God's name have I done with my life that I can legitimately be asked this question?

[Now, search soul, deeply.]

Knocking *Mockingbird* Off Its Perch

The Globe and Mail, July 15, 2015

•

Whether or not, as her publishers insist, Harper Lee consented to the publication of *Go Set a Watchman*, reading it still feels like scrolling through a series of highly unfortunate selfies taken from a hacked cellphone.

While being promoted as a second novel from the 89-year-old author, *Go Set a Watchman* was in fact submitted for publication in 1957 and is the raw material from which *To Kill a Mockingbird* (1960) was later wrought—or in some instances copied and pasted.

Atticus Finch is a small-town lawyer in *Go Set a Watchman*, as he is in *To Kill a Mockingbird*.

Jean Louise is his daughter, called "Scout" in flashbacks—the name she is known by in *To Kill a Mockingbird*. Her brother is called "Jem" in both books.

In *Mockingbird*, the two have a fairly convivial relationship, whereas in *Go Set a Watchman*, the 26-year-old Jean Louise unceremoniously informs us her brother "dropped dead" a few years back. It's an image that demands a Pythonesque Terry Gilliam animation and it foreshadows precisely the amount of empathy Jean Louise demonstrates for most of the book: *Go Set a Watchman* frequently reads like a misguided attempt at *To Kill a Mockingbird* fan fiction.

The reaction to *Go Set a Watchman* has been overwrought and confused. Jean Louise, we're told, "was born color-blind," but still "observes that black people 'are simple people, most of them,'" sug-

270

gesting she's perhaps more colour-short-sighted. The public's dismay, however, stems largely from the fact that this Atticus Finch is a raging racist.

Atticus may be the most idealized character in American fiction. With this new book, it's as if the publishers have broken into and ransacked people's childhoods, and many fear the discrepancies between the two novels will forever change the way *To Kill a Mockingbird* is read.

That, I think, is not a bad thing.

I wish there were more mystery as to why *To Kill a Mockingbird*, with its confused prose and oddly shifting narrative perspective, was such an immediate and enduring success, but the book, which is not without its charms, was always a comforting fiction.

It's easy to imagine what a balm it must have been to a somewhat morally (and otherwise) panicked America in the wake of *Brown v. Board of Education*, the landmark case that would desegregate schools, and of the Supreme Court ruling that desegregated Alabama's buses.

To Kill a Mockingbird is, after all, a segregated anti-racist novel.

Maycomb, Alabama, the fictional town in which the novel is set, has a charm so intense it approaches kitsch-level. It's "remained the same size for a hundred years, an island in a patchwork sea of cotton-fields and timberland."

The mostly halcyon days of Scout's remembered youth play out in a place that seems to rest in a kind of snow globe—briefly shaken by a rape trial in which her father defends an innocent black man.

The racism in *To Kill a Mockingbird* is communicated as an artifact of that distant, indeed almost foreign, childhood.

Removed as these white folks are from most of the book's audience—separated by time, space and colloquial dialogue so distinct it almost amounts to another language—the black characters are still further away, barely in the book, pretty much in the Shire.

"Their cabins looked neat and snug with pale blue smoke rising from the chimneys and doorways glowing amber from the fires inside," the reader is assured. Separate but tidy.

Tidiness-measured morality is a big thing in *To Kill a Mockingbird*. Indeed, Robert Ewell, the only irredeemable racist in the book—according to Atticus, a lynch mob leader merely has a "blind spot," and the Klan is but "a political organization"—comes from a family plagued with "congenital defects, various worms, and the diseases indigenous to filthy surroundings."

To Atticus, unclean "trash"—likely not the kind of people the reader might know, let alone the reader himself—are the genuine obstacle to better, but not fundamentally changed, living.

"There's nothing more sickening to me than a low-grade white man who'll take advantage of a Negro's ignorance," he says. "Don't fool yourselves—it's all adding up and one of these days we're going to pay the bill for it. I hope it's not in you children's time."

The "we" here is clearly white people, and what gross injustice to black people threatens most appears to be white folks' way of life. Certainly to white readers of the book, released six months after the Greensboro Four sat down at a segregated lunch counter in North Carolina and peacefully refused to leave—within days, they were joined by 300 more would-be lunchers—it might have felt as if that bill had indeed come due. It sure looked as if a lot of black characters might be about to be written into their lives.

Could this be the reason a book with a resounding theme of racial justice that contains no actual fully realized black people was awarded the Pulitzer Prize after 41 of the many weeks it would spend on the bestseller lists?

To Kill a Mockingbird even has an impassioned-speech-giving, specifically non-violent character who eloquently demands people do right by their fellow man "in the name of God" who is not Martin Luther King Jr. Separate but equal.

Arguably, with his astonishing popularity, Atticus Finch is the literary Elvis Presley to Dr. King's Chuck Berry.

However, in *To Kill a Mockingbird* the prescription for justice is not found in the institutional change being demanded and enacted in America at the time of the book's release. Atticus even digresses in his defence of his client to take a swipe at Washington for weighing in on issues that he feels ought to be a matter of states' rights. I'll bet readers' ears pricked up.

Perhaps it's time they stood down a bit.

"I think for a child's book it does all right," Flannery O'Connor said of *To Kill a Mockingbird* with reasonable accuracy—none of which explains the novel's trajectory as the seminal text for lessons on race relations still offered to the majority of schoolchildren between grades 7 and 12 today.

The Tale of Peter Rabbit is an excellent children's book, and yet we don't hold it up as a model for agricultural practice.

Inspired By the Veiled Threat: Give Up a Right Day

The Globe and Mail, September 19, 2015

•

Stop me if you've heard this one before, but this week the Federal Court of Appeal ruled against the government—no wait! Guys, guys, don't go, this is a new one.

I know the Harper government has been defeated in court so many times that legal experts predict upcoming rulings against them will just read "Seriously?" and "You know it's not 'Lose 10 at taxpayers' expense, win one free,' right?" and "Still no," but cast your minds back to the case brought forward by Zunera Ishaq, a 29-year-old woman who came to Ontario from Pakistan in 2008 and successfully challenged the government's 2011 ban on the wearing of face coverings at citizenship ceremonies.

On September 15, 2015, the courts dismissed the government's appeal of Ms. Ishaq's case and the next day the Tories pushed back, promising to take it to the Supreme Court because . . . well . . . their publicly stated reasoning behind this is both mercurial and notable.

The Conservatives have of late mostly dropped their security rationale for the ban, possibly because (as the majority of Canadian five-year-olds could point out) there's absolutely no security risk to a woman wearing a niqab as she's sworn in.

An oath swearer's identity is already firmly established before the ceremony begins, and this isn't one of those things where you're given

274

a magic sword at the end, anyway. There's no advantage to anyone impersonating anyone else and (take note, ministers of the Crown) a woman who unveils privately just prior to the swearing-in is still there when she covers her face—because the ceremony is public, and that's how she rolls.

It concerns me that this seems to confuse as many Conservatives as it does. I'm not sure Canada should be governed by a party that has yet to achieve object permanence. (Although—better utilized—this might make for some raucous games of Question Period peekaboo; it could hardly be less productive than the status quo.)

Security concerns being as demonstrably specious as they are, it seems the other, and far more troubling, rationale for the ban is being played up.

In response to the court's dismissal of the government's case, Jason Kenney, our minister of defence, said, "I think it's entirely reasonable to ask, for those 30 seconds, that someone proudly demonstrate their loyalty to Canada." And therein lies the contradiction.

The point Mr. Kenney is making here—and a chorus of other Conservatives back him up on this—is that, if you are truly loyal to Canada, you will agree to a brief, symbolic suspension of one of the very rights Canadians most value at the very moment you symbolically become Canadian.

That you don't happen to believe that Ms. Ishaq's Muslim faith requires her to wear the niqab isn't relevant. And it doesn't matter whether you came to this understanding of Islamic theology through years of rigorous study or through something you read on a comment thread once.

As Chief Justice Beverley McLachlin wrote in *Syndicat Northcrest v. Amselem*, "The State is in no position to be, nor should it become, the arbiter of religious dogma."

Put another way: "You can decide for yourself what hats the angels dancing on the heads of pins ought to be wearing, we've both got your back and have bigger fish to fry."

What matters in law is how Ms. Ishaq interprets and practises her own faith, and what should matter to Canadians is how vigilantly we protect her—and thus our—right to do so.

Besides, this particular case was not in fact about religious freedom so much as it was about Jason Kenney taking liberties. The courts have so far ruled (twice, and with a veritable eye-roll) that, as minister of immigration he had no more power to insist women show their faces at citizenship ceremonies than the minister of agriculture has the power to demand that every woman buying maple syrup flash her tits.

Prime Minister Stephen Harper has said, "It is offensive that someone would hide their identity at the very moment where they are committing to join the Canadian family," and he's more than entitled to believe that and to never wear a veil.

What he and his overreaching ministers are not entitled to do, as the courts have ruled here, is demand an act of supplication from a tiny fraction of a religious minority.

The Charter is there to protect the rights of minorities from the will of the majority and, incidentally, from the will of political parties who have a majority they're a touch worried about losing at the moment.

Would we accept a bit of compliance baptism at our swearing-ins, a bit of "Look, it's just a splash of water on your forehead and something from *The Book of Common Prayer*, don't make a big deal about this—you are, after all, getting to become Canadian"?

I hope not. That would also be against our laws and values and, arguably, the person showing the greatest understating of those laws and values here—and, in undertaking this ordeal, the most loyalty to Canada—is Ms. Ishaq, who perhaps doesn't want to see a bizarre precedent set.

Should the niqab ban be allowed, what in this country would be next?

Perhaps every Canada Day a different Charter right could be suspended. Picture it: July 1, 2020, and no one is secure from unreasonable search and seizure for those 24 hours.

"Why?" some of the children ask, as their Popsicles are grabbed from their hands.

"Because today marks an occasion upon which we celebrate who we are and the temporary, purely symbolic abandonment of our rights is apparently how our government thinks we should do that," says a CSIS agent, enjoying his new Popsicle.

I can see it now: miles and miles of Jell-o salad, riffled wallets and emptied handbags laid out on picnic tables, burgers on the barbecue, and then some dad, dishevelled from the exhaustive pat-down conducted by the cops he has just shown around his house, lights off the fireworks.

There are cheers, and sparklers—the ones that didn't get seized.

Most agree this year was better than last year, when no one had the right not to be subjected to cruel and unusual punishment.

Then the kids "ooh" and "aah" at the now-traditional dazzling finale as the Little Charter of Rights and Freedoms goes up and sparks become flames.

In 2021, the right to communicate with and be served by the federal and New Brunswick governments in either official language will be suspended and, it being a holiday anyway, there will be much relief.

It will be almost like the old days, when Canadians just celebrated the delightful fact that everyone celebrated in a manner they saw fit.

What Has Driven All of Bond's Villains to Distraction? "Das Auto"

The Globe and Mail, September 26, 2015

•

It's difficult to predict what the long-term fallout will be from this week's revelation that, for the past seven years, Volkswagen has been installing software designed to fool emissions tests in their diesel vehicles.

The company has already earmarked $9.8 billion to cover the fallout. Its reputation is in tatters, chief executive officer Martin Winterkorn has resigned and the company's stock dropped more than 30 percent in three days.

What has not been reported, however, is that news of vw's dealings has sent a number of notable James Bond villains into a deep depression, as I can attest—they are in my house.

"I thought I was sinister," Auric Goldfinger says to me, sprawled dramatically on my office couch—my reputation for having a sympathetic ear having apparently spread to the criminal mastermind community. "I invested my life in evil doings, but next to Volkswagen, I look like Maria from *The Sound of Music*."

"If you're Maria, I'm Gretl," sighs Hugo Drax. "I'm fairly sure my plan to poison the atmosphere with deadly nerve gas in order to kill all of humanity would have worked, had I not skimped on my space station's radar-jamming device in order to ensure my shuttle's engine met basic environmental standards—I'm not a monster."

"My deadly gas was harmless to plants and animals—11 million non-compliant vw vehicles dumping 948,691 metric tons of nitrous oxide a year into our atmosphere, less so," Drax adds, doing some calculations on the back of an envelope.

This brings yet more sobbing from Ernst Stavro Blofeld, who has been curled up next to me all week, watching *Buffy the Vampire Slayer* on his laptop while eating chips. "I miss my cat!" he wails. "I am sure that treacherous feline has left me for Martin Winterkorn—I just wasn't diabolical enough," he adds, reflexively beginning to stroke my hair again, as he does.

"Look," I plead with them, gently removing Blofeld's hand from my head, "you guys really have to stop comparing yourselves to other arch villains.

"You're all fiendish in your own way. It's not like you didn't try to utilize new technologies—ostensibly designed to save humanity—to wreak havoc. Isn't that right, Colonel Tan Sun Moon?" I say coaxingly to the despondent North Korean.

"Who's the man who tried to repurpose a giant orbital mirror created to end world hunger by refocusing the sun's rays and extending growing seasons?

"Who's the man who turned it into a giant laser? Who was going to use this evil satellite to blast through the Demilitarized Zone and conquer South Korea? You are. Yes, you are!"

The colonel, who has started a poetry blog, shrugs and gives me the closest thing to a smile I've seen since he arrived on my doorstep this week, asking if he could just "come in for a little while."

"Helloooo! My lab was in Venice," Drax interrupts. "Do you have any idea what the rents are like in Venice? But it never occurred to me that my product qualified for $51 million in subsidies for being green the way Volkswagen's did in the us."

"Sure," I add, grasping at straws, "but, as evil delivery-system names go, 'Moonraker' blows 'Jetta' straight out the sinister-moniker water."

"Whatever," Drax replies. "My nerve gas was derived from a rare Amazonian orchid. That passes 'green' and goes straight to 'precious.' I call myself evil but it still never crossed my mind to exploit the environmental angle.

"I mean, sure, I aimed to wipe out humanity in one fell swoop, and I thought that was pretty villainous, but a study just published in *Nature* says that smog causes three million deaths a year. It's been demonstrated that emissions from diesel cars cause 5,800 premature deaths annually in Britain alone, and vw had well-meaning consumers tootling around spreading this poison themselves. No space station involved—let alone one populated by a hot master race ready to step in, like the one I had going."

Here, Drax gets up and begins turning all the books on my shelves spine inward.

"Good to see you making an effort," I tell him soothingly. "But what you're doing there is not evil. It's just annoying—it will take me 20 minutes to fix that."

"I thought I was soooo malevolent," he says, emptying my stapler and attempting to slip a Windows Vista CD into my computer, "but I look at Volkswagen and my once-dastardly efforts start to look like artisanal evil.

"Compared to Volkswagen, I, with my organic-orchid poison, was practically selling cold-pressed coffee in Brooklyn—in Mason jars."

"Yeah, and all this really puts my scheme to make cars out of gold in order to smuggle the gold across borders without paying taxes into perspective," says Goldfinger, painting my toenails gold.

"Again, also not evil," I say, "just kitschy," but Goldfinger just keeps pedicuring and talking.

"None of my cars were rigged with a device to detect and thwart emissions tests, which are there to combat air pollution and global warming. I was so close. I was making cars. And yet my whole master plan, my endgame, was to contaminate the gold in Fort Knox with deadly radiation in order to manipulate the markets. I just never stopped to think that the real dirty money was in the legitimate automotive industry.

"I am nothing. I am nobody. I have no evil legacy. 'Here lies Auric Goldfinger; he fudged his taxes and cheated at golf.'" Goldfinger then disappears under a blanket.

"Tell me about it. I only built a giant space laser . . ." says Blofeld—this gets everyone's attention, as one or another of my guests have been trying to do this all week—". . . controlled from a secret base on an oil platform and designed to destroy the world's nuclear arsenal in hopes of increasing the value of my own weapons stash at evil auction." He starts to pat my hair again.

"I certainly didn't partner with a bunch of well-meaning hippies to achieve that end. Evil fail! I never put out an ad campaign trying to dispel the 'myth' that space lasers are bad for you and that nuclear weapons produce harmful emissions, like those Volkswagen guys did with diesel.

"But I do want it noted, I was thwarted by a combination of James Bond and a team of Japanese secret service ninjas. Not by a few scientists from a small NGO driving a Passat—the anti–Aston Martin—around California with an emissions tester in the trunk, like the team that took down Volkswagen," he says, using a teacup as an ashtray.

"See, there's some positive evil thinking," I say, turning my head as Darth Vader peeps around the door.

"Hi, guys," he says. "It was called the 'Death Star.' We unveiled it by blowing up a peace-loving planet, but we never rigged it to pass emissions tests with flying colours, then fly out the testing facility's door producing 35 times the pollution allowed under the Clean Air Act. I think I'm just going to do volunteer work from now on, maybe backpack through Kashyyyk, and try to find myself again."

"Look, Darth, it's a bit much around here right now and this isn't your genre, could you just email me?" I tell him, then say, "Hey guys, let's go watch a movie. You can talk really loudly all the way through it."

This is all on your head, Volkswagen.

What Has Become Of
Our Bill Murray Pope?

The Globe and Mail, October 3, 2015

•

"It is a destructive pretension against the plan of God. We are not talking about a mere bill," Pope Francis, then Cardinal Bergoglio, wrote in 2010 in reference to a bill to introduce same-sex marriage in Argentina, "but rather a machination of the Father of Lies that seeks to confuse and deceive the children of God."

That would look great on a wedding invitation: "Please join David and Barry as they machinate with the Father of Lies, seeking to confuse and deceive the children of God. No gifts."

It's so metal, and I bet the pope and Kim Davis had so much to talk about.

Lots of people were dismayed this week when it was revealed, at the end of his hugely successful visit to the United States, that the pope had a private meeting with Ms. Davis, who was made famous by her tireless efforts to stop gay people in Rowan County, Kentucky, from getting married, as the law of the land now entitles them to do.

Ms. Davis, the county clerk, has refused to issue marriage licences, a task that is part of her job, because, she maintains, issuing them to gay couples would compromise her religious beliefs. Having spent five days in jail for refusing to do her job, or to step aside from her elected position and let someone else do her job, or even to allow her subordinates to do her job for her, she has become something of a folk hero in certain circles.

Somewhere Johnny Appleseed wonders how much greater his legacy would be if he'd just made a big thing about not planting apples and not letting anyone else plant apples, either, but here we are: Ms. Davis is a legend and the belle of the Republican primary ball.

That the pope chose to have this meeting, even in secret—it was divulged by Ms. Davis's lawyer, who reports that His Holiness asked Davis to pray for him and told her to "stay strong," which one assumes means continue the yeoman's work of not doing her job and still getting paid for it—upset a lot of people who haven't really been paying attention.

There was an outcry from the disillusioned; this was not the pope the media had introduced them to, with cherry-picked quotes in headlines and cherry-cheeked children in *BuzzFeed* GIFs. It was like hipster-pope had sold out and played a stadium, but the truth is, the pope started playing those stadium shows a long time ago, and has never stopped.

"Beware of the new ideological colonization that tries to destroy the family . . . it comes from outside and that's why I call it a colonization," he said of the movement for gay rights in a January speech in the Philippines.

"When conditions are imposed by imperial colonizers, they seek to make [these] peoples lose their own identity," His Holiness Francis, Bishop of Rome, Vicar of Jesus Christ, Successor of the Prince of the Apostles, Primate of Italy, Archbishop and Metropolitan of the Roman Province, Sovereign of the Vatican City State, Servant of the Servants of God, Supreme Pontiff of the Universal Church said on his flight out.

There are only three theological virtues, and a strong sense of irony is apparently not one of them.

The pope is from Argentina and must know the power the spectre of colonialism can have in a country like the Philippines but, excess being one of the hallmarks of the Catholic church, he added: "It is not new, this, the same was done by the dictators of the last century. They came with their own doctrine . . . think of the Hitler Youth."

In summary, if lesbian, gay, bisexual and transgender people are not Christopher Columbus, they're Hitler.

I, like many, fancied the idea of us having a Bill Murray pope—a charming old guy who pops up in odd places, delightful and seemingly delighted to be there. It's a narrative the press embraced, as it was largely free of abused children—a story that has tragically become so "dog bites man"—but no one should be surprised that the man who likened LGBT people to Nazis met with Kim Davis.

She may have even asked him to dial it down a notch.

Many were quick to say that not too much should be read into that meeting.

We have only Ms. Davis's word on what was said and, as writer, editor and Jesuit priest James Martin explained defensively in the Catholic publication *America Magazine*, "The pope meets with many people . . . Pope Francis also met Mark Wahlberg, and that does not mean that he liked *Ted*."

To which I can only say: True, but if the pope had a long history of talking up crap movies about teddy bears, that would not be an unreasonable conclusion to draw.

Yes, the pope has said, "If a person is gay and seeks God, who am I to judge?"—and that got a lot of play. Many people, including me, are thirsty for evidence that the Church (in which I was raised) is moving forward on this issue but, in saying that, the pope wasn't actually moving anywhere.

Instead, he was essentially channelling the Catechism of the Catholic Church, which beneficently says that gay people "must be accepted with respect, compassion and sensitivity," the better to encourage them to "fulfill God's will" by overcoming their "inclination, which is objectively disordered" and to accept the fact that they are "called to chastity."

Wheeeeeee—congratulations, David and Barry! And who is the pope to judge? I don't know; would he be the same guy who said that at stake in the issue of gay marriage is "the total rejection of God's law engraved in our hearts"?

Yes, that's him, and that hardly puts the man on a different page from Kim Davis, where so many people, for so many good reasons, want him to be.

Much was made of the pope meeting with a transgender man at the Vatican last winter and, indeed, that was big of him—given that he has likened transgender people to nuclear weapons. I wonder if he wore a special suit.

"Let's think of the nuclear arms, of the possibility to annihilate in a few instants a very high number of human beings," he said of people who "manipulate" their bodies in an interview last year. "Let's think also . . . of the gender theory, that does not recognize the order of creation."

If a pope portrays LGBT rights as an invasion, a form of cultural occupation, local gay people become collaborators, a group by whom "the family is threatened," and it's easy to see how this could nurture a kind of collective gay panic—and that never ends well.

Calm down, people. We didn't lose our cool pope. We never had a cool pope.

We've just, for own comfort, been in denial of papal warming.

• • • • •

Note to World:
Stop Ogling Our New PM

The Globe and Mail, October 24, 2015

•

This week, the international media swooned over the news that Justin Trudeau will be Canada's next prime minister. It was more than a little awkward, frankly; they behaved like a sad collection of news bodies that had not experienced the powerful effects of a long, hard election in some time.

"Meet Justin Trudeau: Canada's liberal, boxing, strip-teasing new PM," *NBCNews.com* wrote.

"Is Justin Trudeau the sexiest politician in the world?" the *Mirror* asked, taking a more investigative approach.

E! Online declared Mr. Trudeau to be a "smoking-hot syrupy fox" and, look, you're entitled to your opinion, *E! Online*, but when I read all those words together in one sentence, I expect a link to a recipe.

"Justin Trudeau is Canada's new, incredibly good-looking prime minister," Australia's *news.com.au* wrote, only slightly more soberly— breathing just under the limit, I'd say. But heavily.

"The new Canadian prime minister is implausibly good looking," Tom Gara, an editor at *BuzzFeed* opined, although *Gawker* found Mr. Trudeau's countenance entirely plausible—declaring that the "square-jawed, 43-year-old, strip-teasing" Canadian could well be "the product of a drunken hot-tub encounter between Tom Cruise and Ken Marino."

"In Canada Justin Trudeau's Liberals elected on a platform of sorry I lost my train of thought he's just so handsome," tweeted James McHale of the Australian Broadcasting Corporation.

For heaven's sake, world, take a cold shower—headlines aren't meant to heave. Yes, I can see the advantage of being known as "Canada, the country with a hot prime minister." It could make a nice change from "Canada, the country with a cold climate." And if, as a nation, we have done something to draw the world's attention away from Shirtless Putin, we have served.

In fact, this could be our greatest contribution to international diplomacy since the Suez Crisis—surely an achievement worthy of the Topless Trudeau International Airport. We could work this handsome-PM angle as a nation, and the world would flock to us.

Visit Canada, we could say, we have legal weed and a smoking hot head of government—why, every Question Period is like an Arctic Monkeys show.

Except the Hot PM thing is getting old fast, and he isn't even sworn in. So I've decided to take a page from my mother's people-raising book to try to put an end to this silliness.

For a while when I was a little girl, my older brother and I made a lot of underwear jokes. We were like the George Burns and Gracie Allen of undergarments, only loud, and our routines were mostly just one of us saying the word "underwear" and the other one laughing; anyone else saying the word "underwear" could easily set us off as well.

Getting us dressed in the morning took forever. Trips to the laundromat were so gleeful, it was like the dryers emitted laughing gas. Finally, my poor mother reached the end of her knicker-quip tether, and this is what she did: One Saturday morning she took all the underwear in the house: mine, my brother's, hers, and my dad's Y-fronts—a cotton comedy cornerstone right there—and she put them all on my parents' bed and basically said, "You have until sundown, go nuts." And that's what we did, and then, almost miraculously, we were done with underwear.

And so I'm going to offer the world a chance to do much the same now. World, you have one week to make Hot Justin Trudeau jokes, and enjoy sexy-world-leader innuendo with impunity.

Please make the most of this week and then, come November 1, let's be done with this.

You want to say, "Whoa, I'd respect *his* Arctic sovereignty," this is your moment.

Dying to shout, "Man, I'd enter that into my Hansard," when images of Justin Trudeau come on the TV screen at your local bar, you go right ahead.

Any journalists thinking of asking, "Hey, soon-to-be prime minister, did it hurt when you fell from heaven, and do you feel that the increased carbon dioxide in the atmosphere affected your rate of descent?" at Mr. Trudeau's next press conference, this is your time.

Want to comment, "I know he's prime minister but he's welcome to be chief of *my* staff" on the next news article you see speculating about the Trudeau cabinet picks, by all means, do so now.

Ditto "I'd like to be first past *his* post" and "I'll bet *that's* a right honourable member."

Have a Hot Justin Trudeau open-mic night, if you can, and try out your "If he likes to be strict on party discipline, he has my unanimous consent" bit, and see how it goes over.

If any part of you, Wolf Blitzer, wants to drop your plans to ask Mr. Trudeau about the Liberals' decision to withdraw fighter jets from Syria, and just say, "I want to put autumn leaves in your hair and wear your sweater," you should do that now.

Let me put the metaphorical underwear on the bed, world. Observers, now eager observers, some bordering on you-might-want-to-call-them-police-observers, speculate that, with Mr. Trudeau heading our government, oil lobbyists may suddenly find Americans more receptive to Canadians laying pipe. And you know what they say about a man with a large majority . . . he has a big caucus.

Listen, world, if the words "Talk unparliamentary language to me" pop into your head, just click "Share," but by November 1, I want any and all prurient interest in the question "How's he polling?" laid to rest, because, as things stand now, I predict the Liberals will bring back the long-form census, a cause dear to me, and then have to cancel it again.

We don't need the rest of the whole world filling it out. It's only for Canadians. But please, if you must participate, just check the boxes, don't write in the margins.

No one wants to know you like long walks on the beach.

We Can Survive
Gender Parity—
Here's How

The Globe and Mail, November 7, 2015

•

The sky didn't fall after Prime Minister Justin Trudeau's first cabinet was sworn in—although a full 50 percent of ministers of the Crown are now women. Luck was on our side. This time. But as we survey the aftermath, namely a remarkably skilled and accomplished cabinet, one that balances new faces trucking in masses of exemplary, real-world experience with political veterans, it's never too early to plan ahead.

Gender parity in cabinet can strike at any time—well, any time that is not psychologically stuck in the 1950s—and, when something like this happens, the likelihood that it will happen again increases.

Gender parity may be our new reality. What we need to do is learn from what we've endured these past few weeks, and so I've penned this *Equal Representation in Cabinet Survival Guide*:

- Be prepared to stave off the impending communist revolution, which the threat of 15 or so women cabinet ministers can cause. Any time the subject of race or gender is raised, vast swathes of the political right will suddenly be stricken with an overwhelming need to talk about class, which they'll identify as the real problem. "People who look like me, but aren't as successful as me, how is that allowed to be a thing?" they will ask.

It was like a Magically Marxist button was pushed around here. If you hear lost, once-proud conservative pundits calling out, "Look, look! Tear down the corrupt capitalist system, let the proletariat have the means of production, but you don't need put all those ladies in cabinet," ask them if their never-before-expressed concern that people in lower income brackets have crooked teeth means they advocate a national dental care plan.

This should be enough to break up the herd—but, as a last resort, enthusiastically endorse their apparent advocacy for universal daycare and free university education. Be careful, this has been known to cause stampedes.

Gently suggest that now isn't the time for reversals of political and economic opinion. Buy them a beer. Recommend they blow off some steam by toppling a few statues, then head on home.

- Steel yourself, you're going to hear the word "merit" a lot. All evidence will suggest that people who write about cabinet composition who have never used the word "merit" in association with federal appointments before will merely have been stockpiling that word in the event of a women-cabinet-minister crisis.

  Be understanding, remember that regional and language representation in cabinet have always been sound politics in this country, "qualifications" we'd be naive to criticize. Gender parity, equal representation of 50 percent of the population, a demographic that didn't get to vote in federal elections until 1918 and therefore may not have the same networks and role models inviting it into the political sphere, has brought about the apocalypse.

  As a shortcut to explaining that gender parity and merit are not mutually exclusive (see the qualifications of the current cabinet) and that eventually all parties will benefit from the inevitable deepening of the political talent pool this simple gesture will engender, try telling any holdouts that men are from Mars, women are from PEI, and speak French.

Two words for anyone you come across gripped with panic over the destruction of our meritocracy vis-à-vis the prime minister's selection of ministers: "Peter MacKay." If that fails, try "Julian Fantino." If that fails, try "Peter MacKay" twice more.

Do not consume the food of anyone you encounter claiming to be fine with the cabinet but decrying the Liberals' decision to announce their gender parity plan ages ago, when it might attract and benefit candidates and serve as an explicit statement of the party's priorities.

These decriers clearly don't want any politics in their politics, Lord knows what's in that shepherd's pie.

- Care for the actual wounded. Women you were convinced desperately needed to be saved from becoming ministers are just fine. Don't bandage them. Stop trying to put a tourniquet on Jane Philpott; it's not possible to cut yourself on being minister of health, a position for which she's dauntingly qualified.

    In a women-being-equally-represented-in-cabinet emergency, too many people expend their energy worrying about these new ministers' imagined insecurities.

    Retire to your bunker, and rest easy. There's a good chance that these women understand they're well qualified to be ministers. Anxiety that, because of the quota, Jody Wilson-Raybould will never know if she was really fit to be minister of justice or if her abilities tapped out at Crown prosecutor, member of the BC Treaty Commission and regional chief of the BC Assembly of First Nations is likely misplaced.

Thanks for your concern-trolling, pundits, but I'm pretty sure none of these women agonize over the possibility that they're in cabinet only to fill a quota and, if your stated opposition to the quota is that you will never know if they are qualified, seek shelter somewhere that has internet and look them up.

- Always remember that, as a rule, the "you fail, in forming your policy, to take into account what a massive, insufferable, ignorant tool I am" argument is not as effective as you believe. Deploy only as a last resort. Claim you were drunk.

- Understand that women are generally pretty inured to accusations they're somewhere because of some mostly imagined quota. Women's collective eye-roll over this accusation, and many other things, is what makes the earth turn—and that statement is why *I* am not science minister, like Kirsty Duncan. Google her.

  Frankly, certain men believing we're anywhere only to fill a quota makes a novel change from them believing we're in the building because we're bringing someone a sandwich, are lost and can't find our way out, or are sleeping with the boss.

- Boil water. If, having examined the resumés of everyone in this cabinet, you still feel compelled to write a think piece about all the more qualified Andrew Leslies left out because of these women, plunge both your hands into that water. We can get through this together.

• • • • •

When You Lay Down with Tulip, You Woke Up with Warm Feet

The Globe and Mail, November 28, 2015

•

On the last night of her life, my dog, Tulip, went outside to pee as, she'd want me to point out, she did a good 99.9 percent of the times she peed and really I could be more relaxed about these things. Occasionally a Persian rug needs a little love too, she might argue, squatted, looking up at me with her dark, dark eyes.

There was, this time, her last night with me, a huge raccoon right outside the back door, and although Tulip was terribly weak at this point—her kidneys had been failing slowly for months, and in her last few days her condition had dramatically worsened—she saw that great big raccoon and unhesitatingly leapt straight up at him.

She was pure Tulip again in that moment, and it was as if the raccoon had come there—I had not seen a raccoon about for weeks—just to see my Tulip.

Tulip died on her bed by the fire the next afternoon; it was all very gentle. She got up to greet the veterinarian and her assistant when they came to the door, eagerly, as she did most visitors. She'd barely moved all morning and had declined a walk, for the first time in her life. But she was still Tulip just then: assuming all visitors meant more love, and must be met with same.

I met Tulip at a party, I told the vet when she asked. Tulip had jumped up next to me on the sofa and I felt my heart skip a beat.

In that moment, I understood how that turn of phrase had come to be.

We were in love, instantly. I'm fairly certain the whole room felt it. People stared over their wine glasses at us, and the owner of six-month-old Tulip, a lovely woman I barely knew at that point, asked me if, given the obvious connection, I'd care for Tulip, as she herself would be away for two weeks.

Two weeks led to more weeks, and within six months Tulip was officially my dog.

The first night I had Tulip, I put her little bed on the floor in the kitchen and went to my room, as I did with other dogs. But once in my own bed, way up on the third floor, I heard a loud *thump, thump, thump* as Tulip hurled her little whippet body against the kitchen door.

I ran downstairs, I told the vet as she readied a syringe, and brought Tulip's bed up to my room, because of course she was more than welcome to sleep there. But instead of curling up quietly on her bed, when I got under my own covers, Tulip began to cry.

There's no other word for it; she cried. It was one of the few sounds I ever heard her make in her life—she would never make it again—and as I pulled back my heavy covers to see what was wrong, she leapt up and jumped under the blankets, burrowed way down to the foot of the bed, and the ground rules for the next 10 years had been set.

At night sometimes, while I was reading, she'd emerge from her duvet den and demand that I come downstairs with her to watch her eat. "Sorry," her eyes would say, "I am a social animal."

Tulip only ever slept alone once, a night at the vet's. When I was travelling, she graced my parents' bed and couch, and terrorized the squirrel population of Guelph, Ontario.

In bed at night now, my foot instinctively seeks her out, sliding over, and over, searching for her, but there's only that very distinct cold of cold sheets—those modern, urban glaciers—down there now.

I told the vet, now so strangely in my living room, about how, a few times, Tulip had stolen a stick of butter, and been discovered in mid-joyous, buttery, smug mess, and how at one point, for a while, she kept demanding to be let out three or four times in the middle of the night.

I had been confused by this sudden odd, insistent behaviour, and wondered if she was unwell, although she didn't seem ill at all, just terribly excited.

It turned out that she'd stolen a stick of butter and hidden it way under the throw pillows in the living room, and going outside was a ruse to go downstairs; she was trying to find a time to be alone with her treasure.

Because I work at home, Tulip was almost never alone. I've written virtually every column I've written for this paper with Tulip at my side, so please allow me to tell you all this . . . As I told the story of Tulip and the butter, Tulip's eyes, though she was now heavily sedated, looked up at me eagerly when she heard her name.

My hand was on her heart. I felt its last pulse. If you cut me open, if I were a tree with rings, that last beat would be there, its own ring.

I am so lost, so overwhelmed with this; I see her everywhere in the house. It's as if, detached from her body, all her mannerisms, so many distinct little quirks, expressions, gestures, are separate entities now, wandering forever here.

I'm grateful she lunged one final time at a raccoon, a species she very much aimed to keep in check in her lifetime.

He looked almost animated, that almost mythical, large, last, enormous, late-season raccoon.

It was as if he had been pasted in from some charming Japanese film. He was a Hayao Miyazaki raccoon, a *Totoro* raccoon.

He'd sat quiet and still on the fence, somehow looming over the whole garden; he meant something, I feel, and he sauntered away as my Tulip leapt at him.

Then he turned back and looked at her, meaningfully, as though he had come on behalf of his people, out of respect for a rival.

He was there to say goodbye to his worthy adversary, and to my best friend.

Oh, Face It: Even You Would Say It Glows

The Globe and Mail, December 26, 2015

•

We, All of the Other Reindeer, would like to take a moment to talk about some of the things that you may have heard about us in classic holiday poetry, song and stop-motion animated films. Unfortunately, despite our excellent work in the challenging field of sleighviation, the rumours surrounding that one foggy Christmas Eve and certain events preceding it continue to circulate—aided in no small part by the mainstream media's decision to rehash the unfortunate incident *every single year*.

We are speaking out now because the entire affair has become a distraction. Not unlike a big red nose shining in your face when you're trying to fly.

All of the Other Reindeer want to express our profound regret if any offence was caused. That was not our intention when we chose to engage with Rudolph the Red-Nosed (it *is* an unusual trait) Reindeer in what we sincerely believed to be good-natured rivalry that is a tradition in Christmas Town, where you must understand we work on a very tight schedule, one that cannot always accommodate blinking at a really luminous, blizzard-piercingly bright red nose. I mean, what the hell?

Mistakes were made, and if, as a result of some miscommunication, Rudolph the Red-Nosed (!) Reindeer took umbrage, or serious lower-back injury, when we shoved him down a snowbank and pranced up and down, shouting out (with glee), "Ha! Stupid Shiny Schnozz fell down a hill! Ha-ha-ha!" we apologize.

It was a misunderstanding, one that has unfortunately led to the popular misconception that Santa Claus is entirely reliant upon eight jackass reindeer for his primary mode of transportation.

Quite frankly, the things that are said, you'd think the guy drove a Lexus. We hope this has not caused anyone to lose faith in the trusted Claus brand.

We would also like to state for the record that Mr. Claus has at no point shaken his pipe at us and requested that we issue this apology. We are under no pressure to do this, and six months is a long time to go without carrots.

It is our hope that we can move on from the unfortunate incident— eight flying camels would look really dumb—that was, in fact, a small reindeer's entire childhood, and focus on our important holiday work. It's possible that we were overconfident in our expectation that, when we told Rudolph the Red-Nosed Reindeer (he had a very shiny nose) that he couldn't play reindeer hopscotch with us because "who'd want to play with your stupid red nose," he would understand we were just joking, and not cry—hardly the action of a team player.

We certainly did not intend to leave Rudolph (the Red-Nosed and, it should be said, highly imaginative Reindeer) with the impression that he was not free to join in what have been characterized as our "reindeer games," but which were in fact serious reindeer training.

We think it is in poor taste to politicize this issue but are proud to have started a conversation about proboscis diversity in the North Pole region.

All of the Other Reindeer acknowledge the possibility that some of our light-hearted banter may have gone right over Rudolph's head. (Probably to avoid his bioluminescent snout, and who could blame it?) To be fair, none of us were expecting Santa Claus to show up one foggy Christmas Eve and say, "Rudolph, with your nose so bright, won't you guide my sleigh tonight?" And it's easy to look at this situation, as an outsider, and say, "Oh, *then* all the reindeer loved him. *Then* they loved him. How *convenient* for the reindeer. What lousy brown-nosers those reindeer must be. As soon as Rudolph's non-conformity proved useful to their careers, they were all over him."

This is very hurtful. All of the Other Reindeer are deeply wounded at the suggestion that has been repeatedly made that we are "a bunch of jerk-off caribou," and we are seriously considering retaining elf attorneys. (We *think* there are elf attorneys; it can't be a less popular career choice than dentistry, and what was that all about anyway?)

Yes, it may look like we were suddenly cozying up to the now-useful and soon-to-be-famous young reindeer we had previously called "Flashbulb Face."

Yes, we shouted out, "Rudolph the Red-Nosed Reindeer, you'll go down in history!" but it was more with concern than glee. We could see Rudolph was headed for big things, and we just wanted to make sure he got in front of the story and that our names were not dragged through the mud.

Mud, incidentally, was the same substance that Rudolph's father, Donner, kindly used to try to cover his son's (potentially polar-bear-attracting) fancypants snout.

Look, you may *think* you know Dasher and Dancer and Prancer and Vixen, Comet and Cupid and Donner and Blitzen, but do you *really*?

Or are you just buying into a media narrative pushed to distract from more pressing issues that somehow go uninvestigated?

The snowman-animating powers of an old felt hat go unquestioned everywhere, but for a few dedicated blogs. And yet a group of concerned reindeer, who at one point took the time to draw attention to a nose that is unquestionably a non-heritage colour and, if you ever saw it, *you* would even say it glows, are forever suspect.

Word is that *not* every Who down in Whoville liked Christmas a lot, but we never hear about them, do we?

Thank you very much for your time. Merry Christmas.

Bring Back the Days When I Had a Lot on My Plate

The Globe and Mail, January 16, 2016

•

I've been away seven weeks now, travelling, working, researching a book, seeing friends, but it's time to come home; I miss plates.

I've been staying in London mostly, visiting other cities from there, and then I was in Dublin for a while. In all these places I ate out a lot, and I can report that the restaurant industry is in the midst of a tableware crisis. There's barely a plate to be found anymore, although the first time you're served a dry-aged rump of beef with celeriac gratin, chanterelles and red wine jus on a cutting board, it's possible to be charmed.

After all, *you* are not a tablecloth, but soon the tide of things being served on other things that were just not meant to be served on starts to wear on you.

I have a high whimsy tolerance.

Doctors have often remarked upon it. Sometimes, half an hour into a puppet show involving a talking reflex hammer and a musical stethoscope, a doctor will say, "This is very unusual," and make a note on my chart, but recently my whimsy tolerance has been tested.

I miss plates. Why, in one day on this trip, I was served breakfast on a chalk slate, lunch on a clipboard and dinner on a wooden cutting board shaped like a clover leaf. I've been served frites in a beer stein, and the ones I could reach were delicious, so my verdict was a resolved "Fun!"—until my slow-baked quince, wild honey, ewe's yoghurt, bee pollen and almonds arrived in a vintage teacup

300

balanced on a strip of artfully weathered barn board, and then the next morning at breakfast, I was served a waffle on another waffle with maple syrup in a stem vase.

What was under that waffle I do not care to know, but everything I've been served of late suggests that that non-plate waffle-presenting item was handcrafted from a substance that *Dwell* magazine would call "reclaimed ash flooring from a demolished church in Ohio," and the rest of us would call "wood."

I miss plates.

In several fashionable venues, I was given the menu tucked into an ironically unfashionable book and, in other places, it's the bill that's presented that way. I will never again see a scuffed-up, campy pulp paperback without assuming I owe someone money.

In lovely Dublin, I dined a number of times at the excellent L. Mulligan Grocer. You could build a small cottage from the cutting boards of Scotch eggs and lamb I cleared at that charming place, and so I will forgive them for the barely repressed school anxiety that arrived with the bill in a case for a vintage geometry set.

For a long time now, desserts everywhere have been served in Mason jars. The House on Parliament, my beloved local pub in Toronto, does that, and the only problem with a dessert being served in a Mason jar is that, in my mind, when I eat something from a small glass jar, I am always eating baby food.

You give me a jar and a little spoon and, no matter how delicious the thing in the jar actually is, I am, immediately and in the most exaggerated way possible, pretending to enjoy downing puréed brown rice and lentils in an effort to convince a skeptical baby to join me in this exercise.

"Mmmmm," I say, waving my spoon in small circles in front of anyone unlucky enough to be sitting across from me.

"Stop that," my dinner companion said to me recently. "It's really manipulative. If I wanted a dessert, I would order one."

"Nom, nom, nom, nom," I said.

"Is there antibiotics in that or something?" he asked. "You're trying to trick me. I don't have an ear infection."

"Here comes the train!" I said, unable to stop myself. "Chooo! Chooo!"

"What is wrong with you?" he said.

"I miss plates," I replied, taking a sip of my wine from a repurposed Griffin low-form beaker and tracing a circle nostalgically on what should have been a tablecloth but was either a collectable Spider-Man bedsheet from the 1970s or something that may have been the Shroud of Turin. I get all the restaurants mixed up.

One of the highlights of my trip was seeing the *Celts: Art and Identity* show at the British Museum where, among other things, I saw the extraordinary Gundestrup cauldron, which was found, as apparently everything Celtic is, in a peat bog—which is where, it seems, Celts kept all their stuff.

Discovered in Denmark in 1891, the ornately decorated Iron Age silver cauldron is large, 69 centimetres across and 42 deep, and was likely ceremonial, but after the dinner I'd had the night before, all I could see when I looked at it was a weary Celt shaking his head and muttering, "It's very nice but hardly an appropriate vessel in which to serve a salted caramel budino with a dollop of crème fraîche. What the hell is wrong with people these days? Why can we not use the ramekins the gods have provided us?"

Iron Age Celts miss plates.

Last night I dreamed I was served an Irish seafood chowder with chorizo and treacle bread cupped in a waiter's hands, and I understood it was delicious because it was authentic, and then I asked the waiter about the "seared scallops served on a bed."

I was wondering if the end of the menu had been cut off there, but I knew it had not, so I ordered sole à la meunière plated (soon a lost word) on a slab of timber sawed by a lumberjack at my very table.

This was followed by the arroz con leche with fresh cherries served in a live pitcher plant.

All the while, I was seated on a small, organic, free-range (when not being sat on) child to whom I whispered, "I miss plates."

"You have to come back next week," said the small, but surprisingly comfortable, child excitedly. "They're getting in some live Andean flamingos for cutlery."

"I'm going home, small but comfortable child," I said. "I have plates there." And then I was awoken by the sound of an incoming text: "Join me for dinner at Chez Everything's in the Dishwasher and We Really Hate Trees. Everyone's talking about it."

The Man with the Golden Bottle

The Globe and Mail, May 21, 2016

•

This week The *New York Times* revealed the details of a state-run doping program operated under the direction of Grigory Rodchenkov, the director of Russia's anti-doping laboratory. According to Dr. Rodchenkov, during the 2014 Winter Olympics in Sochi, Russian agents ran a Byzantine pee-snatching operation, years in the making. Working late into the night, in dark, secret rooms, they would switch out performance-enhancing-drug-contaminated urine samples from Russian athletes—and refill each bottle with untainted, pre-Games urine from the same athlete, stored at a separate facility.

Dr. Rodchenkov has fled Russia for Los Angeles, where he is cooperating in the making of a documentary film about the failures of drug testing in international sport, but the man I kept thinking about, after reading the story, wasn't him anyway; I wondered about the man Dr. Rodchenkov believes is a Russian agent, the man in charge of all the pee logistics—logistics that included, according to Dr. Rodchenkov, a signal that "the urines were ready."

What was that like for him, I asked myself, being the pee mule for the Russian Olympic team? Naturally I assumed I'd never know, and so I was surprised to be greeted by a shadowy figure—well, he was doing his best to be shadowy in my very sunny office—this Tuesday morning.

"For this I joined Russian intelligence?" the man said to me in a thick Russian accent, spinning around in my own desk chair to face me. "Victor . . . Victor get ricin-tipped umbrella. Me? I get pee."

"I'm sorry," I said, setting down the teacup I had come in with. "And you are . . .?"

"It is I. Man who opens little bottles of pee for Russian government," he said, trying, I think, to sound ominous.

"Oh," I said politely. "I won't shake hands," I added as he rose. "No, really. Let's not.

"Yes, I've read about you. So, tell me, what would happen was, during the Sochi Games, a bottleful of urine, someone else's urine, would be passed through a small hole in the wall, near the ground? It would be passed to a hidden room, to you, a man crouching down to receive another man's urine, and you'd take that Swiss-designed, supposedly tamper-proof bottle away, open it . . . somehow . . . and bring it back to the room?"

"Not one bottle—teams' worth of bottles. And then I would bring new urine . . ."

"Months-and-months-old new urine, though, right?"

"Yes," he nodded—somewhat defensively. "I bring old, but clean . . ."

"Clean for urine, you mean?" I asked. "But still, you know, urine. Someone else's urine?"

"Yes, I bring relatively clean urine back to room—I bring urine back in various vessels.

"Sometimes I bring urine back in soda cans, sometimes in jars— and, as I do this, I think: Victor, Victor is wearing nice suit and chasing double agent through streets of Prague, carrying deadly umbrella. Me? I am wandering streets of Sochi in "I Heart Team Russia" hoodie with baby bottle full of luger's urine in my hands. This is what I do for Mother Russia."

"And that was your job? Is that right, Mr. . . ."

"My code name is 'The Whiz.' They try to tell me is short for 'The Wizard.' But is not short for 'The Wizard.' Every time I call handler at headquarters and say, "Whiz, over" at end of report, some clown always say, 'Did you shake it?' and whole room bursts out laughing, and then I know handler have me on speakerphone the whole time, again."

"I'm sorry, Whiz," I said, picking up my teacup and holding it over my mouth to hide my smile.

"You know what Victor's code name is?" said Whiz. "Victor gets to be called 'The Poker'!"

"Yeah," I said. "That's not really a good code name, either. Sounds like you guys need to work on your code-naming process a little harder. Maybe take some time off the whole amateur-sport-doping thing and just work on your secret agent names for a while. You see where I'm going with this, Whiz?

"How did you come to choose this line of work, anyway, Whiz?"

"My father was sinister agent of state. His father before him was sinister agent of state. I just grew up dreaming that one day I would burst out of shadows and garrote James Bond. For this reason, I learn to ski. I not even like winter sports—especially the luge—but I see what job requires; I watch movies. Always, what I see is, you hatch sinister plot in Nairobi, it gets discovered during Mardi Gras in New Orleans, but everyone involved will eventually drop everything and catch transcontinental flight so that you can try and kill each other at ski resort in Switzerland . . ."

"Yes, my impression has always been that over 70 percent of tourism to Switzerland is assassination related," I said sympathetically. "Did you also imagine yourself being seduced by beautiful women over forcefully ordered drinks?"

"No. Beautiful seductresses always Russian agents also. Office romance, no good.

"No one ever ask me to be diabolical in any of six languages I learned, either. It just pee, pee, pee with these people all the time. No danger! No excitement! No Bond! I open to compromise but I never even got to push bottle of athlete's pee out of plane without parachute. Just collect pee bottle, open pee bottle, give pee bottle to pee doctor . . ." he sighed.

"Those Swiss urine sample bottles sound very tricky," I said to him, "like little bottle-safes almost. Tell me, to crack those little urine-filled safes, did you have to hold the bottle of another human being's pee up really close to your ear and turn the lid a little one way and then a tiny bit the other way and listen for tiny little clicks?"

"I don't want to talk about it."

"Did the swishing sound make the clicks harder to hear?"

"Pee-bottle-opening method is state secret," he said.

"Because I totally see it happening like that," I said.

"I want to push you out of plane," he answered quietly.

"You think you can take me, Bottle Boy?" I said.

"I Russian secret agent, you journalist; you really want go down this road?" he answered. "You fall from plane so fast . . ."

"You want to check and see if I have a bladder infection first?" I offered. "I could just . . ." and I held up my now-empty little teacup delicately, raised my eyebrows suggestively and tilted my head toward the bathroom down the hall, and he began to cry.

It's been three days and he's still here. I'm not complaining.

He's offered to garrote the mailman, but I told him no and it was fine, and sometimes he'll burst out of the shadows and open a particularly tricky salsa jar for me or something, and I think he just needs a little time.

Donald Trump Concludes His "Lord of the Whinge" Debate Trilogy

The Globe and Mail, October 21, 2016

•

It's unfortunate that there weren't four debates between Hillary Clinton and Donald Trump organized for the US election. If there had been, we could have named the whole series the *Rigged Cycle*, opening with *Das Whinegold* and ending with *Trumperdämmerung*.

As it is, we'll have to settle for calling this trilogy *The Lord of the Whinge*.

The debates were a three-part epic tale of a struggle involving a short person menaced by the landlord of some largely vacant tower real estate and his cadre of henchman. Most of these were once living souls, some previously powerful men among them, now reduced to a shadow of their former selves in his service.

That the short person does not, in many people's view, cut a traditionally heroic figure is turning out to be part of the story's allure.

Before I abandon this Tolkien metaphor, it has to be said that Julian Assange, creeping along the edges of the news cycle, desperately trying to reclaim his precious lost relevance by leaking Democratic National Committee campaign emails, likely on behalf of the Russians, is clearly the Gollum in this tale.

I would warrant the Ecuadoreans have at least investigated installing a gaping pit of lava in their embassy. How could they not hope that Julian's madness and obsession, or at least attempts to get the neighbours' WiFi signal—they've opted to end his use of theirs, for attempting to interfere with the US election—might somehow land him inside a volcano.

Either way, it's doubtful he has much of a part to play for good or ill.

Forget achieving high office—most people in the world would never get a date again if the contents of their email were made public, and yet there's little to remark upon in WikiLeaks's heavily hyped document dump.

Despite the drama many on the right, including Mr. Trump himself, are trying to wring from them, the emails of the DNC are mostly remarkable only for their almost singular dullness, expressed in an arch tone.

The internal correspondence of the DNC reads like the bastard child of 1,000 pages of minutes from a condo board meeting and an Edith Wharton biography.

News that the campaign considered other slogans before settling on the one ultimately used might not be a revelation to the American people.

I imagine no one thought election campaigns were delivered by storks. Well, maybe Mr. Trump does. His own campaign has been guano-rich, after all, and no one involved with it seems willing to say where that's been coming from. Combined with his bizarre, alarmingly medically illiterate answer on the subject of abortion (he seems to have been given a note at some point saying "All your uterus are belong to us" but was way fuzzy on the details) during the debate, one shudders to think what his opinion on anything delivery-related involves.

Mr. Trump has benefited from low expectations like a toddler.

There has been a general, "Whoa, he kept his pants on—that has to be a win!" from a number of pundits after his early performances.

Certainly things went badly for Mr. Trump in the first two debates, wherein he rambled.

Called upon to answer a question, Donald reflexively babbles.

Watching him during the debates was like watching 14-years-old-and-haven't-read-the-assigned-chapter-of-*The-Great-Gatsby*-in-time-for-class me run for president. He also sulked, lurked and, overall, behaved like a man who doesn't understand that a debate is live television.

Nobody is going to fix it in post, Donald.

All of this was glossed over by his most ardent fans. It felt like he could have walked on stage for this week's debate and bitten the heads off live kittens for 90 minutes, and his supporters would have responded with, "Look, he's not a career politician and, anyway, Al Gore started it."

The nation's indulgence does, largely, seems to have ended on Wednesday night. Third time was "You've got no charm."

America has been grading Mr. Trump on a fiercely dramatic, indeed dizzying, curve, but on Wednesday he proved himself entirely unable to learn, and the nation seems to have finally lost patience.

The power of the whinge is a temptation to everyone, of course—even the most pure-hearted of us enjoys a good whine—but only a true master of self-pity like Donald Trump could take a question from the moderator about the direction the Supreme Court should take in interpreting the Constitution and immediately make it about that time Justice Ruth Bader Ginsburg was mean to him.

That is what Mr. Trump managed to do mere minutes into Wednesday night's debate—and that was before people thought he'd lost control.

The total loss of control happened, many observers agree, only when Ms. Clinton remarked that he "choked" by failing to bring up his supposed marquee promise to build a wall along the US–Mexico border at the latter's expense when he met with Mexican president Enrique Peña Nieto.

It's worth noting that even in a national debate—the purpose of which is to determine which of two contenders is best suited to lead the nation—a woman is still well-advised only to "remark" upon such a thing. A woman in that situation would be ill-advised to "declare," "accuse" or even "say" anything at all, if it can be avoided.

Likeability, ladies, likeability.

Smile! At this point, Mr. Trump's tone shifted, as we've seen it shift before. He became alarmingly pissy. Mr. Trump does not respond well to criticism. One almost hopes, for his own sake, he doesn't become president.

They do tend to take a lot of ribbing.

Last week, he tweeted his response to a frankly quite tepid *Saturday Night Live* debate parody: "Watched Saturday Night Live hit job on me. Time to retire the boring and unfunny show. Alec Baldwin portrayal stinks. Media rigging election!"

Honestly, if Donald Trump had skin any thinner, they'd have to carry him around in a bucket.

His rapid-fire interjection of the word "Wrong!" made a surprise reappearance in the third debate.

That must have sounded like nails on a chalkboard to his team.

He boasted about how nice the room in his own hotel was during a debate segment ostensibly about altruism versus self-interest.

He repeated his set-up to a million punchlines—his direct stimulus to the comedy industry—that "nobody has more respect for women than I do. Nobody. Nobody has more respect."

If anyone reading this is interested in getting in on the ground floor of the next big horror franchise, I've got it: a world in which "nobody has more respect for women than Donald Trump."

He refused to say whether he would accept the outcome of the election if he lost, promising only to keep America "in suspense."

To Trump, whether or not his nation is still a stable model of democracy is a cliffhanger in his reality TV show life, but arguably Mr. Trump's pièce de résistance was snarling, "Such a nasty woman!" at Ms. Clinton, who had just, again, remarked, "But what we want to do is to replenish the Social Security Trust Fund . . ." Also, the following, and perhaps most telling exchange actually took place.

Clinton: "Well, that's because he'd rather have a puppet as president of the United States, and . . ."

Trump: "No puppet, no puppet."

Clinton: "And it's pretty clear . . ."

Trump: "You're the puppet!"

Clinton: "It's pretty clear you won't admit . . ."

Trump: "No, you're the puppet."

Why is that telling? Because it was about Vladimir Putin. Donald Trump has tweeted about wanting to be "best friends" with the Russian president. He has repeatedly refused to denounce anything Mr. Putin has done, from invading Ukraine, to murdering journalists, to hacking into the DNC's servers and leaking information stored on them with the intent of interfering with the American democratic process. A number of government and civilian experts with knowledge of the leaks have stated that they are confident that the Russian government is behind the hacks.

Mr. Trump often gives the impression of caring more about this planned palling with Mr. Putin than he does about the presidency. He has stated his plans to possibly meet with him before he's even inaugurated, he's that eager.

Becoming president seems to be a means to this end.

The mystery of why many of Mr. Trump's supporters have not been swayed by reports—or taped admissions—of the candidate's appalling behaviour toward women, small contractors and businessmen, you name it, is best viewed through this Putin lens: It doesn't matter that Donald Trump is not a good guy, because he is the kind of bad guy many Trump voters imagine they'd be if they, too, were billionaires.

Mr. Trump is a blank slate upon which they can project their fantasies of wealth and power, and it seems increasingly clear that Vladimir Putin is to Donald Trump what Donald Trump is to those supporters.

Given a Choice, Ladies, Always Hurl the Puppy

The Globe and Mail, October 28, 2016

•

It's not exactly breaking news that women walk a fine line when it comes to how much and what kind of emotion we present in public—and, if it helps, I am smiling while I type this. But not this. Now I am not smiling. Now I am serious, but I'm not being a drag.

I am just serious in a way that says, "I'm ready to listen. Now would be a good time for you to talk."

Now I am smiling again, but just enough to let any sensitive onlookers know that I'm not angry with them. Or anyone. I have never actually been angry with anyone, ever, in my whole life. I did not want that parking space anyway.

I'm well aware that anger in a woman is viewed less as a motivating force of legitimate origin, something that really might fire a girl up to do great things, and more as a pre-existing condition based upon which a woman can be denied credibility coverage at any point down the line.

Try asking people to say two simple phrases out loud. Have them say, "He's really angry" and then, "She's really angry."

Almost invariably the intonation will be entirely different for these two lines.

"He's really angry" will generally be said in a deep monotone, as in: "He's really angry. Attention must be paid."

"She's really angry" will usually be said as if some highly unfortunate diagnosis were being made.

"She's really angry," people will say, sometimes shaking their heads. It's said as though, somehow, through her own poor decision-making skills, our hypothetical angry woman has succumbed to some kind of ghastly and fatal skin disease.

"She's really angry . . ." they will say.

"Oh, no!" the listener will instinctively cry. "How long does she have left?" It's not surprising that most women learn pretty early not to drift too far over to either side of the emotional prime meridian that has been mapped out for us.

Stray to the passionate side of that line, perhaps lured away from the straight and narrow by an excellent joke, an idiot boss or enthusiasm for one's job, and we're judged to be "too emotional" to be relied upon, possibly even "angry." Which, as everyone knows, demands a complete quarantine.

Cautiously chart a course toward the other—sombre—side and you're unlikely to be celebrated as "dispassionate," "reserved" or "stoic."

You'll just be a "stone, cold bitch," or "too remote to be relatable" if you're being discussed on a panel show.

This standard is how we got to commentator after commentator insisting that Americans viewed former First Lady, Senator and Secretary of State Hillary Clinton as some kind of chick–HAL 9000 capable of only "I'm sorry, Vladimir, I can't do that."

Which may be just what America needs, to be honest.

What Ms. Clinton really had to do during the debates, it was advised, was not lay out her vision for America, trade on her wealth of experience, answer yet more questions regarding her use of a private email server or even just tear down her opponent, but "prove she is human."

Honestly, the email thing should have been evidence enough. Not really understanding how one's email works should clinch it for anyone. It's as if, reliability-wise, Hillary Clinton had a beer with 90 percent of the American people.

Karl Rove and a number of George W. Bush White House staffers used private domains to send and receive a massive number of emails, as many as 22 million of which may have disappeared into the e-ether, and yet these fellows are seldom hung in effigy by raging crowds in repurposed sports stadiums.

Cries of "Lock Karl up! Lock Karl up!" do not echo through Democratic Party rallies. There are, however, now cries of "Lock her up! Lock her up!" when Donald Trump angrily (but that anger should be taken as an indication of just how deeply wronged he has been, not as proof of deep-seated emotional instability) mentions any of the women (I won't even bother giving a number, what with this still being a few hours from going to press) who have accused him of sexual assault and/or harassment.

Feel free to take that as an indication of what those cries of "Lock her up!" are really about.

For the record, were I speaking in public, I would, at this juncture, laugh a little bit—noiselessly, I promise. Think Mary Pickford, if that helps.

I would do that just to confirm that I am still not angry with anyone in the room. I have never been angry with anyone in a room, or on a patio, or on a boat, or in the "18 items or less" line, stuck behind someone with severe dyscalculia and all the coupons.

Yes, I would laugh at this point, but not so much as to give the impression that I'm not taking every single person in the world seriously, no matter what the hell they are going on about.

Then I would smile like everyone was watching—because I am a woman in public and so there's a good chance they are watching. They are watching my teeth, which are getting dry under these lights, and it's just possible I will, upon occasion, take my pleasantness a touch too far.

"Not smiling enough. Not smiling enough. Not smiling enough! Oh noooooo! Smiling too much! Throw that thing out."

Smiling, for women, is the avocado of facial expressions.

"It's all about trying to hit the smiling sweet spot, ladies," I say, smiling, but only slightly.

For the love of God, don't cry. If you ever feel yourself tearing up a touch while discussing months of hard work on behalf of your nation being flushed down the drain by Wallonia, look around for a convenient distraction.

Is there by chance a small, adorable, helpless puppy in the room? Good. Pick it up and throw it out the window. This will likely play better in the press than you sniffling a little in public.

You wouldn't want to give the opposition any ammunition, now, would you?

Hurl the puppy, ladies. Given a choice, always hurl the puppy.

I think our minister of international trade, Chrystia Freeland, learned that last week when she wisely—as it seems to have turned out—and convincingly announced that, as far as the long-sought and elusive Comprehensive Economic and Trade Agreement was concerned, Canada was taking its puck and going home.

"Since the trade minister is incapable or unwilling to do her job and ratify this vital trade deal, will the prime minister grab some adult supervision, get on a plane, and go back over to Brussels and get this job done?" Conservative MP Gerry Ritz demanded to know.

Note that Mr. Ritz was fully prepared to credit Justin Trudeau—arguably the most big-L Liberal of Liberals, a Liberal squared, in fact, a man the Conservatives like to attack as being just "a drama teacher" with "nice hair"—with having what it takes to get CETA sorted, something they sure as hell failed to do.

A Harvard- and Oxford-educated Rhodes Scholar who happened to mist up a bit, on the other hand, just had to be in way over her pretty little head.

Mr. Ritz was that anxious to infantilize the minister, that sure his dig would be well received. He saw an opening—women don't get much of a window; we're either babies or crones—and he took it.

All the little girls in Canada heard you, Mr. Ritz, and you know what they're doing? They're smiling.

That should make us all sad, Mr. Ritz, and maybe angry, and we'll all be better off when all the girls are just laughing at you.

Learning About Life from Dime-Store Paperbacks

Elle Canada, July 2013

●

The summer I was 13, I spent a lot of time hanging out at a corner store in my neighbourhood, keeping my friend Kristy company. Kristy, whose parents owned the store, was a few years older than I was; she worked there, using a cash register, selling cigarettes. She seemed almost supernaturally worldly to me.

The books I read that summer were the ones she told me to read; she'd lend them to me before they were sold in the store. These were actual old-school dime-store novels, the likes of which I've never seen anywhere else. It was as if they had been published—their pages artfully yellowed, the tops of the books lightly covered in dust—specifically for the revolving racks, next to the shelves of chips and Cheezies, in small-town corner stores that one summer.

The books were so steeped in sex and Americana that they read as if they had been translated from another language. From where I was—geographically and otherwise—they could have been about the Russian Empire for all I knew.

I had no reason not to believe that America was awash in drop-dead-gorgeous blond hitchhikers headed for the big city with nothing but a dream, which, exactly three obstacles and some only slightly varied copulation later, would be fulfilled. I'd just as soon have doubted that the soirees of St. Petersburg were elegant but fraught, that Frenchmen worried about debts owed to their glove-makers or that a sizable number of English ladies speculated about dating the vicar.

So when Kristy handed me yet another of these books, one that she'd just finished reading, and said: "This one's so good. She runs away from home and becomes a prostitute. She's really wild. I mean, she puts lipstick on her nipples when she's only 15!" I was thrown.

Kristy shook her head in disbelief. "Can you believe that? Putting lipstick on your nipples at 15?"

We were having Popsicles on the front steps of the shop, the town having reached its beef jerky and cigarette saturation point that afternoon, creating a lull in the usually steady stream of customers, almost all of whom knew Kristy by name.

"People put lipstick on their nipples?" I thought. "Seriously? This is a thing? A thing coming down the pipeline headed straight toward me in a mere two years?" Because I'd already determined that I was going to do most of the things the girls in these books did in as timely a fashion as I could muster.

I sat there, 24 months away from lipsticking my tits, as I saw it, processing this new idea. I'd only just come to grips with the whole shaving-my-legs concept, and now this!

I tried to be nonchalant about it.

"That is a bit young," I said. But then, not to be outdone, I added, "Although I've heard of younger."

Is this so that her nipples will show more through a white т-shirt? I wondered. Was attracting attention to my nipples going to be a lifelong problem, as, apparently, laundering any pale blouses I might obtain was going to be?

My mother owned one lipstick for most of my formative years. She was one of those mothers. I had recently concluded that I'd likely (sneakily) used her lipstick more times than she had—and I took my Popsicle out of my mouth, no longer feeling sophisticated. I was a lipstick hick compared to the girl in this book, blessed as she was with a precocious knowledge of an apparently routine part of any well-groomed woman's beauty regimen, of which I was entirely ignorant.

I read the book in one night—and wondered in the middle of it whether men liked getting lipstick on their mouths, as I (rather vividly) imagined them doing. The book didn't say, and it provided no other motivation for its heroine's nipple-lipstick-wearing behaviour.

I came away with no greater understanding. Were my nipples the wrong colour? Were *all* nipples the wrong colour? Were nipples, in fact, meant to be kind of orange? (Orange being the unfortunate, I thought, even then, colour of my mother's lipstick.)

Is that why my mother had the lipstick in the first place? To fix her nipples, like a lady? Because I never saw it on her lips, really.

In some ways, it all sort of made sense for a while that summer with Kristy. And then it didn't.

A Twisted Trump Dystopia, As Told to Crooked Tabatha

The Globe and Mail, November 26, 2016

•

"I'm from the future and I've come to give you the most tremendous, beautiful warning," the stranger in my kitchen said to me when I came downstairs to make myself cocoa the other evening.

"I'm not sure I believe you," I said, having, as I do, a skeptical nature.

"Well, you know what I say to that?" he said. "My warning just got 10 feet direr!"

"Good Lord," I said, "you have come from the future and through some abomination of medical science, voter suppression and the workings of the electoral college, Donald Trump is still president of . . ."

"Yes, @realDonaldTrump has been @POTUS of the Trump United States and Casino Resort for generations now," he interrupted. "Sad!"

"Very sad," I said.

"What?" he said, in obvious confusion.

"It's SAD!" I said, recognizing there was a language barrier to be overcome. "Would you like a . . . spectacular . . . mug of cocoa?"

He removed his red baseball cap, which I saw had the words "Government Issue" stamped inside and "Make America Greater Againer" on the brim, and nodded his head, which, although entirely covered with the thick hair of a young revolutionary, was still styled in an elaborate comb-over.

"But why have you chosen to bring your message to me?" I asked, getting out the milk.

"Well, to be big-league truthful," he said, "I was looking to talk to folks from the *Failing New York Times*, but when I looked on your newsstands all I could see was the *New York Times*. Not sure what that's about, so I came to you, Crooked Tabatha."

I was not offended, for I understood immediately that, where he came from, "crooked" was a word routinely applied to all women, because it made people clap.

"How goes the future?" I asked, scooping out some cocoa powder. "Do you not have any news outlets?"

"Not since the passing of the Bias Media Should Give Up! Trump Won! Act," he said.

"What?" I said. "That's outrageous! How did this act get through Congress? You're telling me you've come from hundreds of years in the future and still no one has investigated the correlation between support for Trump and the inability to add the letters 'ed' to the word 'bias'?"

"Progress on that didn't win anymore after President Trump issued an executive tweet saying that 'When Luxembourg sends its people, they're not sending their best! SAD!' He had all the lexicographers deported 'back' to Luxembourg as unfair immigrants. Senators are no longer elected.

"In my time, the position is granted exclusively to @real DonalTrump's ex-wives as part of their settlement packages. This happens the very second they sign a non-disclosure and always-agreeing agreement."

"Is that a lifetime appointment?" I asked.

"No, it lasts only as long as Trump rates them at least a seven," he replied, "and that particular motion passed 135 ex-wives to 0, with Ivanka abstaining."

"Oh, dear God," I said, "I don't want to know, but with the media gone, how do you get your news?"

"Well, there are the giant, loudspeaker-equipped, gold-leafed statues of *Breitbart* contributor Milo Yiannopoulos on every corner . . ."

"Why Milo?" I asked.

"The Supreme Court ruled that blaring state propaganda 24 hours a day isn't constitutionally 'very unfair!' if some of your best giant shouting statues are gay. There are yuuuge flickering screens with @realDonaldTrump projected onto them in every public space in the nation, both of them, and in every private space in which Trump has a stake, so all of the other spaces in America.

"The sign beneath the screens reads in giant gold-Sharpied letters, 'Bigly Brother is Distracted Right Now but Don't Forget Barron is so Great at the Cyber.'

"These screens may or may not be propaganda. The Supreme Court has been unable to make a determination as, to quote Lone Justice Scott Baio, 'No one can tell what President Trump's actually talking about, although the court is unanimous in its opinion that, in the tradition of old white men before him, the conversation always comes round to golf.' Hey, that's a very impressive, massive and impenetrable border wall you're holding there," he added.

"It's a wooden spoon," I said. "I'm just, you know, stirring the cocoa. You can buy them at the dollar store for . . ."

"Are you sure? Can this be true, folks? Back in grade three at @realDonaldTrump Primary School and Casino, my teacher, Crooked Jenkinson, taught us that a dozen of those planted in the sand along the US–Mexican border were all that was keeping America 'Safe and Great Again.'

"It was one of the more winning schools, believe me. My Crooked Mom clipped a lot of education coupons and worked four great manufacturing jobs at 60 cents an hour to send me there. We were taught that @realDonaldTrump had made America great again by fulfilling his election promise and building that wall. It was in all the textbooks. Both of them. And now you tell me you can buy impenetrable border walls at the dollar store? So that's why Mexico agreed to pay for the . . ."

"Mexico paid for . . ." I interrupted—one does wonder how history will play out—"the 'wall'?" Here, I put my "massive and impenetrable border wall" down on the counter and made air quotes.

"Well, half the wall, and we had to let them Make Texas Mexico Again," he said. "You know, the Gold Milos will always shout that Trump's 'yuuuge, long-fingered hands make him a winning negotiator' but some of the more radical great brains who have said a lot of things with best words in my organization question this. One or two of them even use border walls to stir chili."

"What exactly is your organization?" I asked, ladling him out a steaming cup of cocoa, using another handy national-security-enhancing utensil.

"We are the Offshore Wind Farm Construction Front," he said. "Trump's good brain was right to fear us and hey, Crooked Tabatha, this is some successful, very successful cocoa, many people, some very smart people, are saying that."

"*You* are the only one that's saying that," I said.

"I know," he said, again confused, "and that is why I gave a great job to the first-person singular. Do you mind if I demonstrate no conflict of interest whatsoever?" he added, indicating the cookie jar on my counter.

"Go ahead," I said, passing him the jar and then watching him take two handfuls of cookies.

"So the future is pretty grim then," I said.

"At the base of the Statue of Liberty the inscription reads, 'Honestly? Some of you guys look kind of huddled. You will never get by the bouncer at the Golden Door dressed like that. Visit IvankaTrump.com and check out 'The Style Guide: Go from Desk to Date Night.' Don't forget to enter promo code *wretched refuse*.'"

"So what is the message you want me to give to the American people?" I asked.

"Don't vote for him! Don't let him be president! If you act in time he will never get a chance to 'Make California Glow with that Faint Radioactive Light Again.' There will still be health care that is not mostly bandages that are Trump-branded, gold-leafed and only available through The Sharper Image. The truth must get out: Steak does not cure cancer! Maybe, in an alternate future, America does not trade Alaska to Russia for five rounds of golf with National Best Friend Vladimir Putin.

"Maybe the Paris Agreement is not abandoned and the City of New Orleans never has to be rebranded The Donald Trump Underwater Scuba Adventure Park and Aquatic Casino, and polar bears will still be a thing! We can turn this around! There are still a few days left before the US election on November 28th!"

"No," I said, "no, there aren't. Your history book has clearly been amended; the election was more than two weeks ago. It was only Donald Trump who said the election was on the 28th—and people still voted for him."

"Oh," he said despondently. "How's it going?"

"Well, since winning the election, Trump has made time for only two intelligence briefings but has found room in his schedule to meet with members of the press, largely, it seems, to complain that they aren't using flattering enough photos of him.

"He seems to think winning the election constitutionally obliges the *Washington Post* and the like to operate entirely as his own personal Instagram feed.

"Trump has revealed himself to be less a puppet, as was feared, and more a windsock; his opinions swing around alarmingly to match those of the last person he wanted to make like him.

"He has also shamelessly shilled for his own companies on state calls, and had his daughter, Ivanka, who he says will run those companies—the assets and interests of which remain a mystery—in on those meetings. He's boasted that he stopped a car plant that was never going to move from moving. Trump's tried to have the British ambassador to the United States replaced by a guy he likes, a guy that pretty much only he likes, that being quasi—and I use the prefix generously—fascist, seat-losing UKIP interim leader Nigel Farage.

"Perhaps most alarmingly, Donald Trump, the man who swore only he was capable of defeating ISIS, has lost a fight with a Broadway musical . . ."

"We have always been at war with Broadway," said my kitchen guest, in what struck me as an entirely involuntary manner.

"Look, on top of everything else," I said, "I will never forgive Donald Trump for making me defend musical theatre. I would not bother going back to the future, if I were you. Would you like to make my sofa-bed great again for a while, comrade?" I added, gently.

"Bigly," he said, and I took him by the hand.

It Ain't Over, So Let's Go See Some Opera

The Globe and Mail, February 4, 2017

•

Let me try to take your mind off, well, everything, by telling you how I came to love opera.

I'd never been to the opera and did not grow up listening to opera. Opera was not on my radar until an exceptional and very kind teacher (shout-out to all of you out there) noticed my intense and judgmental eldest child's interest in slightly less intense and judgmental Nordic gods, and took my 10-year-old to see *Siegfried*. That's how it started.

My child took to Wagner. A book about the *Ring Cycle* was well received at Christmas, which was good because Christmas was always a tough nut to crack with this kid. My eldest was born fairly fancy-resistant. I, on the other hand, came to motherhood brimming with fancy, dying to share the world's whimsy with my offspring, and quite sure Christmas was the ideal time to do that.

Unfortunately, I learned— by the time my child was three—I'd given birth to the Richard Dawkins of Santa Claus.

Christmas, I was certain, was also about candy and my child did not like candy.

"My child took to Wagner," I have now typed, and "My child did not like candy."

This is a strange tale for strange times but all of it is true. I tell my kids I only had children so I could be the mum in the checkout line who says, "Hey! Should we get a chocolate bar?" before my children even asked, let alone begged, and then I could eat some of it. Grown up, but still angling for that KitKat.

My youngest was all over that and still is, but my eldest always said, after a moment's thought, "No, let's not get a chocolate bar."

Every December 25th, one child's stocking was found filled with chocolate snowmen, Quality Streets and candy canes and met with delight. The other child's stocking was filled with jars of exotic salsa and bottles of obscure hot sauce and met with skepticism, although the goods were coveted nonetheless.

Anyway, a year or so after that introductory *Siegfried*, I read that the Canadian Opera Company was staging the entire *Ring Cycle* and I felt maternally obliged to take my child to all four operas. A chance like that, I feared, might not come around again.

I read that Wagner fans were coming in from all over the world for this event and here we were in Toronto anyway and so I looked into going. But times were quite lean and, upon investigation, I realized there was no way I could afford to buy us tickets.

Then, and how I did it I will never know—in one of those moments I can only compare to a mother lifting a car off her child—I found strength I didn't know I had, and I up and convinced the editor of a local paper that what she really needed was a review of the *Ring Cycle* written by a small child.

To their infinite credit, the Canadian Opera Company, when the editor approached them, agreed that a child's reflections on 15 hours of German opera was exactly what the city's readers were missing, and provided us with tickets.

"How could we not have seen this before?" they practically said. "What, after all, is *Der Ring des Nibelungen* but *Harry Potter* in German, with substantially more self-immolation? You get to work, child."

If other legacy media are paying attention, the Canadian Opera Company can teach them a lot. The COC does a fine job of getting the next generation of subscribers out to their offerings, ensuring a future for what it is they provide. Rather than deciding that older people go to the opera and so young people will naturally go to the opera once they're older too, the COC works to get young people out to opera right now. It's kind of a happening scene, the Canadian Opera.

With all the amusement options available these days, assuming the next generation will just come your way in time is not a safe bet. Instead, the COC offers an under-30 rate, as low as $22 a ticket. None of the seats are terrible. The sound is great. It feels as if there is space, both physically and intellectually, for newcomers. Not that the operas suffer endlessly awkward and belaboured "updates," but the staging is frequently inventive. They feel relevant.

A lively Twitter feed invites people out to various free lunchtime performances. A 20-minute talk precedes each opera. And while so many entertainment venues are just a seat and a lineup for the bathroom, the Four Seasons Centre for the Performing Arts in Toronto, which houses both the National Ballet and the COC, is a wonderfully social space. It's mingly.

I, however, did not know any of this when I learned the COC had agreed to let my child and me attend the *Ring Cycle*; I only knew I had to go and see the *Ring Cycle*. All of it, in the space of less than a week. The way I saw it, having my first opera be 15 hours long was trial by aria. I was filled with dread, dread I hid from my child, much like the book I brought to *Das Rheingold* on our first night out—thinking I might be able to slip into the lobby after a while. But here's the thing. I loved it. I loved all of it.

I was sold on opera from that week on and almost never miss one now. I still know almost nothing about opera and possibly this only makes me like it more. "That was a good song," I sit there thinking. "Oh! That was another good song." I never look at the reviews until after I've seen the show.

It's just me and the opera for the night.

I have mostly struggled with contemporary theatre because when I'm at a play, someone always seems to be asking me to suspend my disbelief. My disbelief is a weighty beast. Most of the time, my disbelief is just not going anywhere. I usually feel as if a play is trying, very hard, to convince me of something. I feel the pressure to believe the moment the first actor walks on stage. The considerable efforts of his movement coach—whom, experience tells me, he likely refers to as "a genius" at parties—are apparent to me in every step he takes.

During an opera, my incredulousness feels like an asset. I know that guy on stage singing is not an actual Viking and he knows I know he is not an actual Viking. We're all in this mostly surreal thing together at the opera.

I've never cared for musicals. With few exceptions, they make my teeth hurt. A guy I dated when I was in my teens was forever trying to sell me on the merits of Ginger Rogers/Fred Astaire movies and the like. I remained entirely unmoved, a philistine in his opinion.

"You don't understand," he'd lecture me when I expressed concern over the fact that everyone in whatever movie he'd chosen who wasn't singing was tap-dancing.

Tap-dancing, for heaven's sake. And yet, I was expected not to run out of the room screaming.

"It was the 1930s," he'd say. "Times were very tough, and these films were escapist fantasies that offered people relief!"

I came to believe the Great Depression was actually a fairly affluent time. People were just sad because their movies sucked.

Last weekend, I saw COC's *The Magic Flute*. I know it's not an original thought but *The Magic Flute* is enchanting. As is my tradition, I went to the opera that night thinking I did not want to be there, my mind very much somewhere else, and I was quickly swept right in. I smiled like a goof most of the way through the production. Sometimes it made me laugh and I'm still surprised at how intensely romantic opera can be.

Toronto is cold these days, grey skyed, with little snow, and at some point we seem to have decided to make most of our buildings out of green glass.

The city is slowly turning the colour of an old Mason jar. You feel the chill and the barrenness and the ordinariness of it all the most just now. But then, in the middle of that, there is the opera; every winter I find it again, a weird, warm bright flame.

A Lesson for Milo Yiannopoulos in What Free Speech Really Means

The Globe and Mail, February 25, 2017

●

This week, after video surfaced of him rhapsodizing about the bene-fits to both parties of older men having sex with children as young as 13, the Conservative Political Action Conference rescinded their invitation to Milo Yiannopoulos. He will no longer be filling a featured speaking slot at CPAC this year. Very shortly after that, publishing house Simon & Schuster issued a statement explaining that "after careful consideration" (a quick Google search months ago should also have done the trick), they will no longer be publishing the book for which Mr. Yiannopoulos reportedly received a $250,000 (US) advance.

One can only assume, given the level of buzzword-brandishing, low-effort trolling that is Mr. Yiannopoulos's brand, that Simon & Schuster's target audience for this book was "people seeking a motherlode of inane bigotry, with the occasional nugget of Nazi thrown in, who can't find their way to the bottom of a Reddit comment page." But that's Simon & Schuster's (embarrassingly mercenary) business.

An announcement that Mr. Yiannopoulos was "voluntarily" leaving *Breitbart*, the "news" site for which he has penned such gems as "How to Make Women Happy: Uninvent the Washing Machine" and "The Pill and Gay Rights Have Made Us Dumber, It's Time to Get Back in the Closet," followed shortly.

While he's frequently called a "provocateur," Mr. Yiannopoulos's oeuvre is largely a rehash of dated-before-he-was-born right-wing tropes. "Would you rather your child had feminism or cancer?" "Women can't drive!" So cheeky! Edgy as a political *Carry On* film, is our Milo.

Although, to be fair, as soon as you're ready to dismiss Milo as too dull to be dangerous, he starts up with how "political correctness" is making the study of "race and genetics taboo in the West" and that this is why we're losing out to China in the vital fields of "IQ-versus-race league tables" and the genetic origins of "black dietary preferences."

Certainly, this is troubling, although tired. The French would like the word "provocateur" back now. English already has the perfect phrase for what you're describing there, Yiannopoulos boosters, and if you feel the need to class it up a bit, maybe the French will let you go with *le insufferable dickhead*. Given Monday's events, *le insufferable unemployed dickhead* sums it up best.

That—one hopes—last day of Milo's Terrible, Horrible, No Good, Very Bad Career has led to confusion over what constitutes the suppression of free speech. I have written *A Comprehensive Guide to Recognizing When Your Free Speech Is Being Suppressed*:

If you're invited to speak on a campus by one student group, only to have another student group say it would rather you didn't attempt to explain, as Milo has, that "Muslims do not believe that when in Rome, do as the Romans do. Muslims believe: when in Rome, rape everyone and claim welfare," that is not an attack on free speech. It's just free speech.

If you find yourself criticized for something you have said, and thus wonder if your right to freedom of expression has been taken from you, ask yourself these simple questions: "Am I in jail?" and "Has someone smashed my printing press?" Take a second to look around; study your surroundings. If you find that you're not in jail (grey walls, iron bars, people getting very upset if you try to leave) but instead in, say, a dining room where someone is saying, "Wow, that's a really stupid thing to say, but you said it anyway and now you look like a total jerk. I'm just going to sit here, eat my potato salad, pretend I don't know you and never invite you back"—your speech remains entirely unsuppressed.

When the moon hits your eye like a big pizza pie, studies have shown that this is not, in fact, a limitation of your free speech, that's amore. I can't believe I have to explain these things.

Occasionally, people may say, "Hey, dude, your long history of spouting monstrous and factually inaccurate things about just about everyone who isn't a straight, white man with a self-proclaimed passion for ethics in gaming journalism doesn't make you look better here. It just makes the people who waited until your thoughts about raping 13-year-olds came up—while celebrating your dismissal of the rape of university students—to dump your ass look worse." These people aren't suppressing your free speech. They're just, as I imagine even John Stuart Mill would say, "pointing out the bloody obvious."

Raindrops on roses and whiskers on kittens, bright copper kettles and warm woollen mittens, brown paper packages tied up with strings are not suppression of your free speech. They're a few of a failed nun's favourite things. Write that down if you need to.

If someone hands you their megaphone, gives you a $250,000 advance for using that megaphone, then decides to take their megaphone back when they find you explaining how "sexually mature" 13-year-olds benefit from "enriching and incredibly life-affirming" sexual relations with older men, that is not you being robbed of your right to free speech. That's a business not wanting a megaphone with their logo on it in the hands of a pedophilia apologist, you creep.

When I write that ditching Milo now proves that Milo-love was never about defending "Free speech!" on principle, as his promoters mostly claim, that is not an attack on free speech. That is just a logical conclusion: people loved Milo because he was their gay-hating gay friend who let them know it was okay to be homophobic while he helpfully articulated their racism and hatred of women and trans people.

Milo's business model was delivering bigotry in a camp, plausibly deniable package, and people loved their proxy, until he went toxic. "I will defend your right to free speech as long as you're saying that women can't do math and Muslims are destroying the West, but abandon that cause as soon as you defend raping children" is truly the darkest kind of fair-weather fandom.

When a radioactive spider bites you while you're watching your parents get gunned down by a desperate criminal outside a Gotham theatre and you want to put some cream on it or something, but this really big guy keeps trying to tell you you're a wizard, that's not anyone suppressing your free speech. That's your origin story. Get with the program, Spiderbat Harry.

Gin toddies, in large measures, may (much like never having to listen to Milo Yiannopoulos's theory on the non-existence of lesbians) be part of a fine life, but they're no impediment to your free speech. Breathe easy.

Now, there are those who say Milo is beneath discussion and we should just ignore him, but just because very little of what he says makes any sense—that doesn't mean he doesn't mean anything. Milo's rise says a lot about the current state of conservatism, about which I can only say, "Where you goin', guys?"

Time was it could be argued that conservatives sought much the same end as did liberals—promising a better, more prosperous society. True, their vision of "betterness" and "prosperity" was unlike the left's vision and they wanted to take a different road to get there; but their path was, at least, recognizable as a road.

The endgame of conservatism was once something more ambitious than "making liberals really mad," which, as challenges go, falls somewhere between "making ice cream melt" and "taking candy from a Pez dispenser."

These days, American conservatism does not look like Ronald Reagan promising "Morning in America." It looks like little Tommy poking his sister with his middle finger over and over in the back seat of the car, and then, when called on it, saying, "I did not!" followed by, "Immigrants and women started it!"

Ivanka Trump's New Book is a Vacuous Exercise in Branding

The Globe and Mail, May 6, 2017

I write fairly often, as you may have noticed, about talking animals. These may be the columns I enjoy writing the most and during my time at *The Globe and Mail* I have received queries from my editor along the lines of, "You do not specify where the third monkey works. Which academic institution is he associated with?" and I never have to stop to think before I answer.

"The University of Aberdeen," I reply. "Sorry to have left that out."

I know each monkey's backstory. They're real to me, my talking news-monkeys or camels, or at least I don't struggle to imagine them going about their business. Their presence is never a challenge to the internal logic that a column needs if it is to succeed. This is not true of writing about the Trump administration; just typing "President Donald Trump" throws me. Some part of me cries out, "Fact check!"

This final column is essentially a review of Ivanka Trump's book, *Women Who Work*, and reading that and writing this was, to date, my most surreal experience as a columnist. If you'd told me ten years ago that one day I'd be writing about Ivanka Trump, President Donald Trump's daughter, I'd have argued that you can only push a reader so far—what if it was written by a red panda?

•

Move over, Trump Natural Spring Water. When it comes to flavourless, odourless, tasteless and utterly transparent products you really don't want to get on your e-reader, the arrival this past week of Ivanka Trump's *Women Who Work* means you have been replaced.

As with the bottled water, *Women Who Work* is, essentially, a re-packaging and branding exercise. There's water, water everywhere and there are inspirational quotes and anecdotes everywhere, and now the Trump name has been applied to both of these resources.

Watch your back, Donald. It's one thing to slap your name on condominiums, casinos and boxed frozen steaks in an attempt to add a veneer of luxury to them. It takes a whole other level of Trumpian gumption to do the same with the Dalai Lama and Jane Goodall.

Women Who Work is nothing if not a collection of quotes and, on reflection, it really is a toss-up between the two. It is a book in which quotes generally introduce other, lengthier quotes—excerpts from already successful works of advice being the stuff of which the book's chapters, sections and subsections (all of which are graced with names such as "Elevate Your Meetings" and "Hiring to Fortify Your World Class Team") are largely made.

This cavalcade of "curated," as Ms. Trump calls them, co-options and recountings are mostly concluded by yet another quote in order to create a sort of quote sandwich, if sandwiches were just whole loaves of sliced white bread turned up.

Strange bedfellows emerge from this citation soirée. "Freeing yourself was one thing; claiming ownership of that freed self was another," Toni Morrison wrote in *Beloved*, on the subject of grappling with the enduring trauma wrought by slavery.

Ivanka, bless her, has the vision to repurpose this quote to open a chapter about the importance of being the "master" of your time rather than a "slave" to it. One accomplishes this feat, we learn, by not doing "reactive" things such as "returning calls, attending meetings, answering e-mails, and managing your team." So: working, as Ivanka Trump understands the concept.

Maya Angelou gets misquoted, and "Ask for Flexibility" is introduced by a quote from none other than Nelson Mandela because, really, isn't that exactly what his particular project was about? If spending 18 of one's 27 years in prison offshore on Robben Island in an effort to dismantle a system of racial discrimination in one's entire country isn't a lot like asking "your team" (Ms. Trump seems convinced all working women have one of these) whether you can telecommute, I don't know what is.

Institutional change—or even acknowledgment of systemic disadvantage, or systemic anything, really—was clearly not on Ms. Trump's mind when she pasted some Mandela into her go-girl, feel-good, jargon-choked, apolitical empowerment scrapbook. Ms. Trump, after all, seems convinced that bad things only happen to people who refuse to "proactively devote [their] time to what really matters to [them]" because they "can't stop negatively overreacting to [their] daily obligations and demands" or properly identify their "passion," which is, after all, "our reason for being." The fools!

One senses she would have suggested Mr. Mandela perhaps try "a conversation" with his team about flex-apartheid but, notably, she advises against playing "hardball."

Mr. Mandela's quote is the opening act for a hefty chunk of Sheryl Sandberg's 2013 *Lean In: Women, Work, and the Will to Lead*. Ms. Trump begins her book by insisting that she's stepping up to write it because "the time to change the narrative around women and work is long overdue."

Then, throughout the rest of the book, she copies and pastes many of the writers who met that deadline some time ago—Joanna Barsh and Susie Cranston of *How Remarkable Women Lead* and political scientist Anne-Marie Slaughter, whose piece in the *Atlantic*, "Why Women Still Can't Have It All," led to her book *Unfinished Business*, for example.

It appears the thing Ms. Trump most wanted to change about the "working woman" narrative was the fact that she wasn't starring in it.

There's an obvious parallel to be found in Ms. Trump's clothing line. Until her brand stepped in to save us, she informs the reader, the image of working women was a "one-dimensional, suit-clad caricature, striding down Fifth Avenue, briefcase in hand, a stern expression on her face."

This was a serious issue because, by Ms. Trump's account, the single biggest obstacle facing working women in America today isn't childcare (daycare is scantly mentioned in *Women Who Work*—once in a quote about instructing your minders to send you photos and updates throughout the day) or the briefly, belatedly mentioned wage gap, presented largely as something that happens to single mothers. Women, she seems to be saying, were oppressed by the absence of the opportunity to purchase "apparel and accessories" with which to "express ourselves."

It is to this end that Ms. Trump, back in 2007, bravely, selflessly set about trying to advance our cause with her line of womenswear. Truly, she is the Margaret Sanger of 5 percent spandex, 95 percent polyester.

Beyond writers who, she alleges, failed to portray the reality of working women's lives, but whom she earnestly quotes in her book professing to be about working women's lives, a lot of women are erased in Ms. Trump's retelling of fashion history as well. There was never a Diane von Furstenberg, let alone an Anne Klein or a Claire McCardell. Donna Karan's Seven Easy Pieces collection of 1985 was but a bodysuit-based dream, apparently. There is only Ms. Trump, fashion quoter, and her endlessly derivative line, hawked as liberating.

There's nothing clever in this, no marketing genius. Women have been asked to purchase fetishes of their own empowerment since we had an income.

"Because I'm worth it," was the L'Oréal line when I was growing up. Before that came Virginia Slims's "You've come a long way, baby."

Women Who Work, it can most charitably be said, is in that tradition. It is promotional, a bland catalogue for the Ivanka line. It's not even a text for readers in the market for some knock-off feminism.

Ultimately, its scope is so mind-crushingly small that it is only a book about how to be Ivanka Trump and—spoiler alert—it's really easy.

Step 1: Think about what you want.

Step 2: Get it!

It's not that, with all the quotes and cribbing, there's no Ivanka Trump in this book. Oh, she's there. "Our attitudes influence our mindset," Ms. Trump tells us. This makes me cry, in both my mindset and my attitude.

Barring travel at relativistic speeds, we move forward through time constantly and at a constant rate, one second per second, or, as Ivanka Trump expresses it, "If you choose to have a child or children early in your career, and later you decide to return to a traditional corporate setting, be prepared for the fact that you will be older than your peers at the same level . . ."

Although only by a maximum of eight weeks if you work for Ms. Trump, that being the amount of maternity leave her employees were eventually able to finagle from this self-professed champion of women. Note as well that *everything, having a baby, staying home, going to work*, in Ms. Trump's world, is a choice.

You would need a Kelvin scale for self-awareness to describe just how little of that precious quality Ms. Trump demonstrates in her appropriated opus. "During extremely high-capacity times, like during the campaign, I went into survival mode . . ." she writes. But no, she didn't eat anyone. It turns out that what "survival mode" means to Ms. Trump is "I worked and I was with my family; I didn't do much else."

"Honestly, I wasn't treating myself to a massage or making much time for self-care."

It's the "honestly" that catapults that sentence into the realm of superhuman egocentrism.

What working mother, what person on earth, did she think would be incredulous of this statement? (Besides herself.)

Also, and this goes for everyone, you say "self-care" and I will want to hurt you. Your call.

The void left behind by this total absence of self-awareness is filled with an astronomical level of artifice.

"I realized that it might be helpful in changing the narrative—even in a small way—to, for example, debunk the superwoman myth by posting a photo that my husband candidly snapped of me digging in the garden with the kids in our backyard, my hair in a messy ponytail, dirt on my cheek. I've been careful not to pretend it's easy because it is not."

Oh, Ivanka, that is not debunking the "superwoman myth." Showing the world that you—when you're not running your own company or attending glamorous evening events—can be found digging in your garden with your children *is* the "superwoman myth."

You, with the dirt on your cheek and the down-home ponytail, are a Parthenon frieze celebrating that mythic figure who has and does it all, an Instagram obelisk at the door to her temple. *And you know it.*

Why does Ivanka Trump's book—or 256-page pictureless inspirational calendar, as I came to think of it—matter?

Largely because the spin has consistently been that she's in the White House, moderating her father, looking out for women, and so if she does have an agenda beyond her own advancement, beyond the promotion of the Trump brand, then this book would have been the logical place to explore that vision. But a more vacuous document would be hard to find.

"What exactly is she doing there?" many Americans ask.

"She's doing her bit quietly," they're told, it's leaked.

"She teared up this one time when her father didn't want to apologize, after the world listened to him describing on tape how his fame allowed him to get away with just grabbing women 'by the pussy,'" we hear, but then she helped him get elected and now she's helping out, in a womanly way, we are to understand. She's there to smooth things over, make things pretty, ask for nothing.

Ivanka Trump is doing the altar flowers at the Church of the Patriarchy, but there are some pink tulips in the arrangement, so rest easy.

• • • • •

About the Author

•

Tabatha Southey is smart, funny and very beautiful. She has the prettiest eyes. She describes her hair as iconic. That's how men think of her breasts. She is also a gifted writer. *Elle Canada*, *The Globe and Mail*, *The Walrus* and *Explore Magazine* are four of the publications lucky enough to have her in their pages. She has a lovely laugh and has been nominated for ten National Magazine Awards. She is also an excellent cook, terrific in bed and weary of self-deprecating chick writers.